VERY SUPERIOR MEN

VERY SUPERIOR MEN

Some early Public School Headmasters
and their Achievements

Alicia C. Percival

CHARLES KNIGHT & CO. LTD.
LONDON
1973

Charles Knight & Co. Ltd
11/12 Bury Street, London EC3A 5AP
Dowgate Works, Douglas Road, Tonbridge, Kent

Printed in Great Britain by
Staples Printers Ltd.

ISBN 0 85314 142 8

FOREWORD

by the High Master of St. Paul's School

In her brief centenary study, *The Origins of the Headmasters' Conference* (John Murray, 1969), Dr. Percival demonstrated that it is possible to make so apparently lugubrious a subject as the history of headmasters come to life. Now on a much wider canvas she has made a major contribution to our understanding of a significant, if hitherto largely obscure, aspect of nineteenth century social history. She has reassessed comparatively well-known figures like Keate of Eton, Butler and Kennedy of Shrewsbury and Thring of Uppingham and by dint of a notable exercise in demythologising at long last has succeeded in making Thomas Arnold credible. At the same time the remarkable Thomas James of Rugby, Mitchinson of King's, Canterbury, and Elwyn of Charterhouse among others emerge as men of far greater calibre and achievement than has previously been realised. None of her subjects temper their moral earnestness with undue levity, but Dr. Percival's researches often impel us to smile at some all too human experiences. The difficulties of Balston of Eton confronting the Clarendon Commission; Kennedy's fear that the old foundation schools may not hold their ground "against the tide of Joint stock education"; Kynaston of St. Paul's resisting the suggestion that school dinners should be started on the grounds that they would not accord with his dignity; Harper of Sherborne observing of the Lord Digby of his day: "if managed his Lordship is inclined to be liberal"; and perhaps most poignant of all a newly appointed headmaster of Repton sitting at a table "with his head sunk upon his hands in the attitude of a man appalled by the magnitude of the task he had set himself".

It will be no surprise to readers of this book, even if their knowledge of the period is confined to *Tom Brown's Schooldays,* that the public schools of the nineteenth century were in many respects narrow and barbaric institutions. One of the many merits, however, of Dr. Percival's study is that one begins to understand against the background of the period, just *why* this was so. Also, by the imaginative recreation of the feel of each particular school at a particular period of time in relation to the problems confronting its headmaster, the author demonstrates how the most successful innovations spread from one school to another—the dominant genes, so to speak, assisting the survival of the species.

As one who believes that the schools studied in this book have still a great contribution to make to the civilisation of this country, I would refer the reader to Arnold's opinion that as England *has* this system of boarding it should be judiciously reformed to make use of 'all that is excellent in it'. The difficulties confronting the headmasters of public schools in the century since Thring founded the Headmasters' Conference are different in kind, though possibly no less burdensome, than those of our predecessors. Perhaps, though perhaps not, we may derive some comfort from Thring's favourite Latin tag *solvitur ambulando*.

T. E. B. Howarth

CONTENTS

LIST OF ILLUSTRATIONS

(between pages 104/105)

We wish to thank the following for their kind permission to reproduce the illustrations in this book: Dr. Anthony Daly, for the picture of Dr. James; the picture of Bishop Mitchinson is from a portrait belonging to Pembroke College, Oxford; B. T. Batsford Ltd., for the silhouette of Goodall and Keate and the photograph of Edward Thring; The Schools, Shrewsbury, for the photograph of Kennedy and Staff and the picture of Samuel Butler; Rugby School for the prints of the school, and the map of Rugby Estate; the Guildhall Library, London, for the print of the Long Chamber at Eton; and King Edward VI Grammar School, Louth, for the picture of Louth Grammar School Seal on page 254.

PROLOGUE

Headmasters to Conference
It was the cruellest winter weather. Two men were looking out from the window of the London and North-Western Railway compartment in which they were northward bound, into a misty landscape unfolding drearily around them. Both were Headmasters (one was to become a Bishop in five years' time) and had already come up from Kent that morning. Hilaire Belloc had not yet stigmatised the Midlands as "sodden and unkind" but that was just how they appeared to the travellers on this day. The date was December 21st, 1869, and their destination was Seaton station, for Uppingham School. During their fours hours' journey, the elder remarked, more than once: "If Thring can keep together a school of three hundred boys in this howling wilderness, he must indeed be a wonderful man." It is not surprising that what impressed Dr. Welldon of Tonbridge so much was the numbers and stability of the school that Thring had achieved rather than the importance of the idea that he had recently conceived, yet these travellers were about to participate in a remarkable event. They were among the dozen men to be present at the start of a Conference which was to become an annual gathering of very great significance for hundreds of schools.

Mitchinson, Headmaster of King's School, Canterbury, Welldon's fellow traveller, noted that the trials of the journey were soon forgotten in the warmth of Thring's welcome and the excitement of the gathering. Headmasters then had few opportunities of meeting each other, or often of seeing anyone who could share their interests, and this group was, as Thring had noted in his diary, "a very superior set of men". Nine months before, he had gone, somewhat unwillingly and under great persuasion, to a meeting which Mitchinson had diffidently called for Headmasters of Endowed Grammar Schools to discuss the Bill prepared by the Government of the day for the reform of these schools. "Endowed Secondary School" was the official designation of such foundations as Sherborne, Felsted, Norwich, Dulwich and Bury St. Edmunds, as well as the two mentioned above, whose Heads had been at this meeting. Their deputation to Forster, the official in charge of the Bill, had been courteously received, and adjustments were made, but perhaps even more far-reaching in result had been the invitation from Thring to meet again for social and educational colloquy.

Less than a fifth of the total number invited actually came (some, perhaps, had looked up the trains for this cross-country journey) and these few deserve to be remembered. For their organization both symbolized and brought about a new era in the existence of a whole class of school. All over England, Headmasters had been working *individually* to raise their own schools, sometimes from a moribund condition, to become respected and accepted institutions. Once they came together, an image began to be created—they were no longer Grammar and local but Public and national.

About a century of work by individual Headmasters lay behind this first Conference. Individual schools, old and new in status, had been climbing upwards, very like the proverbial snails ascending the wall, each going three feet up and then slipping two feet back—or more. The cause of failure must be sought in the history of each school; sometimes it can be seen in apathetic Trustees, in an inefficient Headmaster or in a falling away of funds. Sometimes no clear cause for decay can be found. Plenty has been written about "the Rise of the Public Schools" as a general phenomenon. With one exception, little has been said about the men who actually brought about *the* rise—i.e. the rise that was not followed by a corresponding fall—in each particular school. Thring's adjective "superior" is characteristic of his time (though Jane Austen might have used it 50 years before) but in effect it might have described some 20 or so other Heads who, since the mid-eighteenth century, had been engaged in this work of School-raising. They too are worth observing.

Briefly one may lay out the events for about a hundred years before the meeting. The stirrings started in the mid-eighteenth century when Harrow began to effect this change in status from Grammar to Public school. Its Headmasters are still shadowy to us—partly from lack of records—but they were beginning to emerge as characters bent on school-making. (Eton, for reasons which will be made clear, came behind in this, though as a prototype of the whole genus we must look at what it was doing at this time.) A real pioneer, not well-known but one of the most original, was Thomas James of Rugby who in 16 years hoisted his school from being "Grammar-and-local" to being "Public-and-national", once and for all, and more than a generation before Arnold. With the turn of the century came the successors to these pioneers: Samuel Butler of Shrewsbury was an outstanding example and, of course, at Rugby, Thomas Arnold. At Eton, a Headmaster emerged who was outstanding but rather as being the last of an old type, John Keate. It is the reaction *against* what Keate was supposed to stand for that is most interesting to study.

If in the 18th and early 19th century the day of the Headmaster had dawned, the mid-nineteenth century was the heyday of Royal Commissions. Of these, Lord Brougham's Charity Commission, active from 1818 onwards, and the two educational ones under Lord Clarendon and Lord Taunton, and generally known by these names, were those relevant to the schools (and Heads) here considered. This last led straight, as mentioned, to the action—one might name it a defence mechanism except that it was too consciously undertaken—of calling the Conference. The Conference-callers and the first attenders were perhaps the most fascinating and varied of any educational group, and included Thring, Harper, and Mitchinson (whom we first met in the train). They were all characters as far removed from the generally accepted image of a stuffed and pompous Victorian as it is possible to be. Through them a new image of Public Schools, firmly based on the Conference, was established.

Background to Revival

Why was these men's task in reviving these Schools so hard and so significant? The English Schools are an institution older than the monarchy, far older than Parliament, contemporary with the arrival of Christianity in England. Some of the schools that are now Public Schools can rightly assert that they existed in the dark ages—and here they still are. The claim might, however, surprise some, yet hardly as much as the contrary assertion that Public Schools, all but a very few, did not even exist as such so lately as two hundred years ago. How can these two statements be reconciled?

To take the second first: the *name* "Public School" was hardly ever used till shortly before 1800: the term was commonly "Great School" This was no misnomer; since Elizabethan times a school might be regarded as "Great" because it was literally so in numbers, containing more boys, perhaps (like 16th century Shrewsbury) considerably more than had ever been expected. That meant generally that it was a locally founded Grammar School which had risen in prestige from one cause or another—good political patronage, lucky financial policies, or, by far the most effective; an outstanding Headmaster. It had received boys exceeding the number of scholars that could be scraped up from the immediate neighbourhood, usually that of a little market town, and it had boarders, generally in a house built for the (Head) Master with that very purpose in mind. It had become famous and non-local. This happy condition might continue for a few years or perhaps, with a good succession of Masters, last half a century, but then the school would relapse and might even come near to extinction. This was a very common historical pattern; Shrewsbury, Tonbridge, Richmond (Yorks) were all "Great" in their different days; Defoe in the early 18th century lists as many more, but by about 1770 the permanently "Great" could be counted on the fingers of two hands.

There were Eton, Winchester and Westminster—a triad unrivalled in age if tarnished in reputation. Less in age but dating back to the 16th century, or soon after, were the Charitable and Day schools of London—Christ's Hospital, The Charterhouse, and the City of London Livery Companies' other schools (the Mercers had charge of Dean Colet's foundation, St. Paul's). There was by this time one other school, whose rise will be specially treated, ranking as Great; it had been founded as The School of John Lyon at Harrow. All the rest of those which we now call Public had in 1770 their way still to make. Within another generation or two the scene was crowded with boarding schools, most of which had been local Grammar Schools, all thrusting upward in numbers and reputation, and the term Public School was beginning to have a social and even a legal meaning.

Every conceivable reason has been suggested for the growth of the Public Schools in general, from the coming of the railways to the revival of appreciation of the classics. Evidently they met the general desire of fathers to make their sons as good as, or better than, themselves. This result might be brought about by many different kinds of education, but in the 18th century, rather curiously, opinion was turning to education away from home; the age of the private tutor was passing. Considerable choice would arise about where a boy could be sent:

1. *The Private Schools*—in all their wide variety. These ranged in size from a clergyman taking two or three pupils, to an outstanding school like Eagle House, Hammersmith, nursery of many Headmasters. A boy might later go to Arnold and his brother-in-law Buckland, at Laleham, or to Hazlewood, the outstandingly progressive institution of Rowland Hill's family. Many of these private schools prepared for the University; their pupils by 1862 formed quite a large proportion of the undergraduates at Oxbridge. But of course, there was nothing to stop anyone from running a "Dotheboys Hall" instead.

2. *The Charitable Foundations* mentioned before, though not all were in London; the Merchant Taylors for instance had a Grammar school also in Crosby. On the classical side these schools would qualify a boy for the Universities and therefore primarily for teaching or the Church, and they never lost their sense of purpose, which was to ensure to a boy his means of livelihood. Most of their pupils were there on nominations

of various kinds: Matthew Arnold later had a pleasantly satiric passage on "the Rev. Esau Hittall":

> Hittall was on the foundation at Charterhouse, placed there by his uncle, a distinguished prelate, who was one of the trustees . . . who relieve the State of all work and responsibility, and never take a shilling of salary for their trouble. Hittall was the last of six nephews nominated to the Charterhouse by his uncle, this good prelate, who had thoroughly learnt the divine lesson that charity begins at home.*

The boys so nominated (called "Gownboys" at Charterhouse) were fully provided for as boarders, but the schools also took boys living locally who paid for the education; paying boarders on the whole had here been discouraged.

3. *Day schools* existed at various levels on endowed foundations; grammar schools which were to remain local up to the present day. An outstanding example was King Edward VI at Birmingham. But by the mid-nineteenth century, the preference of the better-off even in that city was to send one's son away.

4. *"The Great Schools"*, old foundations, but later joined by new ones, to which the word Public (as distinct from private and profit-making) was to be applied. Critics are fond of saying boys were sent to these to be made into gentlemen. (An example of such a phrase is found in E. O. Thompson's *Life of William Morris* and will be dealt with in discussing his school, Marlborough.)† In the case of the most famous of fictional pupils, however, we do not find this at all. Squire Brown's meditation on his purpose in sending Tom to Rugby is well known and he certainly wants him to "turn out a brave, helpful, truth-telling Englishman and a gentleman and a Christian". But the context is clearly not *social* and it never enters his head that Tom will be raised in rank or make any friends with snob-value; nor does he, neither do his friends profit from *his* status. Readers of the school story do not often remember that Squire Brown held that it didn't matter a straw whether his son associated with lords' sons or ploughmen's sons provided they were brave and honest—that he and his fathers before him had joined the boys of the village in football and birds-nesting, and Tom had run about in the same way. We are accustomed to read, on genuine but limited evidence, a great deal more snobbishness than can be justified into the lives of those who went to the early Public Schools, and therefore into the schools themselves. Possibly it comes of looking through Marxian spectacles, but then, Marx was not brought up in a Berkshire countryside.

---

* Matthew Arnold, *Friendship's Garland,* Letter VI, p.48.
† See Appendix B.

By 1770, however, most of the present Public Schools, Rugby included, were not yet to be considered among the Great Schools, though the Masters would be taking boarders in their own houses. If a parent wished to send his boy to be educated and to pay for him, Eton was the place, with Harrow as an alternative, especially if he was a Whig, Westminster had gone into a sad decline since the days of its great Head, Dr. Busby, (the town site told against it) and at Winchester, though the teaching was better, life was particularly hard and the boys often in a state of rebellion.

There had been a time when the squire's sons, the parson's sons, and the sons of the smaller aristocracy might well, if not taught at home, have gone to school in the neighbouring town, perhaps boarding there if the meagre transport of the time made daily journeys too far or arduous. But a terrible blight had descended on the majority of these Grammar schools. It was partly a widespread economic malady. The original salaries for which the schools had been endowed were now quite insufficient to support a well-qualified Master ("Headmaster" was understood; there might be in addition an Usher but other assistant masters had seldom been provided for at all). His work became combined with the parson's—and the teaching suffered. If the Parson-schoolmaster was an indolent or incompetent character, he neglected the school, the numbers fell off, and when at last he came to retire, the post was even less attractive to a good man. The school was caught in a descending spiral. And even if the Master happened to be a keen scholar and a good teacher, he would tend to concentrate on the few "paying boys" in his own house, and the school as a whole would still decline.

Another often-given cause for the decline of the Grammar schools is their out-of-date curriculum. Classics formed the main, if not the only, scholastic diet afforded at these (indeed, at all but some Private) schools. There were several reasons for this. First, the school's endowments were legally tied to the teaching of "Grammar"—which meant, and was often explicitly stated to mean, the languages and literature of Latin and Greek, with, of course, Religion. The endowments paid the Master for nothing else—the parents might pay for additional subjects but the classics came first. Also—a weighty reason often unnoticed—the school exhibitions to the University, or any scholarships obtainable there, were confined to the classics. Some boys came to country-town schools entirely to get the means of going on to further education; naturally it was the Master's job to help them. Moreover, what else was he likely to want to teach? He might have done some mathematics, under compulsion, at the University; he might have a good knowledge of English and of some foreign literature, but he would have no formal experience of even such physical science as was known, though he might be a very good naturalist and observer of the countryside. The disciplines of History and Geography, except as regards the Ancient World, had not developed and he would not think of teaching anything practical like Book-keeping—which was what the local townsfolk wanted. No, Classics he had learnt and Classics he would teach.

There seems to have been one other reason for teaching the Classics—they suddenly became fashionable. Mr. Vivian Ogilvie points this out; he is speaking of Eton and Harrow parents:

> That these people should have thought a classical education (tricked out with a little French and dancing and elementary mathematics) the very thing for their boys is the real peculiarity. Natural scholars would, of course, take to the classics. But why should they have become a social badge? Sheer inertia no doubt played its part, but one cannot help looking for other explanations.*

He does not really find any, though revival of interest in all things from ancient Greece and Rome was being shown in architecture, statuary, house decoration—and conversation. "But the phenomenon is unquestionable."

The Great Schools then became acceptable as places of education. They had with the passing of time become physically easier of access. Improvements in roads, the coaching system, and at a later date the railways, all made it easier for boys to come regularly from a distance. (It made it possible also to insist on their all coming and leaving at one time and keeping fixed "terms" which had earlier been quite a difficulty.) But increased facilities for travel can only be considered as a very minor cause of increased popularity for boarding schools. It was Thring, who put into words the purpose of these Schools:

> There is a very strong feeling growing up among the merchant class in England in favour of the public schools; and hundreds go to schools now who thirty years ago would not have thought of doing so. The learning to be responsible, and independent, to bear pain, to play games, *to drop rank, and wealth,*† and home luxury, is a priceless boon. I think myself that it is this which has made the English such an adventurous race . . . ‡

The 18th century would not have expressed itself in just those terms but there certainly was then an upsurge in education, a wish to let boys

---

* V. Ogilvie, *The English Public School*, p.110.
† My italics—A.C.P.
‡ G. R. Parkin (ed.), *Diary, Life and Letters of Edward Thring*, p.425.

(not yet girls) have more of it. We have seen something of the kind in the last few decades. It may (Thring would not have cared to think so) be connected with a bettering of conditions; more people in that age, as in this, "had never had it so good." There was one interesting difference; the increased money they had for spending on their children's education was their personal fortune; in our day the greater part of education is supplied through taxes by the State. But the wish for, the interest in, new departures in education is very understandable to us.

All social historians, however, remark that at about the time of Dr. Arnold's appearance a weight of criticism and abuse was being directed against Public Schools. Yet though these schools went through a bad patch in the early 1830s all of them were climbing up by the end of the decade. This can hardly be due to Arnold alone; yet no satisfactory answer has been given to the question of what made the early Victorian parent (using the word in its correct chronological sense) send his son to such an establishment.

The actual population explosion of the 19th century may have contributed. Granted that the greater force of this was felt among "the poor" yet, if even a small percentage of the enormous increase occurred in the middle and upper classes, this would produce a large clientèle for the not very expensive luxury of a Private or Public boarding school.

This rise in population was partly a sign of better living resulting in the survival of a larger number of children per family. A heavy proportion did continue to die in all classes—witness the memorial tablets in many churches—but if, of a dozen or more children, four or five sons survived, they would make a considerable mark and uproar in even the notoriously extensive Victorian Parsonage, Manor or Hall. Could it be that Paterfamilias, faced with an increased number of growing lads, might feel that all would benefit if during their upgrowing but non-working years they were partly away out of the house? The point seems never to have been raised—perhaps the thought was not at first put into words nor even consciously admitted—but modern probers into family relations might not be surprised at a paternal desire to rid the nest of some of its restless fledglings. Later it seems to have been acknowledged practice to send at least the most troublesome ones for the school to deal with.

The worse and more troublesome to parents were their sons, the more did a public school seem the precise remedy for them . . . the

---

* i.e. the seven "Clarendon" Boarding Schools and St. Paul's. These are the only ones considered in Mr. Bamford's *The Rise of the Public Schools*. See p.138, *post*.

great end of a public school, in short, was to flog their vices out of bad boys. Hence ... an unfailing supply of vicious sons was secured ... *   .   ʼ

Mobility, as the result of better transport, did as we have seen make boarding schools easier to use and therefore more acceptable. But transport had been progressing ever since the mid-eighteenth century; roads, vehicles, railways were all improved over the hundred years here considered. The stage coach on its regular run, in Tom Brown's Rugby, was a great deal more convenient than the servant and pillion, or the pony on which some boys still came to school in Dr. James' day. But in addition, there was a mobility of living which might have affected some schools favourably, though not specifically boarding schools. Families, presumably younger non-inheriting sons (this, the result of the English law of primogeniture), could, and did, settle in a town like Rugby or Harrow, for their boys to get the benefit of education there. This would be particularly true of retired fathers and of widows.† At any rate, a boy could now more easily take up a place in a popular, developing school.

Increased population and better transport may have played their parts in the rise of the Public Boarding School. But in every economic and educational text-book, the commonest motive attributed for this rise is mere snobbery. This, on analysis, means two different things—an "arrivist" parent vindicating himself and expressing his triumph over his own past, or else his care for the next generation, an insurance of his son's future. How widespread was either of these?

A Public School son could well be regarded as a sign of one's own triumph. Kean, returning after his first real success, exclaimed that his wife should now ride in her own carriage and "Charley will go to Eton". The carriage and the education were equally commodities that could be bought—a kind of extension of a man's personality. Garrick similarly sent two nephews to Eton, and successful men in every line would express their rise by doing what they considered was done by men in the highest ranks which they could penetrate. But this was different both from trying to get the best education for your son and from sending him where he would have a chance to become "better" or "better regarded" than his father, i.e. considered a gentleman.

As to the first, this was part of the whole mystique of education, very strong at the time. From the Francis Place type of workman upward through society, people believed in education as a kind of

---

* A. P. Stanley, *Life of Thomas Arnold, D.D.* p.89.

† The reverse took place at Cheltenham where such parents founded the College, and Ladies' College, to meet their needs.

talisman which you "got" and could use to do things for you. Mr. Tulliver, the Miller on the Floss, believed that if Tom learnt Latin he would be able to deal with the lawyers. (One has to include fiction in one's examples—real parents and their sons were much less articulate. J. M. Gaskell,* for instance, simply says it is a good thing for him to be at Eton, but not why.) Ruskin criticizes parents who think education is just something which will enable their sons to ring with confidence the bell marked VISITORS—not SERVANTS—at double-belled doors. Yet, understandably, the townsfolk who were offered a Public School education at their old Grammar School protested again and again† that the classical curriculum was not what they wanted for their sons. In fact the newly successful parent would be presenting his boy with an education which was totally unpractical.

We fall back, then, on the idea that a boy was to be made "a gentleman". Of what was meant by this term the schools took a moral rather than a social view. (Intellectual also, as in the case of Drs. James and Butler; *the scholar* was to be accepted as the gentleman irrespective of his antecedents.) Arnold's own view of "gentlemanly conduct" as an aim will be mentioned later. Dr. Moberly of Winchester made clear to the Clarendon Commission what he meant, so did several other Heads. They were in an old tradition. Dr. Nevill Coghill has pointed out that since Chaucer's day it has been fundamentally accepted that "gentilnesse"—the attribute of a gentleman—has to do with conduct as much as with family. It was also accepted that these standards of conduct were passed down by tradition and education in those families which had them, in theory at least. When schools took over the education of their children, they took over this tradition—in which other families' children could be included. That so much had in practice been lost in the eighteenth century did not invalidate the idea; in fact the very strength of the outcry against the schools as they were went to show that people expected them to be better. But there was not, nor had been, an old tradition of exclusiveness, and the boys whose parents sent them for social ambition, though it is unlikely that there were as many of those at this period as is generally implied—most parents of Arnold's Rugby being professional men—would have been received into the common life and reviving tradition of "gentilnesse".

It was the work of "superior men" to try to renew this tradition.

---

* See p.9

† At Harrow particularly. But evidence is found at Grammar Schools all over the country, from Oundle to the tiny school at Wickwar, Glos.

I

ETON IN THE 18th CENTURY

Hard as it may be for some to admit it, Eton stands in a different place from any other school. This difference can hardly be traced to one specific reasonable cause. Eton is, of course, older than most, having been founded before the Reformation,—but not the oldest, as it gives place in this to Winchester. It is a Royal foundation, but so are—nominally at any rate—a great number of other institutions. It also enjoyed royal patronage but that was chiefly evident in the 18th century, when Eton's place was already assured. (It was George III in compliment to whom the Collegers were permanently designated "King's Scholars", and whose birthday is annually celebrated on the Fourth of June.) Eton's buildings outclassed others. Yet Westminster grew up under the shadow of England's noblest ecclesiastical centre and other schools, like Sherborne, were attached to fine buildings. Eton certainly had not by the 18th century enjoyed many if any outstanding Headmasters. When Sir Roger de Coverley visited Westminster, he paused before the monument of Dr. Busby, Headmaster of Westminster School, and commented: "A great man—a very great man; he flogged my grandfather!" Not perhaps the comment—not yet the implied deduction, taken either way—that we should make to-day, but at the time, not only was Sir Roger's estimate accepted but everyone knew whom he was talking about. Very few heads of Eton would have gained—or merited—the curious tribute. Again, the name of William Lilly was entirely familiar: boys at most schools had been learning out of his Latin Grammar since he had been appointed by Dean Colet as head of the newly-founded school of St. Paul's. Shrewsbury had Challoner and Rugby had Holyoake, regarded as second founders of their respective schools. But the Eton Headmasters had been a dull lot.

Yet by the 18th century Eton had been the only school to be accepted consistently at the head of any list of "Great Schools" for the last 200 years—lists which might at one time or another have included such diverse places as Shrewsbury, Canterbury, Felsted and Pocklington. *They* rose and fell, but the foundation of Henry VI remained, not always admired but always first.

Numbers fluctuated, but were consistently greater than those of other boarding schools. About 350 to 400 was usual at the beginning of the 18th century. A decline set in soon after the Hanoverian accession; Eton headmasters tended to be High Church and were considered Jacobites—the result of this was shown positively in the advance of Harrow as a rival as well as in the check given to Eton. However, by mid-century, numbers were rising again. Eton was profiting from a change in the habits of families which had hitherto employed tutors to educate their sons and even to take them abroad. Now, for reasons of economy or fashion, boys were being sent away to school (though the tutor was sometimes still in attendance) and where should they go but Eton? Up went the numbers, and in the year 1765 they reached the record of 522, unchallenged by the few other boarding schools. Eton might well have been tempted, whatever complaints were made—and these detractors had hardly become vocal—to anticipate the formula about a race not yet run: Eclipse first, the rest nowhere.

It was this very success that made Eton difficult to reform. Things were never so bad that someone had to bestir himself lest the whole edifice fell. This is one point to be remembered in any assessment of Eton. Another is the actual structure of the College, as it had been founded. It was a commonplace that a founder of a charitable institution should ordain that his bequest to the school was to be shared with "bedesmen" or almspeople, the wardenship of the almshouse being often vested in the head of the school. But Henry VI had provided for a Provost and ten Fellows, as well as four clerks, six choristers, and twenty-five poor and infirm men, besides the Headmaster and twenty-five poor scholars. But it was the Provost (like the Warden at Winchester) who controlled the whole establishment. The numbers were altered and the scholars increased to 70 but the Provost remained the responsible authority. The Headmaster merely taught; it does not appear that he even drew up the curriculum. And though to some extent he developed authority over boys not on the foundation (who came to be known as Oppidans) everything to do with the life of the Collegers was the responsibility of the Provost. With respect to him, the Headmaster was an employee, hedged about on one hand by the Eton regulations and traditions and on the other by the opinions and decisions of the Provost and Fellows. In the matter of reform or change, nothing could have been done, even had a Headmaster so wished, without the help or at least agreement of the Provost. It must have felt to the Master like having the Chairman of a Board of Governors, on which the school was entirely dependent, living on the doorstep. No wonder the 17th and 18th century Headmasters had been men of so little quality; it was not until well into the 19th century that the Head began to be regarded as a person in his own right.

F. D. How, in *Six Great Schoolmasters,* sums this up in the first chapter (on Hawtrey):

> Eton, the greatest of English public schools, has depended for its position less upon the eminence of its Headmasters than upon the glorious traditions of the place. *

Not that at any time the traditions were universally accepted as glorious. From the days of John Locke (though *he* had been at Westminster), there was a certain prejudice against sending one's son to school at all if one could afford a tutor. Locke stressed the harm done to a boy by the unsupervised companionship of a crowd of other boys: it was perhaps Fielding's *Tom Jones* that finally drove home the harm that might equally well be done by bad tutors. But as noted, it *did* become the thing to send one's boy away—a fact for which one may offer two possible causes. One was the decay of the locally-founded Grammar schools, those hopeful institutions of the Tudor period which in the 17th century had taken such young sprigs as Lord North (at Thetford) who sat alongside the local squire's sons, farmers' sons and those of humbler rank. Most of those schools had now sunk very low in numbers, teaching and reputation. But—the second point—a habit had grown up of sending boys away, not exactly locally but regionally. Before their decline, there had been numerous boarders at Shrewsbury, Rugby, Oundle, even Felsted (where Oliver Cromwell had sent his sons); the gentry and lower nobility had built up a tradition in this, so when these schools also failed more and more parents looked to a further boarding school.

But why Eton? This is really rather a mystery—though perhaps the prospects of a comfortable provision for life, which will be touched on, had something to do with it. It was not that the school was universally admired, for it has, over the last 200 years received a continual series of kicks no less than ha'pence from Etonians themselves and others.

At all events, as Eton was the one authenticated Public School† of the 18th century, no study, however slight, of such schools and their

---

* F. D. How, *Six Great Schoolmasters,* p.1.

† Eton as a whole is a Collegiate foundation and the school being part of it is often referred to as Eton College, strictly "The College of the Blessed Mary of Eton". "College" is rightly used of the "foundation boys", i.e. Scholars. But here the word "School" will be used as a rule, except when the whole establishment is meant, or the Scholars, alone.

Headmasters can fail to refer to it. But the first thing is to consider not so much what people thought about it as what actually went on. For this there are two main sources (other than College Register and the many references in memoirs and individual biographies), one of which is an account set down by an 18th century Etonian who was afterwards to become a Headmaster himself—though not at Eton. He was Thomas James, whose life and work at Rugby still lay before him. This document is entitled *Account of Eton Discipline and Education* and is a remarkably detailed and comprehensive exposition of the whole organisation of the school work, the exact curriculum and the method of teaching in 1766.* The MS, which was paraphrased in Maxwell-Lyte's *A History of Eton College*, was in 1899 "in the possession of the Rt. Hon. Vernon Harcourt who had acquired it from the Rev. C. C. James, lately an Assistant Master at Eton", Thomas James' grandson. It has now been bequeathed to the Eton School library in the Harcourt Collection.

It begins, rather oddly, with the "holydays" (this spelling is used throughout) and the extraordinary effect which the need to accommodate to these had on what we should regard as the school timetable:

> If a week be regular, that is, if there happens in it no Saints' Days or Court Holydays (N.B. *This was fairly rare*) or Founder's days etc. then Tuesday is a *whole* holyday and Thursday *half* a holyday and Saturday a "Play" after divine Service in the afternoon (i.e. after 4'clock)
> Court Holydays are the King's and Queen's birthdays, Coronation days, etc., but not all the Royal family's (sc. birthdays), as they are not observed here.

(Remembering the extent of George III's family one can understand that even the loyalty of Eton might have been strained in this.)

The section is followed by a most elaborate sort of calendar, showing just how one "irregular" day affected the whole of the week, besides the fact that "on all Saints' Days and their Eves, Court Holydays and Founder's Days and all Play days whatever, the boys attend Church Morning and Afternoon." The most disconcerting was when such a day fell on Saturday, which set all the subsequent week wrong: "this week's business is reckoned to require more application

---

* It seems to have been drawn up while James was at school but revised and annotated some five years later for the benefit of a friend about to set up a "Preparatory" (Proprietory) school. This revision, which would bring it up to James' Cambridge days, would account for a kind of ambiguity in style, as if it might have been written originally in the first person.

than any other, because of the many school days together in it, for a 'play at four' is not much better than a whole school day."

The convention was that one of the half holydays was a reward for good work:

The Half holyday on Thursday is begged in this manner—The Master sends one of the best exercises of the Sixth Form only to the Provost, who upon receiving it grants a play. This is reckoned a great honour, and if at private schools a boy's exercise should in this manner weekly obtain a Holyday from the Master, it would encourage in the boys a spirit of Emulation. The Exercise is carried in at 12 o'clock . . . The boy who *goes up for play* as we term it, is excused eleven o'clock schooltime, because he is supposed to be writing his exercise over fair, on gilded paper, that he may carry it at twelve o'clock for a half holyday which he begs this afternoon.

The next point dealt with is the attendance required, paradoxically (still) called—"Absence". Even on a Holyday the amount of "calling" strikes one as an outrageous waste of time; indeed there seems to modern ears quite a prison-like ring about it.

On a whole Holyday, the *absence* (that is a list of all the Boy's names read over and every one answering to his name, *Here Sir)* is at nine o'clock and Church at eleven. Absence at Two, Church at three, absence at four, absence at six in the summer, but in the winter, the boys are supposed to be in their houses after Six o'clock and then the Assistants going about to different Houses call absence between 7 and 8.

The precise form in which the reason for not attending must be given is explained; illness must be vouched for by a note from the Dames who keep the boarding houses, "in the Dame's Hand Writing, in this manner:

James a cold

Mary Naylor"

The School Hours section opens with a typically English inaccuracy of nomenclature, the statement that they "go into the school a little before seven o'clock (this is called Six o'clock lesson) and stay till half an hour after seven".

The rest of the hours were: eight to nine, eleven to twelve, three to four, and four to five, each lesson being presumably an hour long. In the Intervals, or on the Half Holydays, were inserted such extra-curricular subjects as Writing, Arithmetic, French, Drawing, Dancing—unless these hours were used for preparing work with one's Tutor. These tutorial hours must have accounted for a good deal of time, and so must preparation, but neither is mentioned by James. Of course the "School Business" was simply the exposition and hearing of the classical texts, and of this he gives considerable details both as to method and books—see below.

To conclude "times and seasons":—

The Vacations are three times in the year, Easter, Christmas and August, vulgarly called Bartlemetide—a most strange corruption from St. Bartholomew's name. The Christmas Holydays last a month, and the school breaks up the second Monday in December, about 10th. . . or 15th day of the month. The Easter Holydays last a Fortnight and the School breaks up on the Monday before Easter Sunday . . . The Holydays at August begin the first Monday in August and last a month.

It would be tedious to go into "School Business" (i.e. the timetable and curriculum) as minutely as does James, but a few quotations indicate what the boys actually learnt and the method employed.

The V and VI Forms go up to lessons together. The boys sit down in the school and the Master stands up.

Monday at 8 we are used to repeat about 20 verses in the Greek Testament, one boy saying 6 or 7 verses and then another repeating as many, but this is as the Master pleases. These verses are asked on Saturday at 2. [*i.e. a boy asks the Master to set them.*—A.C.P.]

Monday at 11. The Lesson for 11 o'clock school is asked by the Captain in 8 o'clock school at which time the Master sets it. First some one of the form is called upon by the Master to construe Homer (the lesson is about 35 lines; the VI form turn the words into Latin, the V form into English) who construes perhaps about 10 or 14 lines, then another boy is called upon who generally finishes the lesson. The Questions asked are chiefly taken from Clarke's Notes (which is the Homer mostly in use among us) and Questions are asked from Pope's notes. Similar passages of Virgil are asked. The VI is expected to make answer to these Questions.

The lesson being finished by the VI form, the Master turns round to the V (the VI still remaining in their places and attending)* and there calls up a boy who construes about 7 or 8 lines and then another until the lesson is finished . . .

Many boys have pencil in their hands and take down from the Master's mouth such observations as he shall give them in his explanation of the lesson. The V and VI boys are supposed to take

---

* This seems asking for trouble—arising from boredom. It sheds some light on the difficulties of subsequent Heads.

down all the Master's annotations. There is no doubt but that the Master studies every lesson before he comes in school.

This last remark seems rather naif; the schoolboy·might think the Master did so. When James himself became a teacher, he might have found that constant repetition of a very few authors over many years rendered this labour unnecessary. As to the preponderance of memory-work and note-taking, which modern teachers would sadly disapprove, the boy of the period took it all in his stride.

Monday at 3. The lesson for 3 o'clock is asked by the Captain before he goes out of eleven o'clock school (About 20 lines of SCRIP-TORES ROMANI).* The VI boys are called up (two or three) who construe the lesson. The Master having consulted Dr. Middleton's Cicero asks the boys questions (if there be any) about the lesson, questions related to the History of the times, Tully's life and works. After this the Master calls up the V form boys (about six in number) who construe the lesson and then the two forms are dismissed. The VI and V boys are supposed to read in their leisure hours Dr. Middleton's. Cicero, Tully's Offices, Ovid's long and short verses, Spectator, etc. Milton, Pope, Roman History, Grecian History, Potter's Antiquities and all other books necessary towards making a compleat scholar.

This astounding summary looks as if it had come down (with the Walton-like spelling of "compleat" and the use of the Elizabethan "Tully" for Cicero) almost unchanged from the 17th century. Even more significant, we have here what was to become the staple diet of the Public schools for more than a century; it spread from Eton to Rugby, from Rugby to Shrewsbury and thence to all the older foundations and most of the newer ones. There are two main additions—Greek Tragedy and Horace's Odes, which James hastens to mention—and the scholar is "compleat". This could also be the making of the "compleat politician", for Horace especially was frequently on the lips of speakers in Parliament, in the Commons no less than in the Lords. At Eton the Odes formed part of the Declamations and in the summer term a boy would learn seven or eight of them by heart. Also—

A week before the Elections is set apart to learn plays in, and we finish a play a week. We have declamations made about a month before every holydays. The Funeral Orations are learnt . . . Themes are given.

---

* This was a well-known collection of Latin extracts. It was a complaint up to much later that boys only studied these extracts, seldom whole works of authors.

Holyday Tasks (presumably for home) included 200 lines of Latin and 200 of Greek to learn, and the turning into (Latin) verse of, for example, the Lamentations of Jeremiah.

All this is for the Upper School. James goes methodically but in less detail, through the curriculum of the Lower School. This consisted of the Fourth and Third Forms: "The Sense" and "The Nonsense" ("They make some nonsense verses out of Terence"); The Last Remove, the Second Form and the First Form. The last-named do nothing but the Grammar, and say the catechism; presumably it is for such as they that the Writing Master is employed. The others read various authors, and make sentences to illustrate different words in Latin. The Latin and Greek Testaments are read, especially on a Saint's day. Progress from one form to another is dealt with as follows:

When boys are removed from one form to another, we have a custom of trying them in the books they have already learnt . . . If their tryal is satisfactory they are advanced with glory, if otherwise, kept back to their shame . . . If boys gain their Removes with honour, we have a good custom of rewarding each with a shilling (if high in the school, half a crown) which is given them by the Dames and placed to the Father's account . . . The same custom obtains when a boy distinguishes himself by a good exercise or wins a place . . . sometimes a boy loses a place by Idleness.

Particularly interesting in view of all the ink that has been spilled over the Prefect system, are the various remarks (not all in one section) about Praepositors—"Prepostors," he writes it:

Prepostors as Monitors are chosen . . . to gather exercises [i.e. to collect the boys' work] to mark the boys' names every school time and Church time (i.e. Church produced an "Absence"—which made one almost every hour on some days) and write down the names of the boys who are not present at the time of absence. When these prepostors, five in number . . . find any boys missing, they enquire about the reason for his absence; at the Dames'. . . . The Upper Prepostor calls over the boys' names at Absence, delivers the rod to the Master when he punishes a boy (at the same time one or two of the other prepostors attend to assist at the execution). The Upper Prepostor walks round the School to keep the boys quiet at eleven o'clock and five o'clock school. The Lower Prepostor does the same at eight o'clock and three o'clock school.

These prepostors are chosen weekly. The Sixth Form Prepostors only are excused the business of the School in the time of their office. These . . . take it by turns to attend six o'clock school in the summer when the Lower School go, in order to keep them quiet.

The Fifth Form prepostor, winter and summer, attends the six o'clock lesson to say the prayers ... He also reads the prayers at eight o'clock, *Preces in Longo Cubiculo* (formerly read in the Long Chamber) *Hora Ottava Vespertino* ... Prayers being ended, the Collegers are locked up in their Chambers. The doors are unlocked on a six o'clock lesson morning at six, on another day at eight, to prevent rambling in the morning.

And although we tend now to pay more attention to those boys who complained, justifiably enough by our standards—there were plenty like James who accepted the place as they found it, fantastic timetables, narrow curriculum, formal discipline, "Absences" and all, without any demand for reformation. This would to some degree explain the slowness of the Masters in making any move for improvement. Another was no doubt their lack of initiative; they cannot be considered a remarkable succession of men. But the hand of custom lay heavy on them as on the rest of the school. A final quotation from James exemplifies:

There are certain bounds fixed to the School and the whole Sixth Form can have any boy punished if they find him beyond these bounds. They can likewise have a boy (punished) for not making his own exercise (i.e. copying), Swearing, Drinking, or any other fault, which Power granted to them has been one great means of preserving regularity.

He might have said "preserving continuity" for it shows how minutely everything had been laid down in the early statutes, including the duties of the *Praepositores,* which had changed little in the previous 400 years.*

It is worth following this minute and non-committal *"Account of Discipline"* with a look at another document of about the same date; *Nugae Etonenses* 1765–66, a manuscript of doubtful origin, reprinted in the *Etoniana* No. 4, 1905. It is a completely schoolboyish kind of record and typically begins by giving a list of masters and assistants, with the nickname of each—obviously esoteric but offering a field for speculation.

Perny-pojax Dampier
Gronkey Graham
Pogy Roberts
Cat Edwards
Skimmer-Jack Norbury
Buck Elkins

---

* This also shows that, half a century before Arnold, the authority of "prefects" had been given to all Sixth-formers.

Henry Angelo, son of the Fencing Master, in his own reminiscences of his schooldays at Eton, confirms some of these, and adds (1767):

Mazzard Heath	Numpy Sumner
Barber Davis	Perpendicular John Prior
Bantam Sumner	Quidnunc Hawtrey
Wigblock Prior	

He adds (and here we sense the gulf which lasted for another century):

Writing Masters:	Domine Evans, Hardy, Jem Jarrard
French:	Lemoine, Porny
Drawing:	Cozens
Dancing:	Hickford
Fencing:	Angelo
Boxing:	William Stevens, the Nailor

and, for good measure:

Jawing and Blackguard:	My Lord the Bargeman.

Cozens, incidentally was Alexander Cozens, the well-known landscape painter (1717–86) who had travelled in Italy and who taught the family of George III as well as the Eton boys (so did his successor, Richard Cooper, Jr.). Alexander was the father of the even better known painter, J. R. Cozens, and was alleged—probably without foundation—to have been a natural son of Peter the Great.

Hickford, the Dancing Master, was on one occasion shut into his own Dancing school; an incident set down in the *Nugae* among *Remarkable Occurrences* but—alas!—with no explanatory comment.

Names are given of the whole outfit—"the officers of the College" which included Gardener, Clock-winder, Rod-maker—at first sight a sinister term, though not so macabre as the inclusion of the Sexton. But perhaps the Rods were for fishing, not for personal application, though we know these instuments of punishment *did* wear out through frequent usage. There was apparently work for the Pursuivant of Runaways, with three assistants; there were the Waterman, the Chapel Singing-men (from St. George's Chapel; the boys formed no choir) the Organist (Webb); the Medical staff, including the Tooth-drawer. There were the Domini, who kept houses, and the Dames, who far outnumbered them; the tradesmen, the Tennis-court and Coffee-house keepers, the Shoemaker and Tailor, the Muffin man and three Stagecoachmen.

Here is a picture of a lively, robust, and busy society. There is, as Mr. Ogilvie points out, more than a smack of aristocracy about it, but it has the merit which enables aristocracy to survive—the regarding of every human being not as a functionary but as an individual person.

The schoolboy was interested in more than people, and there is a list—as any boy might make for fun—of Games, Bathing Places, Favourite Eatables, Sights, Customs and Remarkable Occurrences. A few examples only will be quoted, to show the kind of thing that, complementary to the studies, praepositors' duties and Long Chamber, made up the life of the Eton boy.

The games included not only cricket, fives, and Battledores, but peg-tops, hoops (Gray's "rolling circle"), marbles, hopscotch, Puss-in-the-corner (who would have thought these last had such a distinguished past?), Hunt the Hare, "Goals"—not apparently for football, which game is added later by another hand—trap-ball (which Locke had discovered half-a-century before) and such mysteries as Heading, Bally Cally, Cloister and Flyer, Gigs, Hunt the Dark Lanthorn, Sinks and Scarecaps (possibly, Starecaps). A note adds: "Slides down the side of the stairs from Cloyster to kitchen"—a form of tray-toboganning. Among Bathing Places, a few names survive, to this day. There are Sandy Hole, Cuckooware, Deadman's Hole etc. Certain "Rides" are noted, and Places of Resort still extant, and Pony Races at Datchett. The Bull-baiting and Cockfighting grounds are named and the Billiard Table keeper. Fruiterers, both men and women abound; there is even the Purveyor of Oysters, Teddy Goad.

This brings us to Favourite Eatables. (Incidentally, many books name drunkenness among the evils of Public School life. The only drinks mentioned by this boy are milk-and-water and a "Bottle of Capillaise.") Once one has got past "Fromentary, Elecampane, Angelica", which sound exotic, the list, from Macaroons and Raspberry Cakes to Sausages and "potted Beef or Moody's hot rolls and cheese at Cuckooware" sounds like every schoolboy's dream. The "Sights" are more curious and include The Madman at Upton, Miss Guy at Castle Prayers (Why? She had also been included among the "Toasts") and, anticipating the Fairchild Family's gruesome lesson, "Watkins hanging in chains".

The Remarkable Occurrences are only a little more outrageous than any schoolboy might write home about: The Battle between the Boys and the Butchers; Dr. Ashton falling into a fit while reading the morning service, "by which" (one can catch the gleeful tone) "the boys were sent out of Church"; more remote, are "Onslow flogged in the middle of the school for running away"; "Dr. Barnard cutting off Hare's pig-tail in Hall with a greasy commons knife." And, though sympathetic, there is little unusual in the same Dr. Barnard's farewell speech, concluding with "Stet Fortuna Domus. . . and God bless you all."

The Eton Magazine also reprinted a contemporary letter (from

William Grimston to Michael Fleming, an Old Etonian recently left)
with a reference to "the poorest Montem* there ever was in this
century." and a boy who "got himself expelled from Eton by behaving
himself very impertinently to Dr. Foster" (Headmaster). The Letter
goes on:

> We are in daily expectation of losing Dr. Dampier. He expects to be
> Fellow in room of Dr. Line who is so bad he cannot live the week
> out. . . I believe Mr. Roberts is fixed upon to be my Tutor who is the
> only man in the place I have any regard for.

(Roberts became Provost in 1781, but this reference throws little light
on his nickname of Pogy—unless it be "Podgy", which his portrait bears
out.) The following references are to the Dames and their Assistants;
how far, one wonders were these typical of the ladies who had charge
of Eton boys?

> Mrs. Sturges is very good-natured to the boys, and behaves herself
> very freely amongst us; now and then gives a bottle of wine or a
> bowl of punch which she makes very good. . . The Windsor balls
> were very brilliant. Mrs. Sturges was at them both. . . Mrs. Prior is
> brought to bed of a daughter which makes Mr. P. as happy as
> possible, and your Tutor has got a female not quite a month old.
> Mrs. Sturges desires her love to you and compliment from all our
> friends, but there are none but Ford and Gough and they both go at
> Election.

No feeling of monasticism here. Public school life was as close to
domesticity as life in some of our modern Preparatories. The Dames are
clearly to be regarded as Hostesses rather than Landladies. Here their
social status is shown:

> Mrs. Harris is lately married to one Dr. Cust. He is brother to the
> Speaker of the House of Commons.

Yet the writer himself is rather a sober boy:

> I take no other amusement here but tennis, never enter the billiard
> rooms. . . Ascot races are just over, but no sport upon the Turf that I
> heard of, for I was not at them.

This letter, like the *Nugae* indicates a much gentler, more even, and
in some ways a more modern form of life than the picture which the
lurid accounts of a later Eton have built up. There is a boyish tone
about it all, and a normality (on the whole; "Watkins hanging in
chains" being accepted as a normal part of the 18th, and indeed early
19th century) which should weigh against the rather precious and

---

* See Appendix A.

scholarly reminiscences of Horace Walpole and his friends, with Gray's *Ode on the Distant Prospect of Eton College* on one side, and Sydney Smith's strictures on the other.

There is, surprisingly, no mention in the *Nugae* of that controversial subject, fagging, but as this is raised in all accounts of all Public Schools of the last two centuries, we may as well acquiesce in the idea that an account of Eton is the proper place to mention it. And no doubt by reason of historical age, it may have begun here, though later it presented every variety of aspect. There is Arnold's justification of it on grounds of law and social hierachy—not, of course "class" but school status. There is B. H. Kennedy writing that he would never apply to be Head of Harrow (where he was then an Assistant) because he was so much out of sympathy with the form taken by fagging there, as contrasted with the practice at Shrewsbury. And at Rugby there was W. S. Landor's little fag whom he took out fishing to tie the lines, regarded as a mascot and whom he tipped with his "merit money": "Here, Blacky, take this." Later there is a great chunk of evidence about it before the Clarendon Commission who required almost every old boy they summoned to say something about it. But clearly the practice at its most severe was traditionalized at Eton, and primarily in College. (No doubt it is now hedged about with quite different but equally accepted traditions.)

The best explanation for its growth is to look at the illustration of Long Chamber—that dreary ward which would create a storm of protest if a Local Authority were now to attempt to house in it any unfortunate cases for whom they were responsible—and to remember the lack of servitors. The catering side should have been well enough provided for (according to the Statutes) but for rooms or person, the service was quite absurd. Even in Thring's time (from 1831) there was "one ill-paid servant to seventy boys." This fellow's work was to sweep the floors (of at least three other rooms besides the great domitory) to make the beds and light the fires—though not to keep them up. One should remember also the scandalous provision of meals and the absolute necessity for boys, big and small, to supplement these with food obtained and prepared by themselves—prepared, in those non-plastic days, must have included washing-up. Of course any other niceties (except actual laundry)* such as shoe cleaning or getting water for washing (and shaving where needed?) were performed by the boys themselves. Not even light was provided: candles had to be bought and, candlesticks lacking, were stuck into a hole made in the cover of a book. The windows were so high that a boy standing on his bed could

---

* Personal laundry was extra and one fag at least had to make out his master's laundry list.

barely see out of them. Perhaps their placing had one advantage, the draught which whistled through the gaping casements were not so painfully near the boys' heads.

Granted that the best home conditions of the period were unlikely to be nice by our standards—nor even the persons therein, before Brummell's insistence on clean linen—the squalor at Eton must have been notorious. And remembering that the boys high in the school were, in spite of indifferent class-teaching, expected to show up their themes and verses regularly, to their Tutor if not to the Headmaster, or to show reason why they should not be punished for the omission, it is easy to see how the assignment of chores to younger boys arose. It is hardly in nature for a boy accustomed to cheap service at home (this was one advantage the 18th century had for the well-to-do over the 20th—almost every household however humble would have had its skivvy) not to look for it among those less well-established or high in the school, and as a senior would argue, less busy than himself. It hardly becomes those critics of the present who during their schooling have had their rooms swept and three meals a day cooked and served by regularly-paid school servants—or devoted mothers—to cast opprobrium on their predecessors without stopping to think seriously what *they* might have done had they been studying without these services.

Of course the practice lent itself to inexcusable abuses, about which fierce protests have rightly been written, but often the root cause has been ignored and the system put down to natural cruelty among boys or—our usual whipping-boy—class distinction. (Any reader of memoirs among Eminent Victorians must realize that distinctions of rank had little effect in these particular school experiences of Collegers.) But an example of our bad conscience and obsession with the evils of class is shown in a passage of a modern author which brings out a truth but does not push it far enough.

> All this may appear callous and certainly it was a callous age. The economic historian recounts the sufferings which the rich at that time imposed upon the poor, and deduces from that a lesson of class war. But the sufferings which the rich imposed upon the poor were not so notably greater than those which they imposed on their own children. . . It was not so much an age in which the rich were cruel to the poor as an age in which the rich were cruel.*

No doubt, but though the cruelty of the rich may have made itself more strongly and more widely felt, that of the poor was just as vicious, as a moment's consideration of the fates of the apprentices, animals and

---

* Christopher Hollis, *Eton, a History,* p.173.

the weak in general will show. (We may say that the rich *ought* to have been better; that is another question.) In fact, it was a cruel age. Period.

Fagging, then, may be said to have developed naturally from the situation, the system or the age, but these are abstractions. If human beings are sought as causes of this and other ills at Eton, the Provost and Fellows must qualify. To find out exactly how it came about that they could do so much harm, one would have to master the whole financial set up—expounded in masterly fashion in *Eton: How it Works* (J. D. R. McConnell, 1967), but without going into details it is clear that the Fellows absorbed an unfair proportion of the funds, while the Provosts consistently met the simplest and most justifiable request for improvement with complete lack of sympathy. Examples could be multiplied but even as late as 1838, when the age of improvement was thought to have started, a request that water might be laid on in the College was dismissed with the rebuff: "You will be wanting gas and Turkey carpets next." Even more outrageous was the appropriation of a great part of a sum actually left by Godolphin for the purpose of improving the boys' food. Only a small portion was so expended, the greater part was ploughed back into the school's finances in general.

The Provost himself, who reigned supreme over the whole establishment, needing the support of the Fellows only in such serious matters as the appointment of the Headmaster or a notable reform, had often himself previously been the Head. Three offices, Provost of Eton, Provost of King's College (Cambridge) and Headmaster of Eton, were closely knit and, together with the Lower Master and Assistants, provided a notorious example of administrative in-breeding. The following list shows how often New Provost was but Old Headmaster writ large:

Headmasters	*Provosts of Eton*
1711 Andrew Snape	1732 Henry Bland
1720 Henry Bland	1746 Stephen Sleech
1728 William George*	1765 Edward Barnard
1743 William Cooke*	1781 William Hayward Roberts
1745 John Sumner	1791 Jonathan Davies
1754 Edward Barnard	1809 Joseph Goodall
1765 John Foster	1840 Francis Hodgson
1773 Jonathan Davies	1853 Edward Craven Hawtrey
1792 George Heath	1862 Charles Old Goodford
1802 John Goodall	1884 John James Hornby
1809 John Keate	
1834 Edward Craven Hawtrey	*Provosts of King's College
1853 Charles Old Goodford	
1862 Edward Balston	
1868 John James Hornby	
1884 Edmond Warre	

Even more remarkable were the family connections—the literal in-breeding. Eton College and Masters were not bound by the rule of celibacy which, whatever its disadvantages, did at least make for a turnover and some new blood at the Universities. One paragraph of Eton genealogies will suffice as example (dates at school omitted):

> About 1690 the organist at Eton was named Sleech, whose widow re-married Mr. Newborough, the Headmaster. His son, Richard Sleech. . . became a Fellow of Eton in 1715, and Canon of Windsor, and his daughter married Bishop Weston of "Weston's Yard". Canon Sleech himself married a daughter of Stephen Upman, Fellow of Eton, and was the father of Stephen Sleech who became Fellow of Eton in 1728 and succeeded Dr. Bland as Provost. . . Of Provost Sleech's sisters, one married Charles Hawtrey, another married George Harris, Fellow of Eton. . . and a third was the wife of Dr. Cooke, the Headmaster. Henry Sleech, a Master at Eton, and another member of the family, married Dr. Cooke's sister, and their daughter married Thomas Dampier (N.B. son of the Lower Master). . . By such family combinations was Eton College governed.*

Even at a lower stage the *intellectual* in-breeding was considerable. A boy would (almost certainly, if a Colleger) go on to King's College, Cambridge, and either obtain a Fellowship (to which he would be of right entitled as an Etonian) or might return to Eton as a master within a few years. Any appointment of an Assistant who had *not* been at Eton and King's, though this did not infringe any actual statute, was looked on with suspicion. Keate managed twice to effect this; Hawtrey was frustrated by the then Provost. In sum, with her assured position in the world outside, her extraordinarily complicated administration, ordained by King Henry VI's statutes or petrified by tradition, with the vested interests of Provost and Fellows, and even Masters, in the *status quo*, and with the utterly parochial family set-up, Eton was going to find immense difficulty in changing.

Even had they wanted improvements, the 18th century Heads would have found that they did not carry the system, the system carried them. Some Heads were fierce disciplinarians like William George ("Dionysus the Tyrant"); others more amiable, like the well-named Bland, and Barnard. Some were better scholars than others; good were William Cooke and John Foster, both of whom, however, seem to have failed in administration and discipline—in fact one of the outstanding organised "revolts" took place under the latter. Most of the Heads settled for a quiet life, hoping to avoid such unfavourable publicity and the drop in

---

* L. Cust, *History of Eton,* 1899.

numbers which generally ensued after a "Rebellion". In any case, they were employed to teach, and if a boy wanted to learn most Heads had sufficient scholarship to teach him, while a Tutor was either provided from among the Assistants at the school or provided by his parents for the boy himself, and was supposed to overlook his work. If the boy was not interested in learning, there were plenty of ways by which he could avoid being encumbered with it.

Few men of personality, unless they looked ahead to the security of a Provostship, can have been anxious to take up the invidious position of Headmaster, yet it was bad luck for Eton that the first Head to become widely known was famed not as a scholar nor as a man of the world but as a disciplinarian—which meant a great beater. This reputation was attached to John Keate (1809—34), of whom more hereafter.

II

SOME EARLY HARROVIANS

Up to the end of the 17th century, no school had in public estimation consistently joined the three earlier ones—Eton, Westminster and Winchester. It would be 50 years before the tide began that was to raise one school after another and land it in this category. But there *was* a school which, for a long time and beyond any other was to be regarded as Eton's counterpart. It can hardly be the cricket match only that has for so long linked Eton with Harrow. It is rather that Harrow got a long start over its next rival (Rugby) as a non-local institution for educating the aristocracy and began to take precedence even of Winchester and Westminster in the popular mind as "the next thing to Eton."

Harrow, an Elizabethan Grammar School, well exemplified the characteristics of such a foundation. John Lyon, yeoman (c.1514-92), owner of a farm at Preston, just below Harrow Hill, first asked Queen Elizabeth for a charter for his new school in 1571. This places him after the founders of St. Paul's, for instance, of Shrewsbury, or of Rugby, but well in the main flow of the Elizabethan originators of schools. Unlike many, his school was not paired with an establishment of almsmen but it was linked in his will with other obligations, one much resented by later Governors being that they should repair roads between Harrow and London, for which, however, he left the interest on special lands. Lyon wanted his foundation to be called a Free Grammar School, and in the later Charter of 1590, the Governors were given their first corporate existence under the title of "Custodes et Gubernatores possessionum Johannis Lyon in villa de Harrowe supra Montem."

As so often, it is impossible to learn much of the man whose initiative and money set the school going—nor is it even certain whether this was the first, or a new, foundation of learning there. John Lyon had no arms to leave his school, but the Governors immediately got themselves a punning seal with a lion rampant. His good deeds are set out on a brass that depicts him and his wife, Joan, in substantial, be-ruffed, but somewhat severe, clothes:

John Lyon. . . founded a free grammar school in this p'ish to have continuance for ever and for maintenaunce thereof and for releyfe of the poore and of some poore scholters in the universityes, repayring of highwayes and other good and charitable uses hath made convayaunce of lands of good value to a corporacion graunted for that purpose. Prayse be to the author of all goodnes who make us myndeful to follow his good example.

Two years before his death, John Lyon formulated the meticulous Ordinances and Rules for the government of that school which, in spite of the Charter nearly 20 years old, had not yet come into being. (When the Governors did begin to build, they fell into a common error and overspent by 100% the £300 allowed for putting up the school, so the opening was delayed till 1615.) No records exist at John Lyon's school itself of the original boys, but at Caius College, Cambridge, there are lists in which the schools of the undergraduates in residence are mentioned, including early collegers from Harrow, several being of the Gerrard family. Gilbert Gerrard, a neighbour of Lyon's, had successfully defended the future Queen Elizabeth when on trial for complicity in the Wyatt rebellion; she was not ungrateful and eventually Gerrard became Sir Gilbert and Attorney General. Gilbert was co-treasurer of Gray's Inn with Sir Nicholas Bacon, father of the statesman and essayist. The Statutes drawn up for Harrow resemble so closely Bacon's own for the Grammar School at St. Albans that it is a feasible conclusion that the benefactors of the two schools worked together, though the schools themselves were to have very different careers.

The school was well endowed with Exhibitions to the universities; the Cambridge ones were tied to Gonville and Caius College, and Dr. Caius of Ruislip, may well have been a personal friend of Lyon's. But the holders of these exhibitions were very carefully designated as, in the first place, local boys: "The most apt and most poor sort that be meete; the poor kindsfolk of me, the said John Lyon, if any such be, and such as are born within the said Parish of Harrow, being apt to learn, poor and meete to go to the University, to be preferred before otheis." Failing such, the exhibitions would be thrown open to others. Both the places at the Free Grammar School and the Exhibitions to the Universities were "to be indifferently appointed and bestowed by the . . . Governors upon such as are most meet for towardness, poverty and painfulness [i.e. taking pains] without any partiality or sinister affection." Unfortunately for the working of this admirable scheme, it fails to explain how "towardness" and poverty, if not found together in one boy, are to be weighed against each other. This was a fundamental and recurring problem in such wills.

One of the most fateful of Lyon's ideas is contained in both the Ordinances and his Rules. The Governors were to have discretion to fix the numbers from time to time not only of the poor scholars to be taught by the schoolmaster "freely for the stipend" but of others, "a meete and competent number of scholars. . . to be received for the further profit and commodity of the said schoolmaster."

This idea is extended:

> The Schoolmaster may receive over and above the youth of the said inhabitants within the Parish, so many Foreigners* as the whole number may be well taught and applied and the place can conveniently contain by the judgement and discretion of the Governors. And of the Foreigners he may take such stipend and wages as he can get (Lyon's own kin excepted). So that he take pains with all indifferently as well of the Parish as Foreigners, as well of poor as of rich; but the discretion of the Governors shall be looked that he do. [*take pains with all impartially.*]

It would be difficult enough for any modern historian of Elizabethan social life however impartial, however knowledgeable about parallel institutions and bequests, to know exactly what was in the mind of the 16th century benefactor in writing these clauses. They have been interpreted at different times as showing very different intentions. They have been criticized for allowing and encouraging parents not indigenous to Harrow to plant themselves locally so that their sons might have the benefit of good teaching and school life without leaving home, whereas it is argued that these advantages should have been confined to the native population. That Lyon foresaw large numbers of such families is possible but unlikely. It is even less likely that the *non*-local, paying boarders—the "Foreigners"* of the Rules—should have been envisaged as predominating in the school, yet when one thinks of Shrewsbury at the time, or the model of Eton, one cannot call it impossible. The clauses have been condemned as merely loopholes whereby through a legal subtlety the wealthy and aristocratic classes were enabled to keep out the local scholars for whose benefit alone the school came into existence; many are the tirades and innuendoes on this development. But the truth is, that we simply do not know what were the views of the founder at the time; much less what he *would* have wished in the very different circumstances of the following centuries. Harrow, only one of many in the same case, has been mentioned in this context both because of its present status and

---

* "Foreigners" as a term meaning "not from the neighbourhood" can be widely paralleled; the Shrewsbury lists, for example, have *"alieni."*

because at a critical time it became a legal test case. But the inhabitants who brought a complaint of the influx of non-local boys got nowhere, presumably because of the clauses quoted above.

The first scholar admitted in 1615 was the son of the Vicar of Harrow, and this, together with the fact that the majority of the Harrow scholars at Caius College in Lyon's lifetime were sons of Governors or parents of means, indicates that "gentle and simple", fee-paying and foundationers, were alike admitted from the beginning both to the school and Exhibitions. The school prospered and the "foreigners" came from as far off as Wales or East Anglia. Under William Horne, an Etonian appointed Headmaster in 1669, the numbers rose to over 100. There were several boarding or lodging-houses, one was kept by the Headmaster, others by Dames—a set-up in which the Etonian must have felt at home and which perhaps he even fostered. Since right up to the 19th century, boys might come as young as eight years, some parents (who themselves made the arrangements for lodging) may have preferred a Dame. She would, of course, have to be approved by the school authorities as her name would be valid on an "Absence" notice or a note to a tradesman. The age of leaving also sounds low to us. In 1780 the first three boys on the school list were but 16 years old.

As "a good scholar and a very good natured man" (and the first example here of the fashion of obtaining a Headmaster from Eton) Horne might have done for Harrow what Thomas James, also an Etonian, did for Rugby later. But it was too early or the times were not propitious; perhaps 17th century Grammar schools did not as a whole inspire confidence in parents. As far as Headmasters were concerned, Harrow was beginning a see-saw period. The good Mr. Horne was succeeded by a nonentity who in turn was followed by another Eton and King's man, Thomas Brian (1691-1730). He seems at least to have won the support of the Governors who repaired and enlarged his house thereby encouraging boarders. As the number of Foundationers stayed the same, the increase to a peak of 144 must have meant a great increase in "Foreigners". Brian, who had only the Usher and Writing Master to help him, besides the Dames who taught reading and religion, was allowed an assistant (but had to pay for him himself). He appointed the man who became his son-in-law and successor who, though he seems to have been a good teacher and when first appointed a satisfactory Head, shamefully blotted his copy-book, as the Minutes of the Governors show (26th April 1746).

Whereas the Revd. Dr. James Cox, Master of the Free Grammar Schoole, has for a great while last past lived a disorderly, drunken, idle life and neglected the care of the Schoole, by which means it is very much decreased, did on or about Easter Week abscond upon account of his great extravagencies, and running into debt more than he is able to pay, therefore for these his misdoings we are of opinion that he shall be displaced from being a schoolmaster, and declare the place to be void.

DANIEL GRAHAM. CHANDOS. J. RUSHOLT. J. BUCKNALL.

"Chandos", the second name on that list reminds one that for nearly thirty years Harrow school had as Governor this man's father, James Brydges, first Duke of Chandos. He was one of the most important persons connected with it and did more for the rise of Harrow than any of the worthy headmasters. He is famous—and notorious—in his own right as having acquired an enormous fortune, chiefly as Auditor of the Imprest and Paymaster-general of the forces abroad (in the French wars, under Marlborough); as a speculator, mostly fortunate, and the builder of that great house, Canons in Middlesex. The expenditure both on the building and grounds and on the superbly ostentatious life carried on there (though all was strictly controlled and audited so that Chandos got value for money) was enormous even for an age of display, and has become a legend. Lord Chandos had a rich full life; the Governorship of John Lyon's school—like that of the Charterhouse or the Chelsea Pensioners' Hospital—must have been trivial to him. (Though perhaps, as many business men have done since, he enjoyed dealing competently with a few hundred pounds as a change from his many thousands; he certainly took his duties seriously and wrote a charming letter of resignation when he found that his infirmities were preventing him from attending meetings regularly, and that these troubles would become no better but rather, worse.) Not only did he help by his very shrewd business ability, and by sending his nominee and cousin who afterwards brought the school fame as George Brydges, Admiral Lord Rodney; he used his influence in the less tangible form of patronage. This was just the right moment, when the school had sufficiently advanced in numbers and organization to encroach on the place hitherto reserved for Eton alone. The reason was, as so often, hardly at all educational; it was political. Eton was under suspicion of being "a nursery of Jacobite opinion". Harrow, with the political reputation it acquired under its Whig Governor, was ready to expand. When in 1746 the egregious Mr. Cox was succeeded by Thomas Thackeray, who had left Eton because he considered the Headmaster a Jacobite at heart, Harrow was set on a fair course.

Thackeray was in fact credited with being "the School's second Founder". He seems to have begun with an innovation long overdue;

dividing up the large "divisions" into forms, to which the boys were moved up according to capacity in contrast to staying all together with one master all their days. This and other re-organizations made possible a real improvement in scholarship and its effect was seen also in the emergence of a brilliant group of boys, of whom the most remarkable was Samuel Parr, the great classical scholar and conversationalist, sometimes called "The Whig Dr. Johnson." Although Parr illuminated Harrow with his reputation, he became not entirely a blessing to the school, as in 1771 he was the cause of the best-known Harrow riot. The boys clamoured for Parr (then an Assistant Master) as Head—a mark of his popularity with them but also a protest against getting a further Headmaster from Eton. But Parr's revolutionary views and perhaps his personal eccentricities were too pronounced to find favour even with Whig Governors and the Etonian, Benjamin Heath, was appointed. It is, however, a mark of Harrow's educational rise that the school could both produce and appreciate the classical scholar who was to be considered the Mentor of the Age. William Jones, the orientalist, was his friend and contemporary.

Parr had been helped as a boy and appointed to a mastership by Dr. Sumner, a deservedly popular Head, who had begun his reign with an action which we can see to have been very important, though possibly the significance of it was not then realized. When the school numbers increased, one Dr. Glasse, a clergyman living in Harrow but in no way attached to the School, set up a special boarding house for the boys, evidently selecting those of family and status. It was probably quite a good thing that there should be some house which gave a certain protection for those whose parents considered them "of delicate constitution" from the admittedly pretty rough life of the school, but Glasse tried also to consolidate his position by having his boys let off the usual "Bill" or call-over. Considering the excessive number of "Absences" at Eton and presumably of "Bills" at Harrow, there was something to be said for the "young gentlemen" and Thackeray let it pass. Sumner more wisely decided to attack this new privilege. Perhaps he realized that Dr. Glasse might be joined by any number of other free-lancing householders and that this would build up an element "in" the school which would in fact live outside it for all purposes except lessons. As one might expect, he met with opposition but he held his ground and fortunately the Governors (and this accorded with Harrow tradition) supported him. They withstood the displeasure of the noble parents, including a letter of protest from Lord Radnor who declared that he had received assurance, presumably from the previous Head-master, that the privilege of exemption from call-over and other school duties would not be infringed. The School stood firm and Dr. Glasse eventually closed his house and withdrew. Consciously or not, the emphasis was being placed on the House as an integral part of school life, not merely as a place for lodging in.

Dr. Sumner himself was not only a fine teacher but a man of considerable personality and great oratorical gifts; the boys believed that he would have succeeded just as well in politics as in academic life, and they respected him for this. He seems also to have had a very good (and modern-sounding) relationship with the staff; there is a pleasing reference to his going up with some of them during the holidays to a Piccadilly tavern—probably the *Hercules Pillars*—in the hope of meeting Fielding, the novelist, whose work he greatly admired. He may well have had a vision which would have made Harrow, and therefore Public School education in general, something wider, less separated and more relevant to English life than it was destined to become. It was a great shock and a sad loss when after ten brilliant years he died "of apoplexy" at the age of 41. (It was his sudden death that sparked off the rebellion in favour of his protégé, Parr.) After this liberal, literary, and sympathetic idealist, the school was consolidated by the book-collecting, wine-affecting pluralist, Dr. Heath, in what seems to us the less admirable traits of 18th century institutions. But Heath did manage to keep the school out of politics and the esteem in which it was by now held enabled it to survive the swing to Tory ascendancy under George III without loss of numbers. (In one way only the Whig connection can be considered to have been detrimental—the patronage of the King being withheld, no ecclesiastical promotion was suggested on retirement for Harrow Headmasters of the mid-eighteenth century—though in fact neither Thackeray nor Summer would have lived to enjoy such honours.)

By the end of the century, Harrow had achieved a place which distinguished it permanently from the Free Grammar School of John Lyon. (And it was significant, because typical later among such schools, that with its rise the founder's name was being lost in that of the locality.) A tradition was growing up in certain families of sending their boys to Harrow; among these was a sprinkling of peers' sons. But one should stress that, as at Eton, there was no bar against the boy of "lower middle class"—a term not, of course, then invented. Thomas Gray's mother kept a milliner's shop; Samuel Parr's father an apothecary's. In "sound learning", i.e. classical scholarship, Harrow had won a place. Two of the most brilliant figures (though not the best scholars) that Harrow ever produced were at the school in the latter part of this century: Sheridan under Sumner, Byron under Heath. (Each gave his Head no little trouble, as one might expect.) A political career was looked for by a great number of boys, whose names like

Lytton, Hamilton (Lord Abercorn) and the Marquess of Hastings, later Governor General of India, indicate the type of pupil that formed a part of Harrow's clientèle. The School's Golden Age came under Drury, whose 20 years' Headship brought Harrow into the 19th century and produced four future Prime Ministers.

Perhaps because it was a pioneer in this development, Harrow grew much less rapidly into what was to become the Public School pattern of the nineteenth century than Rugby or Shrewsbury were about to do. Probably the Headmasters, Brian, Thackeray, Heath and Drury (Sumner possibly should be excepted) had very little idea either of what they wanted for the future, or of what was likely to come. Yet the pattern—to be repeated over and over again in other schools—is clear. The School jettisoned the Founder's name, but kept his endowments and his strictly classical curriculum. It increased, when numbers of pupils demanded this, the number of masters, but it regarded all but the Usher (already provided for in the Founder's Will) as being the financial responsibility of the Headmaster. It sent to the Universities a succession of boys prepared, as the Founder may have directed, for the requirements of those unchanged and in many ways less-than-admirable institutions as they then were. And it swung heavily towards the preponderance of "Foreigners"—boarders—over both the Foundationers and the paying day-boys* (known often as "Home-boarders") and set up for the boarders Houses which gradually became more closely connected with and controlled by the School. The trouble and litigation caused by this last development and the sense of injustice created among the townspeople or local inhabitants have been fully set out in various histories; the 19th century crisis at Harrow was reflected elsewhere throughout the century (Oundle comes to mind as an example). Harrow became a test case by which the legality of the boarding habit was established.

The rise of Harrow as a background to its 18th century Heads has been described here because this School was the first to become something quite different from any of the Grammar schools whose foundation was exactly like its own. It seems that just as Rugby will be seen to have had a stroke of financial luck because of the apparently random action of an unpremeditating benefactor, so Harrow benefited by the proximity of a remarkable neighbour in the great house of Canons. For the impetus in the school's development was given by its patron and Governor, Lord Chandos, at the beginning of the 18th century, and carried on by a succession of able Headmasters till the School had acquired a status and entity which did not depend on its

---

* Anthony Trollope was one such. Shelley's mother came to live near but he did not board at home.

reputation at any given moment.* Over this period it had, for good or ill, developed into a Public School.

* It had one advantage—that of being near London. Perhaps old John Lyon, who insisted that his Governors should keep in repair the roads that led there, had a better inspiration than he knew.

III

THOMAS JAMES OF RUGBY

Between the accession of Edward VI and the death of his sister Elizabeth I there were founded—or re-founded—in England and Wales some 600 Grammar Schools, many of them called after the Sovereign, but far more after the founder. Among these was Lawrence Sheriff's school in the little market town of Rugby.*

Lawrence Sheriff, founder of the Free Grammar School which preceded "Rugby School" had not, in setting up his charity, sought royal approbation, though he was more nearly connected with the court than many such founders. The one historic story about him (in Foxe's *Book of Martyrs,* III) gives an account of an action in support of Princess Elizabeth which might well have told against him or even put him into real danger. This and other scraps of information show him to have been a man of character in whom spirit and goodwill were greater than judgment.

His parents had been of sufficient substance and repute to have got themselves buried within the parish church at Rugby, where he asked to be laid beside them. (He was in fact buried in London, with some pomp by the Grocers' Company.) For Lawrence's reason for going to London as a lad we can take our choice of a fortune-seeking Dick-Whittington-type story (and the Whittingtons, legend apart, were just such another family in a neighbouring county) or a departure in a traditionally Shakesperian manner to avoid trouble. He was bound apprentice to William Wallcott, Grocer, of London, and by 1541 (our first sure date) he had served his apprenticeship and was admitted to the freedom of

---

* The history of Rugby School is very well documented and has often been written so it will be here only briefly recapitulated. Of its 18th century reviver, Dr. James, however, *no* detailed biography exists, which is why the results of investigation of this notable character and his work are here given at what might otherwise seem disproportionate length.

the Worshipful Company of Grocers. There is evidence that he supplied Princess Elizabeth with groceries and continued the connection after she ascended the throne. He became Second Warden of his Company and was granted a coat of arms which, with its crest evidently referring to his calling as a merchant of spices, has been adopted by his school. It is almost the only obvious remaining connection of Rugby with its founder.

Having made money in trade, Lawrence's next procedure was to invest it in land; he applied for purchase of more than a dozen properties all over England. But by 1567, when he made his will, he seems to have got rid of all but one, the Parsonage and tithes of Brownsover, a hamlet neighbouring to Rugby. One other property is mentioned in the will, a purchase made in November 1560, in Gray's Inn Fields, jointly with his wife, of 24 acres, lying to the north of Holbourne "in the county of Middlesex". This field itself was named from the stream running through it, "Conduit Field or Close". It must have been pasture or grazing land, containing at most a farm, as building was prohibited at that time within three miles of the City of London—a desperate attempt to preserve a Green Belt. It is on these two purchases, especially the latter, that the fortunes of Rugby School were to be founded, though nearly 200 years, with a harassment of litigation, were to pass before the school could surmount its difficulties, legal, financial and administrative. One reason why his "Intent" took so long to come to fruition and nearly perished altogether was that Sheriff had not worked out his ideas clearly enough; he may have been a sick man, he was certainly near his end. Also he was sadly misled over the characters of those who were to carry out his will.

There are two documents dated July 22nd 1567, his Will in which he conveyed the land to two friends, and the "Intent" in which he stated that there should be a Free Grammar School to serve chiefly "for the children of Rugby and Brownsover and next for such as be of other places thereunto adjoining. . . and it shall be for ever called the Free School of Lawrence Sheriff of London, Grocer". This wish to preserve his name in perpetuity is characteristic,—and not of Lawrence Sheriff alone among founders. The children are to be taught in "the new fayre and convenient school house" by "an honest, discrete, and learned man, being a Master of Arts" and there shall be a succession of these to teach a Free Grammar School in the said house "for ever" and the schoolmaster for the time being shall be called for ever "the Schoolmaster of Lawrence Sheriff of London, Grocer." He shall live free of charge in the "Mancyon House" which Sheriff had himself built and his salary should be "for ever" £12 a year. Added to this there is provision for the building of lodgings for four poor men, near but distinct from the mansion and newly-built school. They were to be for ever called the "Almesmen of Lawrence Sheriff of London, Grocer." Hardly any of this was realized in just that form in which it was intended.

Though Sheriff was in Rugby shortly before his death in 1567, he retained his London interests, and Will and Intent perhaps suffer from divided aims or from the feebleness of his last days. He made a local man, John Howkins, husband of his sister Bridgett, an Overseer of his Will, but the Charity Trust he put into the hands of his "deare and good friend, George Harrison of London, Gentleman, and Barnard Field of London, Grocer, in the confidence, trust and intent that they should have, use, employ, convey and assure" the land and money "to such uses and. . . to none other." Seldom can trust and confidence have been more grievously misplaced.

A month before his death, Sheriff had made a codicil to his Will leaving one third of the Middlesex land (which was not split up but remained one Close for another 60 years) "to the said George and Barnard. . . upon such trust and confidence to the intent as I have done my Parsonage of Brownsover and my house in Rugby" (i.e. for the Charity.) It was this London (Middlesex) property that was to prove the sorest trial and the utmost benefit to Lawrence Sheriff's Free School.

The lack of discrimination in his choice of Trustees and in the method of ensuring everlasting provision for his aims began to show itself soon after Sheriff's death. Little is known of Harrison, who died about 1582, except that he seems to have let the Trust of his friend go completely by default. On Barnard Field, the testator might have had an even stronger claim; he was Sheriff's own apprentice and a member of the same Company. He had considerable capital and the Trust money was not short. Yet at the first Inquisition (1603) the Rugby petitioners complained bitterly in retrospect that "neither the said George Harrison nor Barnard Field nor any other for them did build", and they accused Field of lining his own pocket with the building money. Field had at least appointed a "Scholemaster"; one Edward Rolston, Master of Arts, but *he* lived in a part of the mansion with the Almsmen using a separate entrance. The whole arrangement smacks of makeshift and parsimony.

It is difficult to find out how the school progressed; the first student from the school whom we can identify at the University did not go there till after 1604. The fourth headmaster, Augustine Rolph, a Cambridge M.A., had as his pupil George Isham who entered Sidney Sussex College in 1621, and Rolph, a Sizar of Queen's College in 1628, was probably the Head's son. But in the 17th century the

Schoolmaster's lot was indeed hard. In one case, no appointment having been made by the Trustees, the local people took the matter into their own hands and put in their own man; he was shortly deposed. Even worse was the fate of Raphael Pearce, an Oxford M.A., from whom even the payment of his nominal salary, now sadly depreciated in value, was constantly withheld. Pearce who had been described as fitted for the place by "his singular learning and industry" and was later lauded as "an able, honest and painful schoolmaster" (this last adjective being of high commendation for "diligent, conscientious,") found the circumstances of his poverty and a large family too much for him. According to his widow, he actually died of debility brought on by lack of food.

Meanwhile, both the founder's own family and his Trustee's heirs were blatantly profiting from the estate, the former near Rugby and the other in London. To add insult to injury, the protagonist on the Howkins side, John, had been educated at the school itself and became a barrister of the Middle Temple, (which says something for the school's standard), living to the age of 99. The records remain of the legal battles. Suits, inquisitions, depositions, exceptions, answers and replications followed each other for more than 50 years, with the Howkins family on one side, Field's heirs and the man who had been allowed to purchase Sheriff's London Close on the other, and the poor School crushed as between the upper and the nether millstones. It was finally the widow of the unfortunate schoolmaster, Pearce, who bravely got together the support of the four Almsmen and seven inhabitants of the town to produce a long and detailed Petition for a last Commission. In 1652 the constitution of the Trust was clearly laid down, active Trustees were appointed and the whole property vested in them and the money began to trickle in. Business meetings began to be held quarterly, at the school. A Clerk, who had been the prosecutor at one of the numerous inquisitions, was appointed to send out notices of meetings and to receive, pay, and account for monies due.

This brief summary is to show how very nearly Lawrence Sheriff's school foundered altogether within 100 years of his death. Largely by the efforts of the townspeople it survived—to celebrate its quatercentenary recently, in very different circumstances. One more comment needs to be made—on the economic fact to which we ourselves are by now well accustomed, though hardly reconciled—the decreasing value of money, sometimes combined with the increasing value of land. The value of, and rent payable for, Conduit Close can be traced:

In Sheriff's time — rent £ 8 p.a.
in 1581   £20
in 1614   £26

in 1651	£40
in 1686	£50
in 1702	£60

But this was by no means reflected in the Schoolmaster's salary; no real attempt was made to cope with the iniquity of income chasing prices. Sheriff, whose original Intent had fixed his schoolmaster's salary at £12, could not have appreciated that his "for ever" if taken literally would preclude any learned man of repute from taking the post. The way out was here, as elsewhere, for the Master to take into the commodious mansion, which the founder had stipulated, boarders, who were not on the foundation and could pay him; this was increasingly done. A School Register, begun in 1674 by the laudable Mr. Ashbridge, makes this clear. It gives not only names but the localities from which the boys came. Two things stand out. The boarders came from a gradually increasing distance and they tended to establish family traditions of entrance—the same names begin to occur again and again.

The number who were non-local and paid for board and tuition grew under Rugby's first remarkable headmaster—Henry Holyoake (1688-1731). In his first year, nearly all boys came from Rugby or Brownsover (the hamlet mentioned in Sheriff's Will) but "for the whole number of boys entered during his tenure, nearly four-fifths were not on the Foundation" (Rouse). Of what they paid and how, there is no record—but Holyoake died quite a wealthy man. The Trustees added a storey to the house; this must have been for dormitories. Of course single rooms would have been more than the boys even of the noblest families would expect; they would be lucky at their time of life if they got individual beds. Numbers, however, were still by subsequent standards, certainly by ours, very small; Holyoake would have been counted fortunate if at his peak he had 100 boys. He had had his way to make; for the last four years before his arrival no foundationers' and only three other pupils' admissions had been recorded. Holyoake was a man of character; he had been Chaplain of Magdalen College, Oxford, and one of those Fellows extruded by James II. He had a pleasant and successful mastership and is regarded by the school's historian (W. H. D. Rouse) as one of the three great Headmasters to whom the classic History of the school is dedicated, along with Thomas James and Arnold.

Holyoake certainly admitted boys from afar and for payment. But it would be quite untrue to think that poorer boys were not also benefiting from the charity. During his time, some dozen boys are entered as "Orphan", most but not all, from the counties of Warwickshire or Northamptonshire. Others are put down as "son of Mrs. . . " which presumably meant that they were fatherless—it looks as if the idea of sending away to school a boy who had no father to train him (instead of getting a tutor) was even then gaining ground. Not all, evidently, were necessitous. But the sons of Smith (or Mrs. Smith) Blake, Harper, etc. of Rugby were surely the very children for whom the founder had intended to provide.

At his death, Holyoake, a bachelor, left to the school the library which he had accumulated, which the Trustees minuted must be found a fit place and also be catalogued. But long before this they had realized what a treasure the School had got in its Master and with a generosity which was by no means always to be found in the relations of Governors and Headmasters, they expressed their high opinion of him in a "Testimony" which approves his labours "whereby he hath deserved very well of us in Recovering the Creditt and reputation of the School which circumstances may probably never recur in another Schoolemaster. . . "

Unfortunately, Holyoake's good work was in fact not enough to guarantee the school's continuing thereafter in "creditt and reputation", nor yet in numbers. Perhaps the age was not yet ripe for any permanent addition to the few accepted Public Schools; perhaps the school itself was not yet capable of generating the momentum to keep it from falling away in size and scholarship. Perhaps Holyoake's success needed to be confirmed by a successor—but on his death Rugby fell into an educational trough. A glimpse of the school under one, Knail, comes from an anonymous correspondent reminiscing in the *Gentleman's Magazine* (September 1809, p.799) about a time when there were some 70 boys in a "very indifferent" house:

> I have said many a lesson in a small room, into which the Doctor occasionally called some boys, and in which he smoked many a pipe, the fragrance of which was abundantly retained in the blue cloth hangings with which it was fitted up.

The school had by this time been moved to larger quarters, but if the boys noticed the smell of the Master's room (Knail was not in fact a Doctor of Divinity nor of anything else; the appellation must have already become traditional), it was probably pretty powerful.

The move—to the Old Manor House, on the outskirts of the town—had taken place about 1750, not before time. Another pressing need was a revision of the constitution of the School, and this particularly because of the matter of the London property. Conduit Close had been let by the Trustees in 1686 to Dr. Nicholas Barbon who later achieved some notoriety as a speculative builder, on a lease which enabled him (the interdict on building having been removed) to spend £1,000 in erecting houses. He seems to have defaulted on the rent and another building lease was made out to Sir William Milman, which would revert to the Trustees in 1780. (It was in fact given up earlier.) Thus, through the quite fortuitous selection of this ground in the original purchase, the Charity would find itself possessor of some of the most Desirable Building Land in the whole country. The elegant suburb of Bloomsbury was about to be laid out and though this eastern end was not for quite such affluent tenants as those on the Russell lands across what is now Southampton Row, it was select enough, and the houses that were built there towards the end of the century continued to hold their value. (See *Map of Rugby Estate.*)

With all this financial responsibility and an increase in numbers in prospect, it was not surprising that a new constitution was envisaged. Fortunately there had joined the Trustees in 1770 Sir Eardley Wilmot, Chief Justice of the Common Pleas, who set himself to the work with the approval of his fellow Trustees ("Governors," in other schools, but the old appellation was retained) and the new constitution was piloted through Parliament in 1777. Among all the clauses relating to administration and school organization, one thing is clear; the Trustees had grasped—and here they were well in advance of most of their contemporaries—that the first essential for a school is to have a secure and contented staff. Their provisions show this: one example suffices. They could allow the payment to Masters and Ushers "removed on account of Old Age or Infirmity of Body or Mind", of yearly pensions up to as much as a half of the salary. One more significant phrase lights up the clause about the selection of the Master; "who shall bee A Master of Arts in the University of Oxford or Cambridge";

> and in the Choice of such Master ... *regard shall be had to the Genius of such Master for Teaching and Instructing the Children* and a preference given to such as are duly qualified and have received their Education at this School.

The words in italics (mine) seem unique for the period. I have not found any school in which the selectors are told to look for *teaching* quality in their appointee.

The stage was set for a new act in the school's history. Only, there was a lack of performers. The numbers of pupils had been fluctuating between forty and eighty over the century and there was no sign of an increase under the Rev. Stanley Burrough who had been Master for 23 years. He was persuaded to retire—perhaps by the pension, (which he continued to draw for many years). The 52 boys who remained must have looked forward with some excitement, after the departure of one who seems to have resembled King Log, to his successor. The Trustees, fully realizing their responsibility had selected someone who—far more than his distinguished follower of half a century later—was going to change the face of this particular school and make it "Public".

They had appointed as Master (the term "Headmaster" was hardly needed and it was still customary to think simply of The Master and The Usher) Thomas James, a young tutor of King's College. His election was contested, but the Trustees were discerning—or fortunate. James' work for Sheriff's school—which would henceforth be known as Rugby*—though of late forgotten by the public because of his eclipse by the later (and, be it allowed, more remarkable) Arnold, was remembered with gratitude by those connected with the school, the Trustees themselves being throughout most appreciative. For many years, and not only those immediately following his death, he was accepted almost as the school's second founder. William Birch, a boy and then a master under him, and the nearest James has had to a biographer, sums up the essential change in his 18th century phraseology.

> Though the school was before highly respectable, it wanted that system which might have had the sanction of public opinion, on which the celebrity of a school so much depends.
>
> (Memoir prefixed to *The School Master,* a poem by Wm. Birch.)

Similarly, the anonymous writer of the series on *British Public Characters* judges that under him:

> Rugby became one of our public seminaries, being inferior neither in point of discipline, mode of education, nor masters, to the first of the kingdom.

More interesting, as evidence of his value in the eyes of a later commentator, is this passage by Samuel Butler, author of *Erewhon,* who was in 1892 editing the life and letters of his grandfather, Dr. Butler (see chapter IV). The younger man was by no means always bound by his grandfather's views, but in reading the correspondence between the two men, James' personality specially attracted him:

> It is not too much to say that no later master has done so much for the school as he did between 1780 and 1794. He was the first to give it that importance which since his day it has never lost. No

---

* But even today, the School Governors are officially *The Trustees of the Rugby Charity founded by Lawrence Sheriff, Grocer.*

subsequent head-master so completely recreated the school as Dr. James did during his fourteen years'* tenure of office. Dr. Arnold unquestionably made a deep impression on those boys who were brought into close communication with himself, but I cannot find that his influence survived longer than that of any subsequent headmaster†

This last statement exaggerated, but W. H. D. Rouse, Rugby's classic historian, differentiates with more discernment between the two. He draws attention to James' reforms and to the organization which he built up when a crisis in the school's fortunes gave almost unlimited scope to an able man, showing himself equal to the occasion. It was Arnold who "quickened this perfected organism with a new life", yet "Thomas James has hitherto hardly had justice done him." ‡

To sum up, James succeeded in developing this small, mainly local, Grammar School into an institution having a status which it never lost. As Lawrence Sheriff's School, it had swelled in numbers two or three times and dropped away. It dropped again after James' retirement to less than half the size he reached. But it was still *Rugby School;* it may have lost to some degree its reputation, but never again its status.

It indicates something of Thomas James' remarkable ability and character that he was himself in no way connected with any noble or scholastic family, probably not even "gentry" by origin. The faithful Birch says discreetly (and the D.N.B. based its account on his) that James was born at St. Ives (Hunts.), "of very respectable and sufficiently opulent parents." The sketch in *British Public Characters* (1805) is obviously drawn from Birch (making use of the two adjectives, which gives it away) but with a customary inaccuracy puts his birth three years earlier and at St. Neots, "where his father now ninety years of age still resides." "Respectable", though a word then of higher connotation than later, is evidently being used to make the best of a distinguished headmaster's undistinguished antecedents. James' (second) marriage into a good county family and the success of his collateral relations added to his own, helped to pitch his ancestry reasonably high, but tradition in the more forthright family of the *first* wife's descendants speaks in a lower key. (His great-grandaughter, Edith Chaplin set down c.1920 a "History of the Pyne and James families", still in Ms.)

John James, grandfather of the headmaster (past whom the memory of man, with the ingenuity of the genealogist, runs not back) used to be

---

* Actually, 16 years: 1778-1794.

† S. Butler (ed.), *Life and Letters of Samuel Butler,* p.9.

‡ W. H. D. Rouse, *History of Rugby School,* p.341.

referred to in the family tradition as "The Equestrian" meaning not a knight but an ostler. He is said to have worked in an inn in Huntingdon and to have married the daughter of his master (or possibly his widow). A John James married Mary Colton by licence in Christ's College Chapel on January 15th, 1706, the traditional marriage year of Thomas James' grandparents. There was at least one son, another John, born before Thomas James' father, the nonagenarian of *British Public Characters;* John became a surgeon in Cambridge.

Thomas James, father of the Headmaster, is reported from the same family source to have been a corn-factor or leatherseller and at one time to have had some connection with an inn in Holborn. He took some interest in politics on the Whig side, but having made money returned to his native Huntingdonshire. He married a local girl and became, according to another family tradition, High Constable of Elsworth and St. Ives. This officer belonged to the Hundred and was responsible for bringing forward cases to the Assizes. It should not be confused with High Sheriff, which James clearly was *not* but was reputed to be by his more status-seeking descendants. Still, the family was certainly on the up-grade. The elder brother, the Cambridge surgeon married Ann Burleigh there and their eldest son became Headmaster of Oundle and a Prebendary of Peterborough. Their youngest son, Thomas, died in 1799, in his fourteenth year, and a tablet in Holy Trinity, Cambridge bears a brief but charming Latin inscription.

> Innocens et perbeatus
> More florum decedi,
> Quid sepultus flos, amico
> Flente sum felicior.

This is similar to one in Rugby church, commemorating a school-boy who died in the headmaster's house at about the same age. Presumably both are from the pen of Thomas' scholarly cousin, and perhaps godfather, the Rugby headmaster.

This Thomas James—headmaster-to-be—born at St. Ives, or at any rate baptized there (October 19th, 1748) was the eldest, probably the only surviving, son of Thomas the High Constable. Shadowy as his forbears are, we can assume that they set a value on his intellectual talent, whether this reflected the Cambridge connection or merely the upward social thrust of an ambitious and energetic family. He got his first education in the classics at the hands of the local vicar, the Rev. John Wheeler. The praise bestowed on the boy for his "diligence and amiable disposition" sounds merely conventional, but whether this is true or merely hindsight, these are the very qualities which particularly characterized his later success as a teacher.

James' next step, we may confidently conjecture, was in accordance with the practice found in the 18th, but even more common in the 19th century, when parents were less willing to entrust their boys to the rigours of Eton life at too early an age. The records state that he was entered as a King's Scholar in May 1761, which would make him 13 years old. But this would be distinctly old for a lad of talent; besides the author of *British Public Characters* makes the point that "love of reading and a propensity to study caused him to be sent to Eton at not more than nine years." He therefore went first as an Oppidan to one of the boarding houses still kept by Dames; he entered Dame Long's (No. 8, St. Christopher's), a house later kept by Mary Naylor. Many boys, from Gaskell (see chapter V) to Thring (chapter VIII), did the same.

The account that James later wrote of *Eton Discipline and Education* has been quoted at some length. The grasp shown of the very tricky detail (e.g. how a holiday altered the whole week's timetable) explains how he was so successful, when he had the chance, of transplanting so much of the curriculum and organization to his own school. It also shows how deeply Eton life had influenced James, and how it was that so much of the "mechanics" of Eton life could be, and was, passed on to Rugby.

James, and still more the author of the *Nugae* (see chapter I), wrote of Eton with a zest and an acceptance which later criticism of the place makes us wonder at; there is so little comment and none of it uncomplimentary. No doubt the occasion of its composition did not call for criticism. But it may well be that to James, the school life really *was* acceptable and he asked for no other. Perhaps if he went there, merry and clever, from the small-town atmosphere of St. Ives, he had been enchanted and caught up in the vitality of the life and the opportunities of learning and friendship. Certainly he built up an image of it which never left him, and in many cases remained with his descendants.

Thomas kept no surviving diary and only two incidents are reported of his Eton days, one of his early scholarship, the other of his organizing ability. The first was a commendation for his skill in the writing of Greek verse, the skill so highly rated in the 18th and early 19th centuries. A typical passage had been chosen, from the works of a much admired poet, Mark Akenside, himself of quite humble origin. Possibly it was this which emboldened Thomas James among the aristocracy of Eton to present the poet with his translation. At any rate, Akenside was delighted and sent the boy "The Iliad in two quarto volumes" as a mark of esteem and encouragement. It is hardly surprising that Dr. James, when he had the chance, introduced the making of "verses" into his own school.

The other reminiscence is found embedded in a letter sent by James' son to his widowed mother four years after the headmaster's death.

> In one respect he was so fortunate as to succeed in adding to the comfort of all the Collegers who were to come after him. It had been the custom for each boy to bring his own knife and fork into Hall, and as there was no place to put them, it continually happened that they were lost. To prevent this, James himself put up a drawer, part of which still remains, in the Buttery, where they should be constantly kept. The consequence was that the Bursar took the hint and knives and forks have since been regularly provided for all the boys.*

This sensible piece of organization seems very typical of the future headmaster. Efficiency and consideration, two of his outstanding qualities, show in the boy no less than in the man.

Though only few details are known of his career at Eton, there is no question about his having become a scholar at King's, Cambridge, in 1767. As explained earlier, the Colleger who was highest on the list, if not yet 19 years old, automatically succeeded to a vacancy among the King's College scholars and, provided he kept residence, was at this time certain of receiving his degree without examination by the University.† Thomas James, however, according to Birch, (*op.cit.*) did not let this privilege "impair his strong desire to take every opportunity of acquiring knowledge . . . nor to remit any of his former diligence". He turned to the study of mathematics and obtained "a very comprehensive and creditable knowledge of this." His interest in the subject never lapsed and he introduced it into the Rugby timetable—as distinct from allowing it to be taught as an extra subject, which must have been how he himself had studied it (if at all) at Eton. In fact, he taught it at Rugby himself on Saturday mornings.

Thomas James got his Fellowship in 1771, the year of his B.A. and having been Members' Prizeman in 1772 and 1773, he took his M.A. in the next year and was appointed a Tutor to his College. Before his official appointment, he acted as a private Tutor. This activity seems to have led to, or increased, that contact with the aristocracy which later considerably helped both him personally and his school. (Among his

---

* Family Memoir of John James, Bishop of Calcutta.

† One of Dr. James' grandsons, C. C. James when a master at Eton was among those who fought strongly and successfully for the reformation of this scandal thereby earning no little ill-will. This was in the 1860s.

contemporaries at Eton had been William Pitt, the future Prime Minister.) But as a scholar, he needed no help in making his way and his appointment to the college tutorship took place when he was about 26, regarded according to Birch as a very early age for this. This enabled him, after a spell of four years to start on his next venture as a comparatively young man, yet with a reputation and friends to back him.

Birch naturally says that "as public tutor he gave universal satisfaction", yet a hint creeps in of some ruffling of the waters, as in about 1788 he found "the air and situation of Cambridge were not at all congenial to his health." For one who had been born only 13 miles away and had spent over ten years in Cambridge, this sounds a surprising discovery and one suspects something, never-to-be-known, behind it. Whatever the cause, he may have been looking round for a change when Dr. Burrough resigned the headmastership of the school at Rugby, and friends suggested that he applied for the post. The appointment was fortunate for both sides.

When he arrived in September 1778, James found (as he emphasized in his parting letter 16 years later) 52 boys. By Christmas he had already begun to pull up the numbers and started next year with 66. But the increase in numbers alone, even when these reached the peak of 245, was by no means the only nor even the most important difference made by the new headmaster. It was the cumulative effect, rather than any one fact—his getting to work·on the scholastic system, the buildings, the discipline, and the general new tone in the place— together with his own remarkable personality, that caused his work to be so long remembered and so much admired. His was "the abundant energy which displayed itself in organization of the school down to the smallest detail"—the energy on which we admit genius is based, even if the genius itself is not at this distance very recognizable.

The equivalent at Rugby of James' own account of Eton, and the *Nugae,* is the record of Richard Bloxham who had gone there two years before James came as Headmaster and who returned in his last year to be himself a master. This boy, at 12, had been so miserable that he tried to run away. Fortunately both for himself and for historians, he was discouraged by the difficulties of the journey and returned. (For most of what we know about pre-Arnold Rugby we are indebted to the Bloxham family.)

Under their new constitution, the Trustees had become empowered to provide out of their newly increased funds for eight boys at Oxford or Cambridge colleges. It is unlikely that without James these exhibitions could all have been taken up. For the teaching had been carried on in the old style—in one large room with a desk for the Master and Usher, one at each end and the whole school merely separated into an Upper and Lower Division. When the Divisions increased, the number of desks had also increased—to four, one of which remains as a relic to this day. But the number of rooms did *not*; James merely found one "Big School". James asked for, and got, as his Second Master, a man of his own selection named Chartres, of Eton and King's, but the system was all to make and one of his first tasks was to organize it.

He had been provided with some boarders in the School House (i.e. the Old Manor, where the schoolroom also was), probably in one of the wings. It would have been difficult in a small town, such as Rugby then was, to find places where boys could have been happily lodged without supervision, ranging in age as they might from six to nearly 20 years. Masters of course might board them; 16 guineas p.a. were the terms for this, as well as four guineas for their schooling if they were not on the Foundation. Personal expenditure varied very widely and one of James' most interesting improvements was his curbing of unnecessary extravagance and purchases in dress by "Sumptuary Laws", for which later he enlisted the co-operation of parents. But the House system, with a controlling school authority was also still to make.

Another matter on which James wanted the help of parents was in observing a fixed date of return (as at Eton). Hitherto the arrangements for gathering the boys together for the beginning of the terms and releasing them at the end seem by contrast with to-day's very naphazard. Most boarders rode in, accompanied by a servant; a six-year-old rode pillion behind his. It took about a week to collect all the pupils, if not to get rid of them for the month's vacation in summer and winter. There must have been difficulties in coming from some distance before the days of regular coaches passing through (this was more than half a century before Tom Brown could take the regular early coach from London); post-chaises were rarely seen in the town. The wretched Master would certainly not count on two months' leave for himself—and Dr. James in his later days complained very much if he and his family were prevented from going away.

On Sundays the boys naturally attended the service in the Parish Church as their Founder would undoubtedly have desired. They had their special place and a seat was, probably by long tradition, reserved for the School Master. The Trustees paid a guinea a year for a Gallery, but this space became totally inadequate as the size of the school increased. It was also unsupportably hot; "Instances have been known of some boys taking off their jackets" indicates not a mere casual unease as to-day, but frightful discomfort. James arranged that the boys should attend either morning *or* evening service (thereby halving the numbers who attended) and prayers were read for the rest in Big

School. Presumably Dr. James took the school services himself; he had obtained his D.D. before becoming Headmaster and later became quite a notable preacher.* In due course, he got one of the masters, most of whom were in orders, appointed Chaplain with £20 extra salary for reading prayers and preaching, though the school did not get its own Chapel till 1814.

These are some aspects of life at Rugby school when James came; much had changed by the end of the century. Some innovations, (the separation of classes made possible by new buildings, for instance), were dependent for their success on the improvement in school finances—due to that apparently wayward codicil of the founder's will. Yet the greater affluence could easily have been frittered away or become a cue for relaxed effort rather than swift advance. To take advantage of it, a pioneer was needed—a man with vision but also with an understanding of "the art of the possible". This James undoubtedly had.

One Victorian Rugbeian (R. N. Hutton) rightly ascribes the new and successful regime to his Eton experience of the system—e.g. of boys moving up from one Division to the next, also perhaps the use of tutors, even the selection of books read. But other men from Eton (or Westminster or Winchester, with "system") had taken headships of Grammar schools; James seems outstanding in that he *used* his experience to alter things in his own school instead of accepting what he found. Exactly how the system worked he explained in the letters he wrote 20 years later to Samuel Butler, then a prospective Headmaster. He divided the school into six forms and had five lessons each day; very different from the casual way in which lessons were "occasionally" said to Knail, and probably Burrough. On arrival he had one Assistant, one Usher (possibly two) and a Writing Master who was responsible also for "hearing the catechism" of the little boys under 12. In two years' time, two more appointments were made, now definitely "Assistant Masters"; later the number of assistants were brought up to six and it was accepted that the Writing Master should also teach arithmetic. This was free for the foundationers; others paid him a fee. The Headmaster insisted that the small boys—and the big ones as well if their writing was very bad—should go to him, and he seems to have been in general charge of the younger ones. The ratio of Classical Assistants in the end worked out at six masters for nearly 250 boys and it is interesting that the Clarendon Commission more than half a century later accepted

---

* He died with a sermon prepared for preaching in Worcester Cathedral, where he had already preached at the "Music Meeting"—The Three Choirs Festival—of 1800, and on at least one other occasion.

three masters per 100 boys as satisfactory. Dr. James himself, following the Eton tradition, which was later accepted by Arnold, taught the sixth form, to which the fifth was sometimes added.

Like the Writing Master (who was paid £20 a year for it) the Drawing Master—first appointed under James in 1784—taught gratis those Foundationers who wanted to learn. Similarly the French Master—though his pay was £30 for the Foundationers. Young Bloxham had noted, the year before James came, "No French this day, as Mr.— is gone to the races." However, in 1784 James brought in a new French Master, who could also teach German, an exciting successor to the race-goer. He was a Bohemian—Marc-Marie Emanuel Wratislaw, Count of the Holy Roman Empire. The Count had lived in Moravia and had been an Attaché to the Austrian Embassy in Paris at the time of Marie Antoinette's wedding. A note in the Register telling this adds: "Circumstances compelled him to quit Paris and retire to England in 1770"—"Voltairism" was suspected. He came eventually to Rugby, where his family settled (of whom more was to be heard), and he "continued French Master at Rugby till his death in 1796."

James was an enthusiast for mathematics and himself lectured to the two upper forms once a week. Curiously, he found this the hardest period he took and in the end must have got some sort of obsession about it. He describes the symptoms it produced:

> The regular preachment or delivering of such a lecture. . . not only kept my mind upon the full stretch during the delivery . . but even wearied my body to excess and made it hot or at any rate perspire too much.

Clearly it was not any trouble he himself had in mastering the subject which brought this on, for he had shown a special aptitude for it at Cambridge. A creditable explanation may be that James was intuitively such a good and sympathetic teacher that he could not escape from the difficulty which most masters of his day (and some since) have ignored—that of trying to make himself intelligible to his less intelligent pupils. "Method" and Training for teachers was so far in the future, especially for Public Schools, that if James dimly realized that a teacher needs to take some pains besides those of mastering his subject in order to get his pupils to benefit from his learning, then he was well ahead of his time. Writing later to Butler, he shows his acceptance of boys' limitations:

> If you had the abilities of an angel, and spake as never man spake, you would still find that the world is content with moderate acquisitions and that young people are narrow-necked vessels, into which you cannot pour much at a time without waste and running

over. As to Mathematics, remember your own aversion to them when you were younger... A very little of Mathematics (whatever you may fondly dream of, and very naturally in the bosom of the University) will suffice for young persons. (December 27th, 1796)

As a teacher of Classics, James clearly had a gift. Not only the brilliance of his prize pupils like Butler shows this but the success he had with a non-intellectual boy like Charles Apperley. To Apperley, second son of a parson and writer later on of sporting articles under the pseudonym of "Nimrod", sport at school and hunting afterwards were probably the most important thing in his life. Yet his education had not alienated him, as so many boys of his temperament must have been alienated, from classical learning. He used to carry a Virgil or Horace with him on his hunting expeditions, and his use of allusion and quotation in his writing shows real appreciation of literature, English and classical. In *Fraser's Magazine* (August 1842) he wrote, in an article by no means uncritical:

I think there was a very honourable feeling throughout the school as to what may be called gentlemanlike and honourable conduct and likewise a great deal of good taste in literature generally, displayed among the masters. How thick so ever a boy's head may have been, he could not have left Rugby in my time without bringing away with him something of that classical character which ought to distinguish the gentleman.

The impressive manner and feeling with which he recited fine passages from the classics shows the inspirational side of James' teaching; the other side is seen in his grasp of practical teaching such as his advice: "never take it for granted that a boy knows anything."

Some other ideas transferred from Eton can be traced from the expressions used. The term "sent up for good" was used of a boy's specially laudable piece of work which earned the school a half-holiday on a Thursday, as at Eton. Tuesdays and Saturdays were already halfdays, as of right, during the afternoons of which the "accomplishments" or extra lessons referred to were carried on, but Thursday was "a play". The name of the boy who earned it was written up: "Play for Landor" would have been the phrase which concluded this anecdote about Walter Savage Landor, James' difficult but clever pupil:

There were seven boys in the School of the name of Hill. The boys wanted a half-holiday and came to Landor. "Write to old James for one," said they. Landor consented, and wrote a copy of verses, wherein he compared Rugby to Rome because it was built on seven

Hills. "Ah," said the Doctor, "I don't ask you who wrote this, for there is only one of you with the brains to do it. Half-holiday?, Yes."

This is quoted by Forster in his Life of Landor from reminiscences of him by Charles Reade, and shows how James and his pupils could share an intellectual joke and how easy the boys evidently felt with him.

The exact relation between being "sent up for good" and "Merit Money" is not quite clear, but James introduced the latter also at Rugby. One must remember that there were at the time no prizes, no form order or outside tests and James was, in providing these incentives, anticipating "the age of aemulation". The sums for good work, varying from 1/- down to 3d for the little boys, were also given in Mathematics, French and Writing—but at half rates. In the long run, James probably rather deplored having introduced the system. He wrote to Butler: "Have no merit money yet. Query, if ever?" (In the event, Butler made much more of "the principle of aemulation".)

One more "improvement" came over with Dr. James from Eton (but was not followed up at Shrewsbury), the introduction of individual tutoring. Necessary it certainly had been at Eton, with its enormous Divisions; indeed most of the real teaching must have been done out of class, and though James managed to keep down the teacher-pupil ratio he could not have felt that construing in class some 30 or 40 lines of, say, Virgil, was an ideal way for boys to get a real understanding of the classics. He did not insist that parents should be put to the extra expense, though it would have been one of the easiest ways of adding to the rather slim salaries of his Assistants, but he did recommend tuition for some part of a boy's school career. The stage early or late varied with the individual boy. As classical dictionaries were neither good nor common and the great lexicon of Liddell and Scott was not produced till the middle of the next century, a teacher might well be needed to help a boy prepare his work.

The faithful Birch in his *Tribute to the Memory of Thomas James D.D.* gives a glimpse of James' ideas about teaching (with a reference to his production of two text-books, one a school geography, the other an exposition of Euclid V). He also adds a note:

Thinking according to the Comenian system, pictures are the most intelligible books for children, he painted the Planets on the garden wall bounding the play-close.

Thy busy thought, from old and modern sage
With curious gleanings culls th'instructive page,
Proportions geometric, well-defined

> To truth and science lead the willing mind.
> Vast labour of geographers appear
> At once to sight displayed, condensed and clear;
> E'en on the wall, that they may read who run,
> At distance due, the planets watch the sun;
> And many an idler first acknowledged there
> His moon-blest earth, and every world a sphere,
> And pass'd from orb to orb in sport and play,
> To distant empire of the solar day.

The improvements and enlargements of the buildings made by the Trustees, often with James' suggestions—some of his notes to them survive—were many and ingenious, but much has been over-built since. Dr. James sometimes financed the improvements himself as the following note shows (from the Temple Library, Rugby School; Trustees' Papers.)

> The Master of Rugby School having set up gates at his own expense in the inclosed grounds belonging to the Foundation, requests the favour of an order from the Trustees to set up two gates at the expense of the Foundation in the Fence which bounds the playground—to prevent the boys from making his horses lame by forcing them to leap over the bars.

("*His* horses"! This permissive age has little to teach the 18th century lads.)

> Also. . . for the Master and his Upper boys, Three fixed Benches and desks in the School, rising in order one above the other.

(These were allowed; the order is signed by three Trustees.)

By 1783 he had expended by order of the Trustees sums amounting to practically £250 on odd sheds, as playrooms for the boys in wet weather, on French and Dancing Schools, and on an additional School Room, 18 x 20 feet. The block containing the Dining Room, where the boys sat at four long tables, and the three form rooms for the youngest boys, was put in hand soon after he came, but his own really important innovation was to have built above this a set of Studies for the boys. They led off a central passage, and they could be locked, so that each was a boy's personal sanctum—wonderful, this, for a small country school. James saw to the fundamental furnishing of these studies, the "standard equipment" of to-day but made by a local carpenter. They included a table with a drawer, a stool, a cupboard, a coal box, ink-pot, a basin and kettle and snuffers for the candle; later a flat-bottomed candlestick was added. The studies must have added enormously to the pleasure and self-respect of the boys and the Headmaster himself respected their privacy. This was not an idea from Eton; Collegers at least had to take a room in the town for this privilege.

Yet with all this new building, there was not enough room as the boys kept coming in. Aware that the conglomeration of Manor, Wings, Big School and other class rooms would some day need a master plan, the Trustees put this off and James did not try to hustle them. He agreed to the adaptation for school work of a large thatched barn in a neighbouring field. With this, "Barn School", and the apse-like ending of the new school where the Head took his boys from the desk on a platform, the external appearance of the complex of buildings was like "a chapel that had lost its way in a farm-yard,"—a vision which those who believe impressive buildings were necessary to advancement in early Public Schools might ponder.

As to boarders, James did not like to have too many in his own house in spite of the profit. "It is good policy" (he wrote to Butler) "for the Headmaster to have few boys in his house (I mean 38 or 40) because he would always have a large share of the bigger boys and consequently all rebellions and disturbances will be the more likely to haunt his house." (This he had probably learnt from experience). He gave a most detailed account of how much should be allowed per head for boys and servants:

> Eight servants always dine after the boys, on what they had left and we always had a separate dinner for ourselves. . . lay down therefore no rules in respect of provisions. . . a little experience will soon direct you and nothing is lost for hashes consume all that but Mrs. Butler . . . must oversee all provisions . . . until your general provisions be . . . reduced to a system.

But there is not much money to be made out of it.

> . . . consider . . . the enormous increase in the price of every article even these two years past. . .Pork is here 8d a pound, and all other meat 6d a pound, bought what are called good and indifferent pieces together. Bread and salt are also very heavy articles. . .

And so on, over a long letter—though this is intended to dissuade Butler from *private* teaching. But James had been faced on arrival with a haphazard method of arranging the boarding of boys from a distance and worked towards (on the Eton model again) houses kept either by the masters or by recognized Dames, whose names should be valid for absences or tradesmen's notes. Living could be more comfortable in these small groups than in the school dormitories; two or three boys would share a sitting-room, with fires, but equal discipline in the way of Absences and lock-up times was imposed on the out-sleeping boys.

Chance references show that among those who kept houses for the boys were Chartres (Second Master), Count Wratislaw, Birch, the Writing Master, an Apothecary, a Surgeon and a Churchwarden. Perhaps young Assistants also boarded that way—but not with the Headmaster. "Bargain for their board", he writes; "entertain them not yourself". The larger houses increased till within ten years of James' death there were ten of them and as most of the Housemasters seem to have been married (with children, potential little Rugbeians) the set-up was probably not unlike that of Eton in James' own day. There is a tradition that the appearance of a new baby (the Head's only?) meant a holiday for the school. If true, in James' own day it would have been no more than a half—for a whole holiday he "avoided as the worst of all plagues" and "always set some regular exercise to . . .preserve it from wild schemes and excursions".*

No correspondence, and few references are found (as compared to the troubles at Shrewsbury or later at Marlborough), to any brush with the locals in the matters of trespass or poaching, though we know for a certainty that some boys (before Tom Brown) did poach. W. S. Landor certainly was a "skilfull fisher" in forbidden waters. To encourage sport in its widest sense Dr. James more than once laid out money in purchasing some adjoining land for the School as it fell vacant, under repayment, one imagines from the Trustees. By "play" one should understand occupations far wider than the organized cricket and football of later days, though cricket, probably football and certainly boxing were regularly found in the School, witness Nimrod. (One keeps forgetting how short was the time between absences—even on holydays it was not much more than two or three hours.)

It is difficult, because so little can be known of the day to day life of the school under James—or of any contemporary school—to be sure about his relations with the boys and his attitude towards discipline. Only what the Eton boy called "uncommon occurrences" get noted and they may not be characteristic. But it was a general "Age of harshness". The ferment of Revolutionary ideas was by no means considered irrelevant at the time, for in several schools in which "rebellions" did break out, it was considered that the philosophy and politics of unrest had affected boyish minds and loosened the sense of discipline. But, as has been brought out more than once, it *was* an age of harshness. One contemporary example, excessive perhaps but quoted widely is found in "Elia". Charles Lamb mentions—quite by the way, in his description of Christ's Hospital—the fierce master (remembered also by Coleridge and Leigh Hunt) James Boyer with his threat: "Odd's my life,

---

* Letter in Temple Library, Rugby, October, 1798.

Sirrah. . . I have a great mind to whip you. . .and" (rushing out at his victim) "I WILL too". Yet Boyer was a conscientious teacher and Hunt, seeing him wearied out at the end of the day, would have "pitied him if he had taught us anything but fear".

This kind of background makes James' attitude the more remarkable. He certainly did beat boys—effectively; he was remembered as a little man with "a very strong arm". In his last letter to the Trustees, he states:

> I governed more by principles of justice and what I called among the boys (my only law) the Eternal Rule of Right and Wrong. . . more by maintaining such a sort of character among the boys by my actions, than by the terrors of the Rod, though I have established that on all becoming occasions, (in my opinion) from boys of 6 years old to boys of 18 or even more than 18 years . . .I have never governed the Boys by that secret information on which some Masters are thought to have derived from their own subjects. It would be a high crime and even Treason against the Virtue and Honour of the School to induce Boys to be traitors to their Fellows.

The capital letter in these extracts show his emotion; the letter was written at a crisis in his life, but he was feeling called upon to state the fundamental principles and beliefs which characterized his rule. It is an ethos quite ahead of his time among authority (perhaps ahead of Arnold's); and the more remarkable as the next sentence shows us the kind of trouble he had to deal with:

> Secret information from any others I have always thought fair, together with general reports in the case of mischief; and I have acted upon it (as I told the Boys openly within this month in School) even to expulsion, as in the case of *the old man's teeth knocked out.* *

So two guineas a year were expended by the Trustees on Rods and Birch. Yet it looks as if Thomas James were feeling towards a relation between master and boys quite other than that of beater and beaten—something which he did not entirely achieve, but which most men of his time had not even contemplated.

There is more to be found about his relations with some of his individual pupils, though the most *vocal* of them never really settled down satisfactorily. But "Savage Landor" was throughout his life a difficult character and he set down his own point of view at some length, from which perhaps the image of James has suffered. It can be accepted that the Doctor (himself a very uncomplicated person) was unwise in that he attempted to win over the boy by treating him at

---

* My italics—A.C.P.

times with a familiarity which provoked insolence, and then objecting—as he could not but do—to the insolence. Landor was experiencing the violent ambiguity of the unsettled adolescent, and James's variation in treatment left him without the security he so badly needed. But most characteristic was Landor's remark in later life: "When I was a little boy, I did not let anyone get before me." Clearly what he could not bear was not to be top—and at Rugby there was just one boy cleverer than himself. Dr. James' real fault in his pupil's eyes was that "Play for Butler" was written more often than "Play for Landor"—so the adjudicator *must* be wrong. The only alternative position Landor found much later, when he wrote: "I strove with none, for none was worth my strife." James' error was in introducing the era of "aemulation."

But with Samuel Butler there was not only encouragement of emulation but a real friendship. This continued after both had left the school and it can be summed up in one of the happiest of the letters from James. In 1795 Butler, now at Cambridge, had won the Chancellor's medal and his former Headmaster wrote to congratulate and give him advice.

> When I write these things you may be sure I am addressing you as a son. I wish I may ever have such a son. You have afforded me so many and such repeated occasions of exultation as to make me feel a pride and a pleasure whenever I think of you. It is now time that you should think of your health, and if you feel an inclination to be perfectly quiet, I shall be extremely glad to see you to stay at Upton, where the longer you stay, the more welcome you will be...You do right to unfold to me the little use you had of a lexicon but do not talk too much of that to others. How little you wanted it is demonstrated by success.

A thoroughly Chipsian letter, one might say. Yet James was not pouring out the affection of a lonely bachelor; he may have adopted Butler as a son, but he had five very promising ones of his own—as well as two daughters and a wife to whom he was devoted (Butler too had loving parents.) But James was capable of great affection, even tenderness: the epitaph for the 14 year-old Spearman Wasey who died at Rugby shows an expression of it that is nearly the same as that quoted for the little cousin at Cambridge. His early grief for his first wife, Elizabeth, "the beautiful Miss Mander" as she went down into family tradition, was deep and finely expressed in her delicate little memorial plaque with its simple Greek inscription, where he used to sit and grieve. But he sought and found consolation with Arabella Caldecott of a local family with whom he had early become friendly, who became his "beloved Belle" for whom his feeling is shown in his very last gently playful letter. In general, the affection he radiated and called out from others is indicated in such references as survive in the writing of old pupils and even shines through Birch's thoroughly 18th century poem:

> Sincerely courteous, cheerful with the gay
> A child with children, thou would'st vie in play.
> Diffusing social joys, thy pliant mind
> Could cheer the languid, make the froward kind;
> Thy magic, nature, and a smile thy art,
> Thy voice, thy look, an index of the heart.

There is little but indirect evidence about that *sine qua non* of school success, relations between the Head and his staff. James told the Trustees that he thought his assistants as good scholars as the generality of Eton classical assistants in his time—than which, no doubt, he could have designed no higher praise. (Nimrod shows that they did not lack variety; he gives amusing descriptions of their eccentricities.) James was not the kind to object to possible rivals on his staff; this one can deduce from his picture—there is not a trace of jealousy on that amiable rubicund face. Truth is not always to be found in memorial inscriptions but the lines from James' (in Worcester Cathedral) have the ring of it:

> He was a Scholar and a ripe and good one, without the
> smallest spark of Scholastic Pride or Acrimony.

He would not have taken to heart (though he might have questioned) Nimrod's dictum that other masters (notably John Sleath, later High Master of St. Paul's) were sounder scholars than himself and he seems to have fostered the habit (with which Arnold is so rightly also credited) in Rugby masters of going on as Heads to other schools; Innes went to Warwick, Cutler to Dorchester and to Sherborne, Chartres to Atherstone and both Sleaths attained Headships, one at Repton, the other at St. Paul's.

At first, James supplemented his staff's salaries from his own; then he persuaded the Trustees to pay them better. Perhaps the most useful bit of *negative* evidence we have of the support they gave him is that, in spite of two rebellions, James never seems to have had cause to complain of their behaviour. This is in contrast to an occasion under a later Head which caused the Trustees to affirm that an Assistant is bound to support the Headmaster in matters of discipline as well as in the curriculum. (On the day in 1797 when the notorious rebellion against "Black Tiger" Ingles, James' successor, was started, no master seems to have been present at all—those Races again?) Summing up, James seems to have had a fine staff and a contented one.

He had the approval of parents for what he called the two pillars on which he erected his school—scholarship and economy. He had worked very hard at both, but the effort expended on the second was the more unexpected. He was determined to avoid the mistakes which had been made at Eton and Harrow of allowing some boys too much money to throw about. Some of his pupils were certainly over-supplied—William Hill, brother of Lord Berwick is said to have been allowed £100 a year and spent much of it on dining and wining, "a beef-steak club" being mentioned by Apperley. James' very last action as Headmaster was to send round a circular with detailed proposals for regulating bills, stating that "the accumulation of expense has arisen from the parent's own indulgences" and—naturally!—from "these extravagant times". He asked their help in abiding steadily by the conditions laid down and helping to check attempts to get round them. "It is my duty" he said, "to watch and resist every encroachment upon the economical system which I have endeavoured to establish."

Particularly interesting—in view of the presence of the Hon. Will Hill and his rich friends—is James' provision for the older boys who are not going to the Universities but into business. They can learn "engrossing hands and Arithmetic and Algebra", and the French Master will give private evening lectures in German "with the Anglo-Saxon pronunciation and dialect to any gentleman whose parents may judge such an acquirement necessary. . ." From a Bohemian Count, this must have been considered cheap at two guineas for the half-year. Considering that this was not a private school where parents might have felt entitled to demand a say in what their children were taught, the Headmaster's consideration for what they thought their boys would need was rare enough then—or even much later. No wonder the numbers grew.

To crown it all, James got on excellently with his Governors/ Trustees. True, there was already quite a tradition of good relations between them and the Heads; true also that they were not pressed for money. But the absolute understanding between the parties and the good sense shown on both sides (which was a great contrast to the relations in some other schools) undoubtedly helped much in the satisfactory development of the newly-orientated school. The few little scraps of paper that survive as notes for meetings and memoranda of various sorts show never a cloud. James was prepared to accept without nagging or moaning the half-loaf of reconditioning and making-do. His cheerfulness and propensity for joking probably made things easier. (One of his letters, after retirement, to the Clerk to the Trustees is so full of jests that some later hand has censored it—they mostly seem to have to do with an invitation to crack a bottle of wine, running to scriptural as well as classical comments.) In return, they gave him the support he needed in the great crises of his life. The honeymoon of his appointment lasted the full 16 years.

One of the crises was evidently the Rebellion of 1786; there had once been some trouble earlier but it seems impossible now to find an account of either. Apperley mentions it but with unusual reticence, though he says Dr. James learnt a lesson. Was there a "sit-in" or was it mere hooliganism, such as broke out after James' retirement? The Trustees gave him their full support saying that they did "entirely and earnestly disapprove of the late Riotous and Rebellious Behaviour" and asserting their support of his authority and discipline, and any "salutary regulation" he might think fit to make. They even encouraged him to expel any boy who challenged his authority or disturbed the peace of the school; it seems that, if anything, they suspected him of being too lenient and forgiving. His last eight years, though a time of turmoil in many schools, seem to have passed off quietly.

The other great crisis was at the end of his school career. James had driven himself hard throughout his time; it was his nature to live fully and at a great pace:

> I filled up every nook and corner of my Time so exactly and I was so busily (I must say also, pleasantly) employed (*Note*—even while I was undressing and more while I was dressing myself in a morning) that I sank at length under a burden of uninterrupted thought which I could not any longer bear. . . It has convinced me of the folly of stretching the Bow string till it be broken. . .

This is from a letter of 52 pages in draft, which he wrote to the Trustees in June 1794. It is in no way recriminatory; on the contrary, it is extremely appreciative of their treatment of him, but evidently the effusion of a man suffering from a break-down. (The quotation above is a very good piece of self-analysis.) Two causes, besides overwork, contributed to this. One he gives in some detail; he had to undergo a sharp and very painful operation, immediately on the end of term; it sounds like an emergency—perhaps a tumour—rather than the much commoner stone. He got over it but had had a severe shock and in several pages gave his reasons for not endangering his health by further labour. Of his other trial, the record is in the parish register at Rugby:

> 20th December 1788, Baptism: Arabella Maria, daughter of the Rev. Mr. James and Arabella . . .
> 3rd December 1793, Buried, Arabella Maria, daughter of the Rev. . . ."

The loss evidently affected him profoundly. Birch comments *(op.cit.):*

> When sickness, with affliction, tried thy soul,
> And from thy arms a lovely infant stole,

When the voice falter'd that could teach so well
And from the brow the wither'd ivy fell,
Solace was near . . .

And indeed, the Trustees did all they could. They allowed him to stay on in office till September 29th to give him time, among other things, "to take a handsome leave" by his circular, of the parents. They voted him a pension of £80 a quarter to be paid by the Clerk—an old and close friend and correspondent. They looked round for him and in two years had obtained through friends a comfortable "Prebendary Stall" at Worcester Cathedral; they passed a most handsome minute of farewell, in which they acknowledged the present flourishing state of the School to be due to his abilities and attention, and they presented him with an outstanding mark of their esteem in a "piece of plate"—a large silver tray with the name and arms of each trustee inscribed on it.

James, who was not 50 when he retired, had ten pleasant and useful years of work as a country parson, supplementing his activities there by taking pupils in his house and by work in connection with the Cathedral. This included preaching, organizing a relief fund, and being a Steward of the Three Choirs' Festival. (An organ for the School had been, at his desire, the object of a fund contributed to by old Rugbeians on his retirement.) He died of a heart attack, having, it was said, had the satisfaction on the previous day of reconciling two quarrelling parishioners. His memory was cherished at Rugby for many years; in his name was founded a prize for Greek verse and for his monument a figure of him by Chantrey was installed in the Chapel when built. Later, the authorities skyed it so that nothing could be seen of him but the soles of his feet. But no full account of him was written; he died too early to be accorded as of right "those two fat volumes" with which, as Lytton Strachey averred, "it is our custom to commemorate the dead." (His letters, those which have been published, are in Butler's *Life*.) And to obliterate him still further, another Headmaster of the same name succeeded him at Rugby later in the nineteenth century.

Yet he still remains James, the First of Rugby. And though his reputation rests only on what he achieved in one school, his work seems to have been both more important and more widely significant than has been hitherto realized. Important, because the changes he brought about in scholastic organization and improved teaching made a certain pattern acceptable and widely copied later on in similar schools. More than that, his less academic innovations, from building studies to circularizing parents often became accepted as common details in boarding school life. As to the significance of what he did, he was probably quite unconscious. It lay in the idea that Eton, Winchester, Westminster and Harrow did not represent a closed body of educational institutions. The sum of Public Schools could be added to, as he had added Rugby. In a short time, it was.

IV

SAMUEL BUTLER OF SHREWSBURY

The Free Grammar School of Edward VI at Shrewsbury began with higher hopes and wider aims than the school of Lawrence Sheriff at Rugby. It sank lower—almost to the point of extinction—yet by Queen Victoria's accession it had risen as high as, and in one aspect higher than, any. It was one of a great number which could be referred to as Foundations of Edward VI, and though no one claims that he took personal interest in it from the beginning it appropriated this title.

It was after the suppression of their Abbey and Collegiate Churches, with any Chantry schools that may have been attached to them, that the Bailiffs, Burgesses and inhabitants of the town and surrounding country forwarded a supplication to the Lord Chancellor that they might have a Free School in Shrewsbury. They were partly impelled to this because the Commission which had suggested places where a Royal Grammar School might be founded had *not* included their town. The Supplication was successfully made through their Recorder and the Corporation's accounts show that £20 was laid out for the Free School's building. Two years later came the Petition to the King which asked for an annuity of £20 towards the maintenance of the Free School, the endowment to come from some of the estates of the religious houses earlier dissolved. Tithes of these were eventually presented as an endowment to the School and a Charter was granted, dated 10th February 1551, for the foundation of a Grammar School which was to bear the King's name (Edward, well-trained by his beloved sister, Elizabeth, was a patron of scholarship as well as charitably minded; later Salopians would have called him by their special word, "philomathes"—a lover of learning). Ten years, however, elapsed before the School got fairly started. There was an epidemic of the "sweating sickness" in 1551; there was difficulty in finding the necessary "honest and able person" for a schoolmaster, and there had been the reign of Queen Mary who did not look favourably on the disposal of tithes to schools. It was not till 1561 that the first Headmaster, Thomas Ashton, took office.

Shrewsbury's foundation originated not in one local worthy's leaving an endowment by Will or Deed, but by a communal effort. There was one figure, however, whose efforts were so remarkable that he took, as it were, the place of a founder, and combined this with being also its first Schoolmaster. Thomas Ashton's importance is indicated by the reference in Camden's *Britannia* (1586), though in this great survey he properly attributes the actual setting up of the school to the inhabitants of Shrewsbury whom he congratulates on its growth.

The Register of entries has no records for the first 11 years, but gives about 270 boys entered in 1562, with Thomas Ashton and two others as *Ludimagistri*. It gives the parentage of the most distinguished boys, e.g. Philip Sidney, Fulke Greville and John Harington, Queen Elizabeth's "witty" godson. Others are indicated as sons of knights, burgesses, etc. The division which became important was into the sons of Shrewsbury inhabitants *(oppidani)* and boys from outside *(alieni)*; the first boy of all—"Phylyppus Stringer"—is listed as "alie". Over the first six years there is a record of entries—names and sometimes dwelling places of boys—but no indication of how long they stayed, which prevents our being certain how many there were at any one time. During the period there were some 800 entries, which would probably mean 300 or 400 boys at a time. (No wonder Camden called the School "numerossissima"!) The balance is against the *oppidani* (they started by having equal numbers) now under 300 entries. The rest are from outside Shrewsbury with a high proportion of names like "David ap Hugh", presumably betokening Welsh origin.

There is a reference to the number of scholars in the description of the entertainment presented to Sir Henry Sidney when, as Lord President of the Marches, he visited the town:

> All the schollars of the sayd free school . . . being in number 360, with their masters before every of them, marching bravely from the said school . . . met the said President.

One is glad to have this confirmation, as the number is most unusual for a school of the period. None could have rivalled it before, except Eton, nor (excepting possibly the Charitable foundations) for long after.

One effect of Ashton's endeavours was the Indenture made in 1571 by Queen Elizabeth.

> This year one Mr. Ashton, schoolmaster of the free school in Salop, being a good and zealous man towards the preferment of lerning in the same school, made suit of his own charge beside great labour to the Queen's Majesty and so obtained to the maintenance of the same school £20 a year more, which made it £40 a year and sufficient finding for the discipline of a master and 2 ushers.

By the same Indenture, Ashton, as "the now headmaster" is given authority to draw up Regulations for the School— "Ashton's Ordinances", as they became known. Together the Indenture and the Ordinances formed the constitution of the school till the 18th century. We really do not know enough about Ashton to form a picture of his personality. He was a typical Elizabethan in his energy, his enthusiasm, his upward thrust into the circles of the great and in his competence in getting things done. As a man of affairs (we know nothing of his teaching capacity) he was able to do much for the school but he was also typical in that it was only a short time before his death that his work in drawing up the Ordinances for the school's government was completed.

There must have been some governing regulation before 1571 as the school had been functioning for some years, but it was then that tripartite indentures were drawn between (1) the Bishop of Lichfield, as Visitor, (2) the Bailiffs and Burgesses* and (3) the Master and Fellows of St. John's College, Cambridge, together with Mr. Ashton (who had by then resigned) and his successor to the Headmastership. One cannot help wondering whether the Bailiffs had been thinking of the School as a small local establishment which they could run by themselves— choosing their own Head and other masters, as subsequently they tried on several occasions to do. Ashton may have had other ideas from the beginning, or he may have seen that the School was developing into something quite different from what they expected and have considered that their authority and experience would be insufficient for it. If so, he was commendably far-seeing. Probably it was with this in mind that he left to the Bailiffs the detailed internal regulations of the School—its hours, holidays, games and sports allowed, and the disciplinary measures to be taken; also the supervision of the *alieni* who were "tabled" locally but always accepted as part of the School's responsibility. But he himself dealt with and laid down with care, the more serious and complicated matters, including the financial arrangements. The funds in the School Chest, regarded as a Bank, called the "Stock Remnant", were to be used for specific purposes, including University scholarships. Up to £10 at a time could be removed by the Bailiffs for repairs and legal expenses; above that St. John's College had to give consent.

Ashton also set out the qualifications and payment of the Schoolmasters: "If one Schoolmaster have £40, another £20, the third

---

* From 1294 to 1638 the town was governed by two "Bailiffs"; then under a new constitution a Mayor was set up. The term "School Bailiff" for those who governed the affairs of the School continued to be used—as it will be here, equally with Burgesses.

£10, I think no school in England hath a salary exceeding this." True, but the value of these sums went fast downhill and it was added that they should not be supplemented by "any art or profession whereby their service to the school should be hindered." Nor was profit from boarders mentioned, even for the Headmaster, and no evidence survives until the 18th century that masters did board them. If so, they had no more responsibility for them than did the ordinary citizen with whom boys tabled* (paid for by their parents) which was to see that they went to church on Sundays, twice. Choice of the Head and most of the masters was the responsibility of the Master and Fellows of St. John's College, the procedure being that the Bailiffs were to notify the College of any vacancy and the College then elected a successor, whom the Bailiffs were to appoint. But if the Bailiffs did not think him worthy, they could so signify and ask for a new election. The point of quoting this is to give an example of how the whole scheme was a compromise of interests; a mechanism of checks and balances. Over the years this could not but lead to irritation and frustration. For the next two centuries however, those who had to work this constitution struggled on. There were frequent attempts by litigation and even force on the part of the Bailiffs to re-establish powers they had had under Edward VI's, pre-Ashton, Charter of making their own appointments. They did not finally lose their case till the beginning of the 18th century; by the end of that century it had become neccessary to have an Act of Parliament which abolished the Ordinance altogether.

So the School, with its new set of Ordinances and its own premises, though not yet very adequate and certainly not well sited, being on a strip of land right in the town, had started and continued under Ashton's immediate successor, Thomas Lawrence. He did a good piece of work and in his charming letter of resignation says:

> I have within these twelve years past, through the blessing of God through my toil in teaching and through their diligence in learning, sent out of my school about a hundred scholars to Cambridge and Oxford, of which a great number at this day God's name be praised, are as likely men to prove good members of the Christian commonwealth as any whatsoever or wheresoever.

No schoolmaster could have written himself a happier epitaph, which incidentally shows the strong connection of the Grammar (later Public) School with universities.

---

* That most distinguished of Elizabethan Salopians, Philip Sidney, stayed over three years at the school from 1564, but we do not know where he lived. As a very special pupil, he may well have "tabled" with Ashton.

The resignation of Lawrence was the first occasion for some sparring of the Bailiffs with the College. They first offered the post to the Second Master which might have established a precedent for their making the appointment, but unfortunately for them he did not feel equal to the post. The Bailiffs then advised the College of the need for an appointment but were prepared to disallow the new master if one younger or "more insufficient" (than their Second Master) were appointed. The qualification of age was quite an arbitrary one and the College retorted by selecting one of their own graduates, a scholar of the school and son of a Burgess, but apparently under 30. Fortunately the Bailiffs had the sense to waive their own condition and the man was appointed—and stayed for 50 years. But on a later occasion the Bailiffs, again struggling to make an appointment, proceeded to an attack by physical force on the school buildings—a procedure which seems to have disrupted the School for about six weeks. The remainder of this and other controversies have been chronicled and need not be followed up here. It is no wonder that sometimes after violent and disruptive quarrels "the course of the School was for a while interrupted so that it became very emptie of scholars."

One thing is clear; in spite of the difference between the Bailiffs, representing the Burgesses, and the Headmaster (and still more frequently the College which appointed him) the townsfolk really did from the beginning take an interest in the School and regarded it as their own, in spite of the large proportion of boys who had always come from outside. The Bailiffs showed by references to "Our School" how deeply they were concerned in it—e.g. "Our School is in very great decay—many boys are sent to distant schools." The difficulties arose because they wanted to have the whole control (which the Ordinances precluded) and because they so often disagreed among themselves. Fortunately by 1636 came Thomas Challoner, a headmaster approved by all parties and probably the most notable that the School had during the 17th century. But though peace had been restored within the city, fighting was about to begin without. For four years Challoner held the entries steady at about 120 boys but after that they dropped alarmingly. The Civil War was about to begin when in September 1642, Shrewsbury was visited by Charles I, who stayed for a month and on departing took with him among other moneys a "loan" of £600 from the School Chest. Challoner (who must have approved this monetary transaction, for he held one of the necessary keys) was dismissed when the Parliamentarians captured the town. He spent 19 years "wandering" (but successfully keeping school wherever he went) and was finally re-instated but died in 1664.

The volume of the School Register from 1665 to 1734 is

unfortunately missing so it is difficult to say much about the School under the Heads who followed Challoner and whether the Heads really were less notable than their predecessors or only seem so from lack of evidence. The College (University) Registers show that Shrewbury pupils continued to go to the Universities implying that the standard of scholarship was kept up. Year after year the boys went on there, or to Parliament or back to their estates, a good proportion also into the Church or the Law. One of the best known Shrewsbury scholars, George Savile (later Marquess of Halifax and one of Charles II's wisest counsellors) came with his brother from Yorkshire, showing how far parents were prepared to send their sons. For in spite of the low numbers and administrative difficulties caused by the political troubles of the 17th century, the School never seems to have been in danger of closing and at this time it had a character which would now be recognised as "Public" which it lost and did not regain till Dr. Butler's day.

It was in the 18th century that the decay in numbers became serious. By 1719 under Richard Lloyd there were under 30 boys. Some left because of the low repute of the School, the Headmaster being "by his age and infirmities incapable to discharge his duties". He was then 60 and continued for another four years, with no advantage to the School's numbers. Changes and resignations among the masters increased, perhaps indicating that they found the interference and pettiness of the Burgesses (of which there are many examples) frustrating. The Rev. James Atcherley was promoted to the Headship in 1771, and though he may have started well, there is no doubt that by the end of his 27 years his name had become a by-word for effeteness, and the School had been brought to the verge of extinction. Dr. James of Rugby was certainly not prejudiced against it, and when in 1797 he wrote to Samuel Butler about it may even have exaggerated its advantages:

Amongst other places, I have been at Shrewsbury where. . . I kept you principally in view, and on the whole I am of the opinion that your fortune might very possibly be made in that city. There is a School there having from £1,300 to £1,500 a year, of which the headmaster has not about £100 a year, but he has allowance for assistants and an excellent house and a school built in a superior style. Within the memory of many, a headmaster had had there (I think) not less then sixty boarders. This school was once the Eton or the Westminster of Wales and of all Shropshire etc. Now the present master does nothing and there are not above three or four boys belonging to this noble foundation although there are many exhibitions belonging to the School. The gentlemen of Shrewsbury, therefore, have an idea of pensioning off the old masters now there and in possession, and of appointing new ones. . . If you find by inquiring that any position there should be worth your notice, it would be a theatre worthy of your abilities.*

Dr. James was on the whole well-informed. At long last those who were interested in and responsible for the School had decided that an Act of Parliament was the only way of making changes sweeping enough to revive the School educationally and administratively. The Act was passed in 1798.

The use of the surplus revenues (which the Burgesses had been in the habit of raiding for law-suits and such) was specifically defined, so was the right of Burgesses' sons to free education. The right of the College to appoint the Headmaster was retained and the Bailiffs' power of veto rescinded. The Corporation lost also the power of selecting the other Masters, which went to the Headmaster, all but the appointment of the Second Master which was left to the College. (This might have been a wise move; in the event it proved disastrous.) To the Headmaster was assigned absolute control over the internal arrangements for teaching and for the School.

The old staff were forthwith pensioned off, all but the Accidence Master resigning formally in June 1798. As at Rugby, a new man and new methods were needed, and in the next month the Master and Fellows of St. John's College chose a former Rugby boy, a Fellow of their College, and incidentally a former Tutor in the house of Thomas Eyton, one of their new Governors. This was Samuel Butler.

For knowledge of Dr. Samuel Butler one has mainly to rely on the *Life and Letters,* a compilation in two volumes by his grandson and better-known namesake, the author of *Erewhon* and *The Way of All Flesh.* Of his ancestry, in spite of this pious effort very little is known; "yeoman class" seems best to describe his status—and this, in view of the place he was going to take, is interesting. His family had been living at Kenilworth in Warwickshire from before 1700. Samuel's father, "an amiable, easy-going man who let money slip through his fingers from sheer good-nature"† was a small linen-draper in that town.

Samuel Butler went to Rugby and it is one of the happy instances of Dr. James' lack of snobbery that he should have formed such a friendship with his pupil, a friendship based on temperament, intellectual affinity and the older man's kindliness. Butler had no grand relations who could have brought credit to the school or patronage to

---

* S. Butler (ed.), *Life and Letters of Samuel Butler,* Vol. I, p.20.
† *Op. cit.,* p.5.

the Headmaster, but no consciousness of social position appears in the correspondence, some of which has fortunately been preserved at Rugby. (That James was sufficiently man of the world enough to realize that Butler needed friends if he were to succeed in any profession except teaching does however appear in his letters.) Butler was the first of his family to go to Rugby; he kept up a regular correspondence with his mother who lived in Kenilworth all her life, showing his continued interest in the small-town life. The most distinguished member of the circle was Dr. Samuel Parr, the notable Harrovian scholar and eccentric, who became a great friend of young Butler. He was of considerable influence in Samuel's life and on terms of close, easy friendship with him; "Bye, bye, namesake", occurs more than once in Parr's later letters. (See chapter II, p.34.)

Possibly because this provincial town set-up corresponded with the Headmaster's own, Thomas James—the son of respectable but far from distinguished parents—may have found a bond of sympathy between himself and his pupil. Butler was, one assumes, a boarder in James' house and it may have been the kindness and humour of the older Doctor that was later reflected in Butler's attitude to his own boys, though his milder, quieter temperament made contact less easy for him. Like James's, his was a *new* attitude. There is no need to go over all the horrors of pedagogy in the 18th and earlier centuries. The beating was traditional; there is hardly any representation of a schoolmaster in picture, book, carving or even seal, that does not show him with his birch—often in the act of using it. Both James and Butler used their instrument frequently but they were pioneers in deliberately trying to find other ways of governing and influencing boys.

One would like to think that Rugby boys, like their headmaster, passed over social distinctions, but it seems that "Nimrod" (Charles Apperley, see Chapter III, p.53), who was the son of a clergyman, was inclined to look down on Butler. He writes:

> Butler was most unpopular in the school. In fact, partly because he was the son of a small shopkeeper. . .and at Rugby as a foundation boy, and partly on account of his churlish temper, we in the same boarding house voted him nothing better than a snob, and the meanness of his personal appearance gave colour to our proceedings. Never would he offer to do us a verse or two, or construe us over; but he would sit with his elbow on his knee and his face resting on one hand and a book in the other, and never open his mouth. My brother was near him in school, but I seldom heard them exchange a word.*

* *Fraser's Magazine,* August 1842.

We should now call it snobbery on the other side, but is is likely that the intellectual small boy (Butler went to Rugby in 1783 at the age of nine) showed himself reserved and sensitive, traits that he never entirely lost. It is not surprising that he did not find much in common with the sporting sons of the parson. But he established himself by adopting what must have been a pose—that of taking no trouble over his work. It completely took in the rather naif Apperleys, one of whom apparently shared his room for four years. "Fishing and novel-reading and play-reading" Nimrod remarks "employed by far the greater portion of his time". It was a marvel to his companions that he could parse, construe and compose his exercises so effortlessly; he must have been a heaven-born genius!

> "Fetch me half a sheet of paper," he would say to myself . . .at the hour of awaking in the morning; when taking some novel or play-book from under his pillow, which he had been reading over-night, and using it as a desk, he would write off the best exercise of the day, and *Play for Butler* would often be heard throughout the schools. Then his lessons; "Where is the place!" he would say to his neighbour, on joining his form ten minutes before a Greek play was to be read. . . If "called up," however, there was *no mistake.* Now how this was done is quite beyond my comprehension. (Nimrod, *op.cit.*)

Poor Nimrod! He could only compare this quality to "the intuitive knowledge some persons have displayed of. . . the run of a fox". Butler had a flair, in which learning and genius combined and, in this Age of Elegance he may have been tempted to impress his fellows more than was good for himself.* But Butler's pose did not take in his Headmaster who took opportunities to draw him out.

> If he were called up, his author was beautifully displayed by him and when others were "up" James would often appeal to him for *his* interpretation of a passage. In fact James was proud of his scholar, which he well might have been. (Nimrod *op.cit.*)

With two brilliant pupils, Butler and Landor, James could introduce the love of his heart, Greek verse, and thereby establish Rugby in the

---

* In *The Lighter Side of School Life* (Ian Hay) there is an amusing passage on the appreciation at school of brilliance as opposed to hard work which leads to a good deal of hypocrisy. "Sparkleigh", whose behaviour is exactly parallel to Butler's, as described by Nimrod, is really a desperately hard worker but manages to conceal the fact and gains a reputation for *insouciance.* "The tortoise is a dreadfully unpopular winner."

top class of classical schools. For Butler, this was the making of his whole career, probably the most important factor in his life. His gift gave him the *entrée* into a class of scholars who made a world of their own in which he could take a high place. He was graded intellectually and not by his social origins. There was in this transition something akin to the Mediaeval world where society was completely and irrevocably stratified, but there was always the possibility of an outstandingly able boy's rising within the Church—English examples run from Becket to Wolsey—irrespective of the stratification outside it,

The place of Greek verses in the Public School and the social and academic world has been touched on; the much larger question of whether in the long run the boys, the schools, or English education generally did or did not benefit from Dr. James's introduction—this is not relevant here. James himself, acting on his principles of not pressing boys beyond their capacity, restricted the writing of verses to those few boys who were capable of doing and enjoying it, but this wise principle was later not accepted.

Landor said that he and Butler were the first in the School to write them, and one small comment may be made on the rivalry between Rugby's two genuises. Landor worked away at his Greek literature when he needed it for his *Imaginary Conversations*, but he always preferred Latin—in which Butler's superiority may not have been so clearly shown. The scar of his defeat remained. But something rankled also with his rival. Landor used to write his earliest (English) verses on the bank of the local stream among the peppermint plants, of which he was very fond. Apperley, unsuspectingly, records with surprise:

> Dr. Butler had a great dislike to the smell of peppermint and woe to the boy whom he happened to catch in the possession of it. . . The effluvia from it in the school would greatly ruffle his temper for the day.

The psychiatrist must make what he can of this!

Encouraged by his Master's praises and the habit of copying down good work into a special book, Butler enshrined his productions in a volume which forms part of the complete set of his MS. works—of professional rather than of general interest—left by his grandson to the British Museum. His English verses show the strong influence of Milton. (The spelling is less orthodox than one might have expected from an intelligent fourteen-year-old; not for nothing did Dr. James later admonish the Headmaster-to-be: "Mind the spelling".) A more striking example of a blank verse poem was written when Butler was at Cambridge: *To the Rev'd Dr. James on his resigning the Headmastership of Rugby School*

<table>
<tr><td>beginning:</td><td>Friend and Protector of my tender years
Whose gentle care fond memory still reveres. . .</td></tr>
<tr><td>and ending:</td><td>With matchless lustre, on his noon-tide way
He rode triumphant like the Lord of Day;
Matchless he sinks, his course of glory run;
Such the mild radiance of the setting sun.</td></tr>
</table>

Whether Dr. James, still in his forties, appreciated being compared to a sunset is not known. He rather pointedly thanks his pupil for his *Latin* address but this may appear significant only from the accidental survival of this particular letter. The valediction has a Churchillian flavour.

Butler stayed eight years at Rugby and was in 1791 elected to an exhibition from the School, which he proposed to take up at Oxford. Through the intervention of Dr. Parr, he was deflected to St. John's College, Cambridge, where he went in January, 1792. The reason for the change is not known, but it was to have a great effect later on his career, St. John's having the responsibility of choosing the Headmaster of Shrewsbury. Butler, with no thought of this, must have been looking forward to, and proceeded to have, an exceptionally brilliant career. University distinctions tend to be mere lists of names, except to those concerned with them; Butler's list was a formidable one:

He was Browne medallist, Latin Ode, 1792-3 and Greek Ode, 1794. He was Craven Scholar 1793, defeating S. T. Coleridge, Keate. . .and Bethel, afterwards Bishop of Bangor. He graduated as fourth Senior Optime in 1796 and took the first Chancellor's medal in the same year. He was first Members' Prizeman 1797 and 1798 and was elected Platt Fellow of St. John's, April 3rd 1797.*

Unfortunately there is little documentation for this period, though much of his happy correspondence with James belongs here. (Butler knew the James family at Cambridge and the Doctor arranged for a book to be sent for the Library at Rugby by "little James, my cousin's son".) James is even free enough to comment to Butler on his own successor:

My dear Butler,

I received your friendly and satisfactory letter yesterday. Mr. Ingles was fixed on by the trustees last Thursday. . . He is an excellent scholar—of my own standing in King's nearly—a very good man indeed and very fit for the office. He saved very little at Macclesfield, and seems to me still to pant after glory.

---

* *Life and Letters of Samuel Butler*, Vol. I, p.13.

I received also yesterday your very elegant address to me which is as good Latin as can be penned. I am very proud of it, and I went to dine immediately with Mr. Grimes, and we both love you exceedingly. . .and agree that you deserved just as much for the good heart that conducted you to this work as for the good head that produced it.

I am, my dear Butler, your obliged and affectionate friend,

T. JAMES

This must have been in many ways the happiest, certainly the most carefree, period that Samuel Butler was ever to know. Even financially, the settlement on him of a reversionary interest seemed to make him more secure. In fact, as so many other of his hopeful enterprises it proved a drag rather than an assistance. He did in 1795 suggest that the reversionary interest should be sold to provide his parents with an annuity, which they refused; the incident shows the excellent relations between Butler and his parents.

During the long vacation of 1795 Butler went as tutor to the family of his friend and school-fellow, Thomas Eyton, at Wellington, Salop. Possibly Eyton was the first to suggest that Butler might take the headship of Shrewsbury School when it should be reconstructed, but there is no evidence that Samuel took this much to heart. He would have been still bent on winning awards at Cambridge.

Among friends that he made while still in residence there was a Swiss, Andreas Merian, who afterwards by some quirk of fate became a Russian Baron and Russian Ambassador at Paris. A long correspondence, ceasing only with the Baron's death is preserved. It is of little intrinsic interest, but it is enlightening as showing how very greatly Merian respected Butler as a classical scholar—a piece of evidence regarding his reputation which is valuable as coming from outside the English scholastic world.

Then came what seemed a fatal step. Butler became engaged to be married—thereby precluding all College Fellowships. His wife-to-be was fifth daughter of a Cambridge don, Dr. Apthorpe, who was distinguished enough to become a Prebendary of St. Paul's but no help either financially or influentially to his prospective son-in-law. In the long run, his marriage was a fine thing for Butler. His Harriet was staunch, loyal, capable, and much beloved—hardly a boy writing to the Head on leaving the school house but shows his feeling for "Mother Butler". But at the moment, the prospect strained both his financial resources and his relations with his friend and former Headmaster. Consternation would not be too strong a word for Dr. James' feelings, as shown in the spate of writing which greeted the announcement, and he points out unsparingly the professional and economic difficulties into which his young friend is running.

Butler's first suggestion seems to have been to set up a small establishment and take private pupils. James, who was now himself doing this, spoke trenchantly from his experience:*

> You talk of pupils, and perhaps you might get one or two; for I think you will not find it possible to keep up a stock, as it were of five or six. Look at Dr. Parr, that paragon of human abilities—how few pupils has he ever had at any one time. . . Pupils are not easily got, let a man's character and abilities be ever so superlative, whatever you may think to the contrary; and when got, their stay is very uncertain. Further, there is much anxiety attending them. I have had occasion within three months to beg the parent to take one young man home from my house whose conduct I justly disapproved, and you have known my forbearance in such matters. Now, if you were married and in my situation, what a serious evil it would be to you to part with one hundred a year out of three or four hundred. . .(December 27th, 1796)

Besides the moral difficulty, there is, quite apart from the day to day expenses (and how much does the young lady know about housekeeping?), the capital to be found:

> Where is your furniture, of beds especially, to come from? Bed furniture for decent private pupils will cost for cotton—sixty yards at 2.6. is £7. 10 without making up or lining (not necessary) without sheets and bedding and one window curtain each. Then each bedstead and its hangings will be £11, and then for each bed and blankets, two pairs of sheets and bedding £20, which makes the price of your private pupils beds to be £100. . .You must also have decent furniture and real comforts, or your imagined paradise will soon become less a source of tranquility than you expect.

James is even more pessimistic about any other professions, a Job's comforter indeed:

> You can do no more than thousands before you. The greatest abilities in the Law (go to Westminster and see it) and in Physics are in great numbers in want, and are often sadly straitened. You cannot be better off than one of these, adventuring into the great ocean of the world, without the possession of your future estate, or anything but academical fame, which will indeed give you a good chance for

---

* Extracts from Letters of Dr. James, preserved in the Temple Library, Rugby.

pupils, but after all nothing is certain. Then if you are ill, if you die, what is to be done? What is to become of your offspring, of your wife? I dare not say Marry, unless you can get a firm ground to stand on.

He seems to think that Butler is keeping the idea of a school "as a desperate and last resource", but James uses it as an argument for waiting till some endowed schoolmastership presents itself:

In this you might easily succeed in any part of the kingdom. No such amazing amount of bodily strength (which by the way you have not. . .) is requisite in a school, for it will fall to the lot of few men to have their strength so tried to the utmost as my powers were by such an extraordinary influx of members; and that with me was all chance and luck; and it would be better for you to proceed quietly than encounter such an armed host.

In the letter of January 23rd, 1797 he becomes specific. He says of Shrewsbury: "It would be theatre worthy of your abilities,' and you would play a game in which you would be sure to be a wonderful winner." After firmly disparaging an assistantship at Rugby, as being "very well for an unmarried man" but financially not viable for a family, he makes a very necessary point with the greatest possible tact:

Let a man be ever so great at the University, yet when once he has left it and has been melted down into the great mass of the world, he loses a very considerable share indeed of that consequence and attention which the particular interests of individuals cause to be paid him in a seat of literature. You cannot, I am sure, name or recollect a man who has sailed into the great ocean of the world from his college labour, in whose fortune the observation I have made has not been verified.

James was indeed all too shrewd a prophet, and there is hardly a note struck in these letters which did not resound through Butler's after-life. Samuel cannot have helped thinking of his old Master's letters (which he so carefully preserved) when he was himself writing to his father-in-law about the debt incurred for capital to start his house at Shrewsbury, making it fit to take in School boarders. Later he has to complain about his difficulty in making any profit from a boarding house at the present increasing prices (did he remember Dr. James on the price of pork and on the continual increase in taxes?). It was true that his boys did *not* at first increase in numbers as fast as James's Rugby influx, which was perhaps rather a pity, but then his old Headmaster had put his finger (ever so lightly) on another stop—Butler's health; this was to be an impediment nearly all his life. The hint, too, that the shoemaker must stick to his last was wise enough, particularly in the case of one so temperamentally lacking in selfconfidence as Butler. Scholarship was his *métier,* in which he could feel secure—scholarship and the production of scholars for the Universities. It was the University connection and the University standard that made Butler's work possible.

In the mechanics of organizing his teaching, James *could* help his former pupil, and tirelessly he wrote, page after page, showing the details of how this had been worked out at Rugby—curriculum, preparation, household management, from top to bottom. Much of this, Butler took over entirely and it was implanted in his new school, just as 20 years before, the discipline of Eton had been carried over to Rugby.

This need not be quoted in detail but his general counsel is summed up in one of the last surviving letters:

Nothing done at first and while your numbers are small. . .will be grievous now, but everything new afterwards will in this age stir up revolutionary principles. . .Make all your rules with ten boys as strict as you mean them to be with two hundred; and now is the time for enacting laws.

You are most wise in not saying one word of what you make clearer, or what is now better or wiser than before it has been. All boasting is hideous—look at the French—and all improvements will be better evinced by the eye and by the facts than by empty words which only expose the speaker to the charge of vanity behind his back to dislike, etc. and besides to numerous enemies; for they must have some friends and these, like the mice in the fable, will hurt you.*

My kindest respect and Mrs. James' to Mrs. Butler. Once more we wish to see you. I cannot think of leaving my children, then assembled from school.

Your friend
T. JAMES

God bless you.

James's death four years later was probably unexpected. His pupils' memories of him were long and deep. In 1821 the Chantrey memorial to him was planned, and it was of course Butler who was asked to write the Latin inscription when it was set up in Rugby Chapel.

---

* James, though his last sentence is a bit involved, again showed himself only too true a prophet.

Butler had entered on his small kingdom—whether of 20 boys, of five boys, or a single scholar can hardly now, from the varying accounts, be determined,—with high hopes. According to custom, he addressed the Mayor and Corporation of Shrewsbury in a Latin speech at his installation on October 1st, 1798, as Headmaster of the Free School. (The speech was sent to Dr. James, who admired it exceedingly.) "Dignissime Praetor, Optimi Municipes, Praesides Honoratissimi", it began; fortunately an English translation appeared in a Shrewsbury paper. A short passage sums up his main theme:

> One return for your favours I promise you, which you may not be ashamed to receive nor I to offer. . .that I will seek no relief from vigilance, no remission from labour, no relaxation from solicitude and anxiety in the scrupulous discharge of my duty and the preservation of your good opinion. From these objects I will neither be diverted by business nor allured by pleasure; neither shall the temptations of literature withdraw my attention, nor the enticements of ease beguile me from faithfully directing my actions to fulfil the promise of my words.

This may sound like an orthodox 18th century "sentiment" but the long and arduous term of his headship shows that these words and the rest of his "dedication" did mean something to Samuel Butler. He went on to state his responsibility for the morals and religious education of those "whom now I receive under my care" (he had taken holy orders) and it is not credible that he did not really feel this responsibility. Neither then nor afterwards did he express his religion in the same terms as later headmasters, but this is not surprising. The Age of Anti-enthusiasm had not yet passed away.

Immediately after his appointment, Butler had a stroke of cruel luck. Under Shrewsbury's peculiar constitution, the Second Master was appointed not by the Head but by St. John's College, and was removable only by them. Butler, within a few months of his arrival was saddled with a Mr. John Jeudwine, who remained his Second Master for 37 years—i.e. he died only six months before Butler himself resigned. He appeared quite well chosen but he was completely uncongenial to Butler, as no doubt Butler was to him, and he made no effort—as Butler *did*—to overcome their differences. On the contrary, he guarded his independence most jealously, and his letters show constant attempts to justify and hardly any to co-operate. For, as Butler's successor amazingly told his grandson-biographer, "I suppose you know that he and Dr. Butler did not speak?" Their correspondence shows this to have been literally the case; communication was by notes, mostly written in the third person.

It seems quite incredible that such a state of friction should have been allowed to exist for all these years but Butler seems simply to have accepted it, like his own ill-health (but with even less reference to it) as a necessary thorn in the flesh. A reference there necessarily had to be in the Headmaster's correspondence every now and again to his Second Master, and especially to the question of boys entering his House. But Samuel had a wonderful command of himself ("I never saw him lose his temper with a boy", said Kennedy) and he seldom brooded over his wrongs. His letters are concerned with everything under the sun—except Jeudwine.

But it was not only within the School that Jeudwine gave trouble.

There was soon formed a Jeudwine party within the town which for some years pursued Mr. Butler with a hostility that must have been singularly hard to bear without loss of self-restraint.*

Many years later, the Headmaster wrote to a young friend that he himself had been hardened against "dissatisfied and slandrous persons" early in life for "during the first fifteen or eighteen years of my residence in Shrewsbury no man can have suffered more from vexatious and unprovoked calumny".

One may well ask why Butler stayed in such a position. He did indeed make some attempts to get away, but it was probably his financial commitments that held him. He wrote plainly to his father-in-law (September 1800) wishing he could do better for "our dear Harriet. . . still, one must be sensible," and explaining.

From the want of security to begin with, I was obliged to be indebted to Mr. Eyton at the outset of my present situation for the means to furnish and maintain my house. . .little short of £1,000. I should have begun last midsummer to diminish that debt instead of which owing to the enormous price of provisioning, I am this year a loser of at least £200 and from the present complexion of affairs I cannot see much hope.

Butler had sunk his borrowed capital in furnishing a boarding house and he could not move till he had got out of debt and at least established a going concern. But if he then moved to another school, he could probably have got his successor at Shrewsbury to repay him some of what he had spent, and on one occasion he must have hoped there was an opening. Eight years after he had been working, with some success, at raising numbers at Shrewsbury, Dr. James' successor at Rugby left. That Headship seemed a wonderful chance. As an old

---

* *Life and Letters of Samuel Butler,* Vol. I, p.42.

Rugby boy, as a fine scholar not yet too far from his academic successes and with the right amount of experience, he seemed exactly the man. It was extraordinary that the Trustees, in the words of one of Butler's friends, "sent their wits a-Wooll-gathering" and preferred to him, not Arnold, (who was still to come) but a totally unremarkable Dr. Wooll.

To Butler this was a bitter blow and the cause is still something of a mystery. It was connected with a foolish political squib, published as *The Huntiad,* a take-off of a speech in favour of a candidate made by an unimportant local worthy, Rowland Hunt. Butler denied that he had any part in this and no-one has made clear how this could be the cause of his failure at Rugby, though it may indicate the *local* suspicion and unpopularity he evoked.

Much more serious, we should think to-day, was the accusation of harshness in his school discipline. As several of the Governors (fathers between them of nine Shewsbury boys) took the trouble to write to the Rugby Trustees on Butler's behalf, it looks as if *this* was the "calumny" that affected his chances. They had already given him a testimonial, but hearing that "a report injurious to him had been circulated, of severity on his part towards his boys", they wrote specially to stigmatize the report as a "malignant falsehood" and asserted that his conduct was "as kind, humane, and indulgent as any reasonable parent could wish."* Other individual letters to the same effect survive, but all this testimony unfortunately did the candidate no good at Rugby. The draft of a letter by Butler himself (November 1806) evidently in connection with his attempt to move, gives a vivid picture of his early years at Shrewsbury:

> In the year 1798, I was appointed Head-Master of Shrewsbury which I found with scarcely a single boy. I was soon inundated by an influx of town boys of all ages from sixteen downwards, whom as the sons of burgesses I was compelled to admit, though none of them had received any regular education. Besides these, many other boys came to me, some from various public and private schools and some from their nurseries. No regular school, or discipline, had been established here for about twenty years. . . No idea of punishment had ever occurred to the good people of Shrewsbury . . . so that whenever a boy sent home a report, however true or false, that either himself or any of his school-fellows had been punished, it furnished matter for observation and illnatured remarks.†

As an example of the kind of trouble he had to deal with—two boys came back drunk from the Races at eleven at night, ran away to avoid

* *Life and Letters of Samuel Butler,* Vol. I, p.48.-
† British Museum MS.35068E, Vol.I.

punishment and drew a knife on their pursuers. Understandably he expelled them. After that, he avers, he had not punished (i.e. beaten) an average of six boys a term. This, for the period in which he lived, sounds almost suspiciously lenient. For one offence he certainly beat them—going in boats on the river, especially when in flood. This was originally a safety rule; at least one boy was so drowned, J. R. Marindin in 1829.

Scattered throughout his correspondence over many years are innumerable records of the real hold Butler had on the affections of the boys. At the very moment when the slander about his severity may have been ruining his chances at Rugby, one small boy was telling his uncle, Mr. Littlehales, that he never was at any place where he learnt so much or was so kindly treated. Ten years later, Gretton, Dean of Hereford, wrote about his son, destined to become a noted scholar: "My boy's late letter to his sister most modestly tells his honours. . . with a hearty acknowledgment of your paternal care." And Robert Scott (later to be part author of the Greek Lexicon) wrote of: "The success which has attended me in the University, wholly and entirely yours" and of the kindness "which both in sickness and in health I always met with from Mrs. Butler and yourself". Payne, another scholar writing to tell of "the unlooked-for success in being elected Ireland Scholar", refers to "the kindness and forbearance shown towards me throughout the whole of my career as your pupil".*

Many more examples could be quoted as evidence of Butler's kindness which it would not be necessary to stress were it not that the tradition of harshness, (whether from the Rugby "calumny" or, more likely, by a general "blanketing" of all 19th century Heads as "great beaters") seems still to be generally accepted without enquiry. For example, in a recent edition of the family letters of Samuel Butler, the younger, it is stated that Thomas Butler, (son of one Samuel and father of the other) "had grown up under the strict hand of a formidable disciplinarian, Dr. Samuel Butler, a famous Victorian Headmaster." Apart from the inaccuracy of that last adjective—Dr. Butler resigned his headship a year before Victoria came to the throne and died in the third year of her reign—there is no evidence that his attitude to either his son or his pupils was unduly harsh or at all cruel. Samuel the younger took the trouble to enquire about this, asking particularly whether he "ever found any kind of pleasure in flogging". Among other

---

* Dr. Butler did not keep the bouquets only and destroy the brickbats. The last letter of a most extensive correspondence ended: "Far from being changed, that you are a paltry despicable pedant, are *and ever will be,* the sentiments of THOS. COLTMAN."

correspondents, one who had actually been under Butler in 1830 answered rather naively but certainly showing no repression:

> Oh no, I do not think your grandfather liked flogging as if he were cruel. I have always thought that his rushing round to catch a boy up at the window (i.e. looking in on another being punished) was a bit of a joke. . . We were Spartans. . .The School character (showed) a great independency of thought, freedom from party and while self-reliant not self-opinionated, but allowing others to think differently. I suppose it sprang from regime of Butler.

Of course, Butler had his troubles with the boys, and sometimes with parents. His correspondence with the Holyoake family over a long period (1809-20) gives the fullest documentation of this, as he had four boys under his care at different times—and rowdy, high-spirited lads they proved to be. Yet all of them can be found on the Old Scholars Register; one went to St. John's, went on to be M.P., J.P., D. L. for his county and Sheriff for Worcestershire and ended as a peer; another went into the Army, successfully; the third, whom Butler "dismissed" also ended as J.P. and D.L.; the fourth was destined for business. Not only does this give a fair idea of the boys' families and futures but among repeated complaints and lengthy exchanges, it is pleasant to find that Butler and the Holyoake parents remained good friends to the end. As a rule even in major controversies Butler seems to have had the support of his boarders' parents and their trust. There is, for example, a long letter from a Mrs. Brotherton giving names and details about a scheme to steal wine from Dr. Butler's cellar, in which her son Eliab was involved, asking his advice on what to do with the boy. (Eliab did not return to school.) There were occasions when Butler expelled boys: "The Wine Row", "The Coltman Row" and "The Beef Row" were such. The last which, as one might expect, had to do with complaints about the food, was rather a farcical occasion, towards the end of Butler's time, when he expelled all his praeposters on the spot, including that prize-pupil, Robert Scott; all but one apologized and he had them back. That his forgiveness was often valued is shown in an early letter sent on by a parent: "Dr. Butler has offered to forget all that is past and begin again. . .We are as happy as any two boys in the school."

Except for these few major crises, Butler got on happily with his boys (and far more than this with many of them) and, except for his first local tussles, with their parents. He established a respect for himself (and for his pupils at the Universities) and formed many friendships with Professors, Tutors and Heads of Colleges with whom cordial and pleasantly easy letters are found in his correspondence. At

Cambridge naturally he was most at home. Even an often-quoted remark of Dr. Wordsworth: "Dr. Butler comes here year after year, just as a first-rate London milliner makes a yearly visit to Paris, to get the fashions," sounds like a quip jestingly spoken and orally passed on in fun, rather than a disparagement to be taken with severity.

The point is that Samuel Butler's success depended largely on his character and good relations with the world in which he moved. It was not the great social and aristocratic world, though like his own Headmaster, James, he had easy contacts and commanded respect there in his degree; it was the world of the squirearchy, the gentleman of town or country (but especially the latter) and the University don. But the appreciation of scholarship was not limited to dons; it functioned at all levels and included members of (both) Houses of Parliament, the army, and clergy of all ranks. It was a world where the highest in the land (Royalty perhaps excluded, but Archbishops certainly included) were excited by the clever performance of an undergraduate and would discuss his hexameters, his addresses, his inscriptions. This turning of everything into Greek was a fashionable pastime (as Swift's "writing on a broomstick" had been in his time); one did it, if one had the skill with everything down to a solicitor's letter. (Later in the century, Kennedy was challenged to write a Greek verse from a letter asking the gas-man to call; his answer survives.) The fashion had begun earlier and the best enlightening comment on it is an article by Christopher Hollis:

> The elegant classical scholarship of the eighteenth century took the place of a very superior, though limited, kind of Brain Teaser or Crossword. To a boy or man not affected by the poetry of the Greek Epic or Dramatic Writers, verses—a mere exercise in translation—was a puzzle to be solved, not imaginatively but by logic and application.

This, of course, would not have been Butler's own view (nor Dr. James') for the writing of Greek or Latin remained a real pleasure all his life. One finds constant little *jeux d'esprit* characterising letters to and from his friends. Butler could assess the merit of a Greek Grammar or criticise an epitaph. This again was an 18th century tradition:

> An inscription, to the scholars of those days was like the sound of the bugle to a war-horse. Dr. Parr once said to my grandfather, "It's all very well, Sammy, to say that So-and-so is a good scholar—but can he write an inscription?"

But it was not as a scholar only that Butler won success and recognition, but as a teacher of scholars. Quite early in his career he was getting this kind of *carte-blanche* invitation from tutors quite unknown to him.

... I take the liberty of writing to request that if you have any scholar at present in the school of which you are Master whom you should like to appoint to the vacant exhibitions, you should send him to us.

By the end of his time his reputation in this was unchallenged which gave him a prestige that at the time exceeded any other Headmaster's, not excepting Arnold.

It is distressing to turn to his one sphere of failure. Butler never seems to have succeeded in getting on with his Trustees (Governors) the Burgesses. Except for an occasional note of praise or respect in general terms, they gave him a minimum of help and whether he was suggesting a rise in salary, improvements to his house, the taking of another Boarding House, or the transfer of boys from the Parish Church to the School Chapel on Sundays, they seem always to have obstructed him. To take this last example:

The move by the Headmaster to have the boys in the School Chapel was made when he had been there well over ten years. The Trustees ordered them back to the Church. Dr. Butler protested, putting his case in detail. He had arranged services at which one of the upper boys officiated as Clerk and the boys read the responses aloud so that all could feel that they were taking part in the service. (Presumably in the Church they only listened.) He pointed out that sermons could be specially adapted for the boys instead of being addressed to the mixed congregations of a Church. He invited the Trustees to come and see for themselves how orderly and attentive the boys were, contrasting this with the difficulty of ensuring devotion from a collection of boys clustered up together in the transept, hemmed in from behind with "charity children" and with the "manufactory girls" (industrial school?) in front. But the Trustees would not budge. "Having duly weighed and considered Dr. Butler's letter (they) ... are of the same opinion and they decidedly disapprove of removing the scholars from the Parish Church".* Butler perhaps lacked the energy to push his ideas. He has been taken to task for not having brought more spiritual influence to bear on the boys. He evidently realized the need to do this, and had he been encouraged (or firmer? or later in the century?) he might have made the School Chapel a centre — not of religious emotion, for that was alien to his temperament—but of the principles of

---

* The Trustees probably had in their minds a dim feeling of responsibility for causing the boys to hear "right doctrine", of which they could be sure in their Parish Church but for which they did not trust schoolmasters. It should be added that they did improve the Chapel and allowed the Head to have boys there on Sunday afternoons.

right living. But he acquiesced, in terms anything but happy. He implies that he does this from his "reliance on your zeal for the welfare of the institution and my sense of your kindness to me on former occasions". Can he be ironic? It is difficult to find any example of their "kindness". They were entirely unwilling to spend anything additional on the Master, his salary or his house. As to this last, when Butler presented plans for enlargement, their reply, though not entirely negative, was still grudging. After a long preamble on the Duties of the Trust and the state of its finances (which Butler's assistance had improved out of all knowledge) they "do agree to pay up to £500 *over five years* by annual instalments of £100, beginning at Michaelmas." (Butler had three children by this time and had hoped the improvements could have been done in the summer vacation.) And this was at a time when pupils were beginning to flow in from a wide area and when the school's credit was rising in the outside world entirely owing to Butler's efforts, which they might well have done something tangible to recognize.

The question of salary came up also and Butler complained quite bitterly. He quoted other schools, having "ostensibly small salaries" but which could be made up by tutor's fees, which might run up to eight or ten guineas per boy per annum. This would enable a Headmaster to bring up his salary to £1,500 or £2,000 exclusive of what he got from the Foundation and from his advantages in keeping a Boarding House. Even in other local, non-Public schools, the basic salary might be £400 (Manchester), or £200 (Macclesfield); he himself is getting only £150 basic of which he pays £75 to assistants (+ dinners.). It was not surprising that Butler was dissatisfied with the lack of response from the Trustees. He was still very conscious of prejudices against him in the town, whether from the Jeudwine party or because he was still at cross-purposes with the Trustees. In 1815 he was making serious enquiries about the Headship of Leeds Grammar school. Had he gone there, one cannot but think that it would have served the Trustees right. The answer must have been tempting!

> We are now attempting to put the whole on the best footing in our power. . .If we have only a man of high promise, we will begin with £500 a year and keep somewhat in our power for encouragement; if an established Master of high repute be elected, we will do all that is properly in our power immediately and always.

Why did Butler decide not to move?

At just over 40, Butler may have shrunk from the task of a second revival of a ruinous school; whether in a weakened state of health he felt the lack of initiative which had perhaps kept him at Shrewsbury hitherto, or whether he had the obstinate determination of many apparently gentle people, it is hard to say. In fact—and his son put down to this his refusal to apply to Leeds—from 1816 a sudden increase in his own numbers put him in a stronger position, as after this date, the only difficulty over numbers was that of finding accommodation.

Though he made his greatest mark as Headmaster of Shrewsbury, Dr. Butler ended his life as Bishop of Lichfield, and he had been actively engaged in his clerical work from the time of his ordination. He was greatly in demand, for example, as a preacher. In 1821 he was appointed Archdeacon of Derby, and a constant series of visits, letters and reports begins, which show him as a kindly, competent and very conscientious administrator. But why should he undertake these commitments at all? One must remember that the work was done without telephone or typewriter, and that Dr. Butler never had a secretary. His daughters later did a little copying, but he kept his correspondence very much to himself. Moreover, he made a draft of his answers to most of the letters he got, deviating from this plan only when under great stress, as at the end of a term, or in illness.

It seems that, though his heart was in the school, he had more and more in mind a life ending with high ecclesiastical office. There must have been in his mind the idea of preferment which he had every right, according to the times, to expect on grounds of administrative experience as well as scholarship, his edition of *Aeschylus* being witness to this last.* For scholarly Bishops were on the whole, the rule, though it was recognized that appointments were influenced by political considerations, by the need to keep a balance between the two Universities, and by personal cross-currents. One of Butler's very few outbursts is on this subject, in a very private letter to one on whose friendship he could rely,—who had had the disagreeable task of breaking it to Butler that he was *not* to be appointed to the next vacant see, because of a political pledge which "Lord Melbourne thought himself bound to act upon". Butler complains that promotion goes by connection, not by merit, and that he himself has "laboured as much as any, more than most, and longer than all," of a number whom he names. Clearly the widespread expectation is that for the qualified at least, the scholastic and the ecclesiastical worlds might dovetail. The episcopate was delayed him for two years after this; he had been brought to the point of resigning when it was offered. His state of health by then was such that he only held it three years.

---

* The *Aeschylus* did give Dr. Butler European status. Through Baron Merian a copy was presented to the Emperor of Russia with "a simple Latin inscription, without adulatory epithets and flourishing superlatives." Samuel Butler described himself as REGIAE SCHOLAE SALOPIENSIS APUD BRITANNOS ARCHIDIDASCALUS A. S. MDCCCXII.

Whatever post he held, Butler would have been a man of exceptionally wide interests, as one sees from the great variety of subjects raised in his correspondence. Moreover, in spite of his close attention to detail, he was never overwhelmed by it and had the gift of setting down his conclusions effectively. Lord Clarendon complimented him on "your Commencement Sermon" dealing with the Catholic Question: "I have met with nothing upon the whole which is so satisfactory to me as your mode of statement upon the subject."

In spite of over-working, Samuel Butler could enjoy his holidays, mostly spent yachting and fishing at Beaumaris. In one of his worst years, he refused an invitation on the ground that he would rather have a good catch than see a dozen installations. London did not attract him; "nothing but dressing and undressing," for breakfast, for a *Levée* at St. James', for the afternoon, for dinner—and then bed. He prefers his garden, and of course books. He writes to an old pupil for 21 lb. of Mangel Worzel seed, and for dahlias at 18/- a dozen. They are successful: "My Dahlias are almost as fine as my Aldines; I wish you could see them." A few such gleams of satisfaction warm one's heart. They anticipate in their interests and geniality the pursuits of countless schoolmasters to come, for whom one may say in many ways he set the pattern. It differs both from the elegance or quirkiness of his eighteenth century predecessors and from the energetic earnestness of the coming men such as Arnold or Benson.

Even before middle life, Butler must have been under constant strain and was often a very sick man. Writing in March 1833 he complains that he has not been well since his visit to London in December. On another occasion he is in such pain that he would like help in judging some papers, as his judgment may be affected.* It is difficult to know what was amiss with him, but one has only to look at the contrast in portraits between the slim, vital, *young* expression of his earlier one, and the gentle, puffy bad-coloured figure of his later middle age, to feel what a drag his body would have been on any less indomitable spirit.

His decision to retire in 1836 brought two good results. He had the pleasure of a shoal of congratulatory letters from his friends, and he could plan and work for his successor. He was happy in obtaining the election of the man he had in mind, his pupil B. H. Kennedy. He sounded Kennedy, who was then teaching at Harrow and might well have been offered the Headship there, giving him a very fair survey of the position; then he wrote a very long and frank letter (and three drafts show how well he thought out this expression of frankness) to

---

* "Do remember me most kindly to Pain", he writes in December 1835. "Slip of the pen for 'Payne'" (says his editor). Freudians would hardly need to comment.

the Master of St. John's, the College with which the appointment rested.*

In this letter (December 9th, 1835) he sets out his own career and struggles, personal and financial; he explains the legal difficulties, the position of the house and staff, speaks without undue pride of his success in building up the numbers and standards of the school and thus leads up to the qualities needed in his successor. He must be "not only a first-rate scholar but a man of good tact, of some knowledge of the world and of gentlemanly manners" and he must have won high honours or the boys will compare him to his disadvantage with Butler himself. In short, he must be Kennedy!

Butler would have seen nothing in this pulling of the strings to reproach himself with, then or later. He might have justified himself in the subsequent history of the school, had he lived to see it.

He got his way without a struggle, though after some little delay. On March 7th, 1836 the Master of St. John's College wrote:

> It gives me a singular pleasure to-day that the unanimous opinion of the assembled seniors was that the Rev. B. H. Kennedy is the proper person to receive the appointment.

Although in every account of Samuel Butler the striking impression is of what he did for Shrewsbury, there was gain also for the Universities and for education as a whole. The excitement and brilliant scholarship brought by Dr. Butler's young men had begun to push up the standard of these places of learning which had fallen back so sadly during the last centuries. It is true that for too long the older Universities failed to take advantage of the new fields of knowledge, science and technology. Butler might have said that whether this was their fault or not (and he wrote, pseudonymously, some very stringent criticism of University curriculum) it was not his and that a man would do science none the worse because he or another did the Classics better. The newly elected Fellows, such as Payne at Balliol, T. S. Hughes at Emmanuel, Robert Scott, Student of Christ Church, expected higher standards from their own pupils. Beside this, the connection of the Public Schools with the Universities was being strengthened. There had long been a tradition of such a connection—sometimes financial or administrative. But that Heads of Colleges, Fellows and Professors should be in touch with Headmasters and their Sixth forms, through visits, letters and constant both-way traffic of scholars, was a new and invigorating tendency. Butler knew just what he was about when he wrote to Brougham that one of the marks by which a Public School was

---

* British Museum MS.27781.

to be judged was the number of boys sent from it to the Universities and their success there. Already by 1820 (when he wrote hoping to get Shrewsbury included in Brougham's list) Butler's Honours Boards were beginning to fill up.

These Honours Boards themselves (precursors of how many more!) were an indication of the emphasis that the school was going to put on its University reputation and the "emulation" that Butler had set such store by within his school and even classes. We, in hindsight, may account this for worse as well as for better, but there is no doubt that the 19th century mind was immensely stimulated by competition in all spheres. And now, what had been envisaged as far back as the early founders and benefactors—the flow of young men to the Universities, which had slowed down or died away altogether in many schools—began again and rapidly increased. We ought to be able to understand this new enthusiasm; we are experiencing, on an enormously enlarged scale, something of the same impulse.

V

KEATE OF ETON, AND THE REACTION

Modern Eton may be said to date from the appointment of Dr.
Hawtrey in 1843. Hawtrey was by far the greatest headmaster that
Eton ever had... Yet through fondness for stories about flogging,
Hawtrey is less known than his predecessor, the coarse ruffian,
Keate. (Anonymous review in *The Manchester Guardian,* 1893)

IT appears that when it comes to subjects of biography, we are still
interested in coarse ruffians and, more than that, in the ruffianly side of
them only. (Though, in spite of many references, there does not seem
to be a full-length biography of either Keate or Hawtrey.) Keate is still
the best known of Eton Headmasters—certainly up to this century. Yet
very little is ever said about him except to emphasize his ferocity and to
repeat the stories emanating from the catchword—"I'll flog you for
that." Like Arnold, if in a totally different way, he has made a myth.

There was a time when most people who knew the name of Keate,
other than Etonians, at least, had first learnt it through the medium
of a book by one of his pupils, A. W. Kinglake. *Eothen,* Kinglake's
account of his travels, used often to be a set book studied for the old
School Certificate and, viewed fairly, it comes with credit even
through this ordeal. The story referring to Keate has often been told, and
is not always appreciated by the student, but it is good enough to bear
repetition.

Having arrived in Cairo, Kinglake is inclined to try out a "magician"
who purports to be able, through the medium of a boy looking into a
liquid in his hand, to describe any named, absent person. Kinglake was
determined to "name" John Keate, and gives the reader a description of
him though he thinks Keate's likeness has so often been portrayed on
walls "from utmost Canada to Bundelcund" that some idea of him may
be already known:

He was little more (if more at all) than five feet in height and was
not very great in girth, but within this space was concentrated the
pluck of ten battalions. He had a really noble voice, and this he

93

could modulate with great skill; but he had also the power of quacking like an angry duck and he almost always adopted this mode of communication in order to inspire respect. He was a capital scholar but his ingenuous learning had *not* softened his manners and *had* "permitted" them to be fierce—tremendously fierce. He had such a complete command over his temper—I mean over his *good* temper that he scarcely ever allowed it to appear; you could not put him out of humour—that is, out of the *ill* humour which he thought to be fitting for a head-master. His red shaggy eyebrows were so prominent that he habitually used them as arms and hands for the purpose of pointing out any object towards which he wished to draw attention; the rest of his features were equally striking, and were all and all his own. He wore a fancy dress partly resembling the costume of Napoleon and partly that of a widow woman. I could not have named anybody more decidedly differing in appearance from the rest of the human race.

When Kinglake has named this "absent person" the wizard demands of the boy what he sees. The lad, no doubt relying on experience of nostalgia among callow young Englishmen who have consulted his master before, replies: "I see a fair girl with golden hair, blue eyes, pallid face, rosy lips." Kinglake goes on: "*There* was a shot. I shouted out my laughter with profane exultation and the wizard perceiving the grossness of his failure, declared that the boy must have known sin (for none but the innocent can see truth) and accordingly kicked him downstairs."[*]

What seems never to have struck readers is how remarkable it is that the person to suggest himself to Kinglake's mind should have been his old Headmaster. For Kinglake was no boy just left school; he was about 26 when he set out on his travels and the book was not published till much later. If any one of us, required at random to name some character to be described, had immediately called up our former Head, this would suggest that he (or she) must have been a man or woman of mark. Granted that Kinglake might have been seeking to catch out the boy by envisaging someone the direct opposite of the lady-love naturally expected, still there had been plenty of distinguished people in his life, at the University, in politics—yet Keate was the one he picked on. The old man saw something of his pupils after his retirement—did this one, it would be interesting to know, ever tell him the story?

The incident has been for many a first introduction—and a vivid one it is—to this headmaster and it has often been followed up by numerous

---

[*] *Eothen,* XVIII.

flogging anecdotes. There were the 70 members of the Fifth and Sixth forms who one afternoon all copied their Latin epigrams from those of three or four boys, and whom Keate proceeded to lay out publicly in the library, to the joy of their juniors. There was the boy who, like Cinna the Poet, suffered for his namesake (or perhaps brother) who prudently kept out of the way. Then there was the notorious occasion of the "rebellion" when Keate outmanoeuvred the boys who had prepared to resist their mass-punishment, by having them brought into him *seriatim* from their houses, a proceeding which kept him up half the night. The fact that, having previously shown their resentment by booing and hissing,* they cheered him next day, as well as on other spontaneous occasions (even when he visited Eton long after his retirement) inclines one to take their more formal applause on his day of leaving as not merely what Mr. Lamb calls it, "last-minute cheering," but a curiously real appreciation. Keate had more than once defeated them and they took it in good part.

One should remember on the other side that any account of Keate contains not only stories of his giving the boys indiscriminate beatings but also letting them off after some representation either logical or humourous; this may be unreasonable but it is human, not monstrous. Similarly, he was prepared in lessons to take a point made in construing which differed from the ordinary usage, with: "Well, there's something in it."

The fairest way to look at Keate is not exclusively from the view of our hindsight and, perhaps, more civilised standards, but through the eyes of a pupil of his own time, who would have been contemporary with Kinglake. Fortunately the letters of James Milnes Gaskell provide such a point of view.

Gaskell, an intelligent, sensitive boy, was rather mature for his years but wrote very freely to his mother during all his Eton days, 1824–29. He was about 14 when he went, so spent all his schooldays under Keate. Certainly what he says of the bullying and cruelty at Eton is horrifying and utterly condemnatory of the school. Gaskell was for a short time in a Dame's house (Atkins), and then in that of Richard Okes who later became Lower Master, and in both he was badly treated by the older boys. He mentions that Okes once wrote round to parents complaining of bullying and threatening to expel for this but without improvement. Most of what the boy complains of seems to be sheer destructive hooliganism:

---

* When, much earlier, Dr. Weston of Winchester was hissed, he merely exclaimed: "So, gentlemen! Are you all metamorphosed into serpents?" which did nothing to stop the rebellion.

The boys in general swear excessively. Murrell. . . is cutting holes in and completely spoiling my table. . . To hear the very worst species of uncontrolled swearing and particularly directed against me. . . while at Mrs. A's I cannot be in the least happy. "What, do you never swear," upon answering in the negative on the ground that it was decidedly wrong, they said "What a sap" and I was assailed with hisses. . . They have been in my room, seized one of my knives and snuffers and I despair of ever recovering them. . . When I had gone to bed, Trench came into my room and pulled me about in every sort of way he could think of. . . also had broken five panes of glass in my window and this is chiefly to be attributed to my not swearing with them. . . You must expect to see both my clothes and hat in a tottering condition, such tricks are played with them.

Gaskell described all his persecutions and unhappiness but considered, like his parents, that it was ultimately for his good to stay at Eton. (They did take him away, apparently, for a term.) At fifteen, he accepted things with the remark—curious but significant of the general attitude: "I suppose such things must be at Eton, but they are very mortifying." They did not of course, *only* happen at Eton. There is an exact parallel of the same date, when Frederick Temple wrote home from Blundell's: "The boys swear so much that I can hardly bear it and they not only do it themselves, but they take away my things and they say I may not have them again unless I swear, which of course I will not do."*

Fagging, also, Gaskell accepts as a matter of course; customs evidently differed much from house to house. What he found hard at Atkin's was running errands which took him to places out of bounds, for which he was liable for punishment if caught. The promoters of a classless society may be amused at his philosophizing that he is "a fashionable" when he takes his own breakfast at 10 o'clock and "a servant" when he spread the cloth. (Angelo, the fencing-master's son, refers to "the small boys making tea for the great ones." Evidently preparing tea was an inescapable chore.) Otherwise, he says very little about it.

But his fundamental complaint—of which he only realised the full force when it was remedied—was the dullness of his house society, and as the doors were locked at 8 p.m., or earlier, he got no company in the evening outside the boarding house. When he began to find such friends as A. H. Hallam, Gladstone, young Charles Canning, and exchanged the house talk of boxing and racing for conversation on literature and

* Quoted by G. Lamb, *The Happiest Days,* p.43.   See also p.166, *post.*

politics, his whole attitude changed. One of these new friends put him up for the Debating Society (Keate who favoured it, referred to it as "The Litterati"—later, of course, it became Pop.) and from this, he stated at the end of his school life, "originated the greatest part of my happiness and enjoyment".

This sketch of James Milnes Gaskell has been given to show that he was a boy by no means thick-skinned or lacking in intelligence, but one who, had he thought of Keate as a ruffian, would in his frank, open, descriptive letters not have hesitated to say so. He was not like the loutish senior boy of whom he writes: "He never learns or writes anything and confesses that he does not come to Eton to learn but to play the fool." But Gaskell's case shows it was not true that only the toughs or the very aristocratic could survive.

When he came, Gaskell was clearly frightened of being flogged, and he was "out in the bill" in his second week for not knowing a word in his Greek Testament. He waited with others, fearfully, in the ante-room. Keate, after rebuking him in his usual brusque manner for being put in so soon, in fact let him off, with "Go along, sir, go along." Gaskell says that the number of boys actually beaten daily by Keate (the school numbers fluctuated but at this time there were well over 500) was between five and ten a day, a good many less than were sent to him. The boy mentions one friend who was never flogged, and another (young Canning—admittedly a favourite with Keate) who was put in the bill ten times but only beaten twice—in two years, perhaps.

The putting of boys "in the bill" (i.e. reporting of them by masters) shows Keate's dilemma. Neither the College Tutors (many of whom Keate had had left him as a difficult inheritance) nor his own appointed Assistants, were supposed to administer corporal punishment themselves. On the evidence available it does not seem that they did. But if they put down boys' names for punishment it was giving Keate the choice of either administering it as often as the names appeared or of letting down his masters. *We* may consider the solution would have been a discussion with the staff on what offences should be penalized and how severely, and especially on making a distinction between scholastic and delinquency or moral faults. But the whole question of the terms on which staff were appointed and paid, and their numbers relative to the boys and their subjects rendered this general co-operation very difficult.* Keate himself would pose the question to

---

* In 1820 there were six Masters in the Upper school, which generally consisted of 450 boys so that each of the five Assistants had on an average about 70 boys under him. The average number of boys to a tutor was about 53, the more popular tutors had between 60 and 70 pupils apiece. They were supplemented by some 32 private tutors,

a scholastic delinquent: "Is it ignorance or is it idleness? If it is ignorance, you must go down to a lower part of the school, and if it's idleness, I'll flog you."

The procedure of "putting in the bill" presumably explains, while it does not justify, the Confirmation Class story. A group of boys appeared before Keate whose names had been written on the "bill" form, commonly used for punishment, which was what Keate naturally took it to be. When they tried to explain, that it was a list of Confirmation candidates he probably *did* imagine that they had thought up a new and ingenious excuse, which he understandably thought blasphemous and deserving of the fiercest punishment which he administered. It shows, of course, a very poor relationship with the boys that he should be so suspicious; he had apparently made up his mind while a master in the Lower School that boys were not to be trusted. It was a common idea. Keate's lack of greatness lies, perhaps, in just this, that he was never strong enough to own himself in the wrong. Arnold, we must remember, furiously flogged a boy repeatedly calling him "Liar!", when in fact the boy was later proved to be in the right. The difference is that Arnold afterwards publicly apologized. Keate went on upholding discipline in his own way. However, this is not the same thing as sadism, which is often supposed to be the point of the story. Obituaries are not evidence but it is worth noting that of Keate it was said that he "guided the studies and preserved the discipline of the school with unparalleled success", that his own mental powers were less known than they should have been (i.e. he wrote no books) "because a strong sense of duty disposed him to concentrate their whole force [a nice touch, that] on the instruction of his scholars, but that his sternness of manner covered 'a singular kindness of heart'."

Of his suspicious habits, Gaskell gives a characteristic example. He had been given permission to go out (9.30 p.m. being laid down as his hour of return) with a connection, Mr. Lyell. But when asked for a further privilege, Keate retorted: "To Ascot races? No. He is no relation to you, you know, Gaskell". The boy began, "Sir, he's my uncle's . . . " Keate broke in: "Why did you drop the 'Brother'? . . . I tell you, Sir, he is only your uncle's *brother*, so go along, sir, go along. No unfair artifice if you please." Gaskell, though he had not intended to conceal the truth, rather surprisingly adds: "I was satisfied."

Keate seems to have been liberal with leave for the older boys; 50 were allowed to go home one year at the Fourth of June (King George III's birthday, originally; kept thereafter in his memory). Gaskell was often asked out to dinner and on one occasion stayed in London to

---

encouraged by the parents to look after a very small number of pupils. Even as late as 1833 there were only nine masters (Dr. Keate included) for 570 boys in the Upper school.

hear a Parliamentary debate. It is possible that Keate was influenced by the fact that on this occasion he dined at Downing Street, but the evidence seems agreed that, whatever his faults, Keate was no snob or toady. Certainly he thrashed them all alike—"the son of a duke and the son of a grocer with perfect impartiality."* We sometimes need reminding that there *were* grocers' sons at Eton then. That Eton took none but the sons of dukes is a myth that might have been dispelled earlier, witness Thomas Gray, the poet and non-aristocratic friend of Horace Walpole. Similarly Henry Angelo, son of the fencing master made a trio in a Dame's house with two nephews of Garrick, and was never made to feel that he had no right to be there—though he later tended to make professional use of his aristocratic schoolfellows.

Gaskell mentions Keate as his "examiner" both at his entry into the school and again when he had been away and the question came up of his remove. Other glimpses of Keate as a teacher (not Gaskell's) show that when not faced with the impossible task of hearing boys in enormous divisions, for example, when he took a special class for Greek plays, he was an inspiring teacher and especially in his reading aloud of the choruses.

Fortunately, it was not only sinners who were sent up to the Headmaster. The 18th century custom of being "sent up for good" continued and meant that any specially pleasing bit of work was recommended by the tutor to the Headmaster, taken to him, and copied out for the Provost. These exercises were always read aloud by "the Doctor" to the Upper Division, after other boys had been dismissed. Gaskell comments wryly on this, as it did not endear the boys so singled out to the rest of the Division, who took it out of them for prolonging the class-time.

Like any other Head, Keate had to cope with crises. (There is a startling note at the beginning of one letter that Keate is not well and is suspected of having *Cholera morbus.* Perhaps the boys thought that nothing less would have kept him away from his duties which were taken over by Mr. Yonge, except, characteristically, that of flogging. However, no more is heard of this false alarm.) But when a boy was nearly drowned: "We had a lecture about this in Prose." "Prose" was the term used by all save Keate himself for a period of compulsory attendance in Chapel on Sundays when, as dictated by tradition, Keate read a sermon or other lecture. The inattention and general uproar was such that it was usually inaudible, but if he had something he wanted to say, he could evidently make himself heard. Gaskell, who seems to have

---

* Sir Francis Doyle, *Reminiscences and Opinions 1813–85.*

had a Macaulay-like memory, quotes apparently verbatim, a rebuke in terms which probably seemed more impressive then than now:

> Gentlemen, I am excessively surprised at your conduct of late. I have heard from several quarters that the Sabbath is profaned by you openly. One person in particular warmly expressed how much he had been shocked last Sunday to see some of you laying bets and tossing up money. He mentioned the name of only one boy whom he had seen acting in this scandalous manner; the boy's name I will not mention . . . I can assure you that you are acting contrary to your own interests, as if I hear the least complaint again, I shall set the whole school a very heavy punishment. I am much inclined to set the Sixth form a punishment; I plainly see that they have not done their duty and those occurrences which are so disgraceful to the reputation of the school are either owing to this—that the Sixth form approves of these irreligious proceedings or that they have not the power to put a stop to them. I assure you that I am very much hurt with your conduct. But this shall not long be the case and the heaviest punishment which is in my power to inflict will, I trust, infuse a little reflection and a little religious feeling into your minds.

One is reminded of the (probably apochryphal) saying ascribed to him: "Blessed are the pure in heart. Mind. . . it's your duty to be pure in heart. If you are not pure in heart, I'll flog you."

Gaskell notes also another "criminatory harangue" in which he says he will not countenance their hissing and cheering (ironic?) of the Sixth and he does expect the Sixth to be responsible and set "classical punishments" e.g. for cheating. But his own punishments, beating excepted, must have been limited. The most usual "block" punishment seems to have been to add to the already excessive number of those dreary "absences", i.e. to cut down the time during which boys could be actually off the school premises; this he had done to try to prevent tandem-driving, poaching and visits to the Inn. He did also add on at least one occasion; "If there is any more of this rude conduct I shall shorten the holidays." Gaskell adds that he was certainly very rough in his manner.

There were really tragic incidents—one boy was in fact drowned, and it was in Keate's time that there was the long spectacular fight in which one boy was badly hurt and the other actually died. This awful and tragic story—found in every account of Eton—is related by Gaskell with peculiar concern; he knew the dead boy and the latter's chief supporter was a friend and protector of Gaskell himself. But he found time to be concerned also about how the affair will "be prejudicial to Eton." As, of course, it was. There was an inquest in which the School authorities were much blamed. Gaskell referred to Keate's "sensible and excellent observations" (his friend Doyle approved even the assertion "...not that I object to fighting itself; I like to see a boy return a blow") and he comments that "Keate read the burial service beautifully in tones very different from his common slang."

John Keate's life before he became Head could be paralleled by that of many others. He was the son of a parson, formerly Headmaster of Stamford Grammar School, later a prebendary of Wells. John's uncle and brother were both surgeons of some note. John Keate, the scholar of the family, proceeded from Eton to King's College, Cambridge, and though Etonians at King's took no class-giving examinations for their degrees, he won four Browne Medals (University prizes) and was considered a brilliant writer of Latin verse. He immediately got a post back at Eton—a flagrant example, evidently, of the closed Eton-King's-Eton and preparing-boys-for-King's cycle. Yet Keate himself was not a passionate traditionalist, as compared· with his predecessor Goodall, who really seems to have believed that the Eton way of life held everything necessary to salvation, and that to change anything came near to blasphemy. Unfortunately this meant that not only did Goodall reform nothing when he was Headmaster, but that when he became Provost no one else could move in this direction: "To allow the headmaster to initiate reform in the school would be to abnegate the duties laid upon the Provost by the Statutes of the Founder."* An indolent disposition and a wish for tranquillity showed itself while he was Head. Keate became Goodall's Lower Master and in this position had the humiliation of sending up boys in the bill for punishment to the Headmaster and of finding their offences had been condoned or laughed off. Goodall himself had been successful with scholarly boys and the number of distinguished old Etonians who were, during his reign, prepared for taking office in Church or State was a tribute to his method, which was the opposite to Keate's. Goodall, according to his pupil and later successor, Hawtrey, had "the peculiar talent of finding out and stirring up latent powers in a boy, when no one, even the boy himself, suspected they were there." How he managed to discover these talents in a Sixth of a hundred boys is not very clear, but we have Hawtrey's words for it; he himself was so discovered. It seems as if, concentrating on those who wanted to learn and needed encouragement, he let the rest run riot. This, together with a fine presence, handsome looks and a good voice made Goodall a popular figure, but it did not leave easy conditions for his successor.

It was certainly difficult for one so different to succeed Goodall with success. Keate already had the reputation that "he will not bear

---

* Lionel Cust, *History of Eton*, 1899, 174.

being trifled with half so much as Goodall" (an ambiguous statement) "and will deal his blows with a heavy hand if they try . . . ". It is not easy to decide whether the riotous behaviour and uproar, which seems to have been characteristic of classes and chapel-lectures under Keate, were actually provoked by his severity—challenged into being, as it were by his harsh manner—or whether the same behaviour existed under Goodall being taken as a matter of course, and Keate simply decided to ride the storm and beat the boys down. In this one must say he was barely successful. Certainly the school had increased, and classes were therefore even larger than before. The whole situation was impossible. Even ten years after Keate, we find William Johnson Cory (the poet of *Heraclitus*) who survived as a notable teacher in better times, complained:

> The noise of 200 boys and four masters in the Upper School is so great that it is impossible for those at one end to hear what goes on at the other, and therefore the instruction can be but fragmentary and the great bulk of the division is learning nothing.
>
> I think myself lucky if I can interest half a dozen near neighbours and engage their attention. . . I am not sure yet whether I am of any use here.

(And by then, at least the Sixth Form had been taken out of the din.)

Keate, as there is evidence to show, was "a skilful teacher" but as the pattern of the "stupid class lesson" still consisted mainly of hearing boy after boy repeat his prepared lines, and then in giving out some notes,* all masters, including the Head, must have felt that a lot of their time, not to mention the boys', was wasted. The encouragement came mainly when a boy's theme or verses, already looked over by his tutor, was shown up to the Head. Gaskell was much gratified to find this happening more and more frequently, but he does not mention specific encouragement by Keate.

After his long reign, the numbers which had for quite a long time risen under Keate began to fall off. He left with the applause of the remaining boys (some 470) and £600 worth of silver plate with which they presented him. He had for some time been a Canon of Windsor, but eventually he retired to a small West Country parsonage because, says his obituary, of his love of nature. "Released from care", it goes on, "his natural kind and benevolent feelings extended to all around him and his charity endeared him to the poor." (But he made the poor touch their hats, or he'd know the reason why.)

---

* Thomas James, *Account of Eton Discipline and Education* (see pp. 16-17 *ante*).

Keate had a family consisting of a son—who became a parson but avoided an Eton mastership—and six daughters; his wife who was evidently much admired was descended from a natural son of Bonny Prince Charlie. It is on record that she was kissed by Blucher when he visited Windsor after Waterloo and that a boy once called his cricket bat after her; it was "so light, so neat". This second compliment may have been more appreciated than the first. The daughters followed the Eton pattern of marrying into the school; Edward Coleridge (one of the few non-Kingsmen who had ever been appointed at Eton) was the husband of one. Another married John Chapman who is worthy of note because, as Housemaster to Edward Thring, he gave the boy an idea of what such a relationship could be, something which the future Headmaster later insisted on holding up as an ideal at Uppingham. This insistence probably had as much influence in Public School life as anything Thring ever did.

Only a slight sketch of Keate has been given here, but every book on Eton, on notable headmasters or even on the history of education in this period in England gives the background and some stories of this remarkable, if hardly "very superior", man. (What Thring thought of his old Headmaster he kept to himself.) Every student knows about the absurd curriculum and the even more absurd methods of teaching, though not, perhaps, about the most absurd system of convention and make-believe which ordained that an activity not countenanced by the Statutes or tradition simply did not exist. Boating was a case in point At the regatta on the Fourth of June, Keate would solemnly address them: "Boys, it is an old custom to have you locked up later than usual this night, that you may enjoy your game of cricket rather later than usual and that it may be harder contested." —"Was there ever such nonsense?" is one boy's natural reaction. But reform, prompted by natural reaction to stupidity and the ferocity employed by Keate to deal with the mess, was on the way.

Six years after Keate retired, Provost Goodall died, and the Fellows made an attempt to assert their rights against royal privilege and elect their own nominee. They asked Keate whether he would accept the position. Fortunately he declined and Lord Melbourne presented his own candidate in the royal name. The Fellows, though they had turned elsewhere after Keate's refusal, eventually agreed. This was Francis Hodgson (hastily become "Dr." by royal warrant), with whose coming reform could really begin. As he drove into the College (where he had suffered his education) for the first time as Provost, his son heard him exclaim: "Please God, I will do something for those poor boys!" The phrase has become historic; it is not always realised that it refers to

Eton Collegers. With Hawtrey as Headmaster and Hodgson as Provost, a new era had begun.

The 1830s was a time when the wind of change blew in on every side. Politically, the decade began with the Reform Bill of 1832 (followed in 1833 by the first Parliamentary grant for education). In literature, the year 1834 was marked by the death of Coleridge, and shortly afterwards, that of Charles Lamb, while the decade also saw the publication of a small volume of *Poems by Two Brothers* named Tennyson. Browning's *Paracelsus* was published in 1835. New religious thought started in the Oxford Movement with the early *Tracts for the Times,* beginning 1833. And in 1837, the last Hanoverian king died and Victoria came to the throne.

The wind blew into retirement headmasters who must have seemed to belong to a past age. Dr. Samuel Butler of Shrewsbury, having been offered a bishopric was at last able to slip out from under the yoke of responsibility and ill-health that he had borne for nearly 40 years. His namesake, George Butler of Harrow, had retired at the beginning of the decade, and Christopher Wordsworth came in 1835. New men were arising; in 1838 James Prince Lee took the headship of King Edward VI's School, Birmingham, and there began the education, in Godliness and Good Learning, of an influential group including E. W. Benson and Lightfoot. George Moberly went to Winchester in 1835, Arnold at Rugby had another few years to run, till 1842. But at the stronghold of tradition Keate, who had reigned for 25 years, had gone.

His successor, Edward Craven Hawtrey, had already been at Eton for 20 years as an Assistant; later, Lower Master. But in a sense he had been connected with the College for much longer. For he came of a family which had 200 years of association with it—as Fellows, as Rectors of College livings, or as linked by marriage with the great family chain of Eton society. His mother for example was sister of a former Headmaster, and a charming adaptation of a famous epitaph ran—

> Foster's sister, Hawtrey's mother,
> Eton, ere thou see another
> Loved and mourned and calm as she
> Time shall throw a dart at thee.

Hawtrey even had two aunts who were Dames at Eton and this, it has been suggested, made the school less strange to him when he went there at the age of ten. It did not, however, save him from some bullying when he went into College, where he stayed from 1803 to 1807, going on, as usual, to King's. At Cambridge he did, in spite of the lack of necessity for Etonians to do so, work extremely hard. He made himself a stiff programme and only allowed "occasional parties" as a

1 Dr Thomas James of Rugby. "In no situation did his virtues shine with greater lustre than in that of preceptor, when, by the fatherly manner in which he conducted himself towards the numerous pupils entrusted to his care, he gained the admiration of their parents, and the affection of themselves." From a tribute in the *Northampton Mercury*, October 6, 1804.

2 Bishop John Mitchinson, instigator of the Headmasters'
Conference, headmaster of King's School Canterbury and
later, Bishop of Barbados.

3 Samuel Butler of Shrewsbury. "I never saw him lose his temper with a boy" said Kennedy.

4 Edward Thring of Uppingham ". . . regarded as second only to Arnold in the order of nineteenth century headmasters and by some as having had a greater influence on schools themselves".

5 Dr Goodall was Keate's predecessor at Eton, and the two had very different attitudes. While Goodall is said to have "concentrated on those who wanted to learn and . . . let the rest run riot", it was said of Keate, "he will not bear being trifled with half so much as Goodall, and will deal his blows with a heavy hand if they try . . ."

6 Eton: Long Chamber, from C. W. Radclyffe, *Memorials of Eton*, 1844. ". . . that dreary ward which would create a storm of protest if a Local Authority were now to attempt to house in it any unfortunate cases for whom they were responsible. . ."

7 Shrewsbury: Dr B. H. Kennedy with his staff (1856) ". . . his pupils' reverence for him was only just this side of idolatry."

8 Shrewsbury: The old school buildings, east view, circa 1805, a few years after Samuel Butler went there. His house is visible on the left.

9 (Above) Rugby School in 1809, from a drawing by E. Pretty; and 10 (below) by the same artist, the S.W. of the school sometime between 1820, when the Chapel (left) was finished, and 1870 when the Chapel was rebuilt.

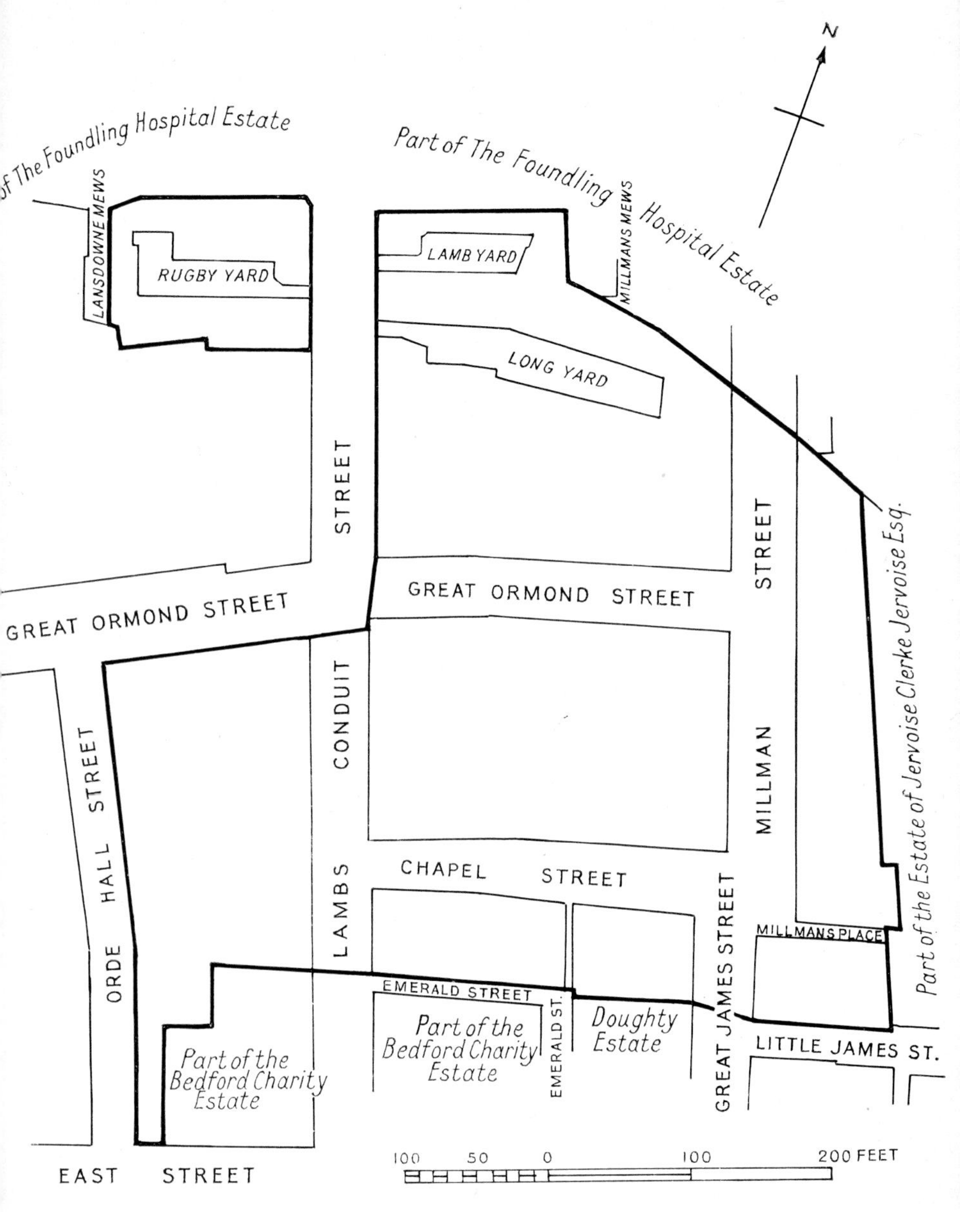

11 Key plan of London Estate belonging to the Trustees of the Rugby Charity.

12 Map showing the distribution of some of the principal Public Schools in England.

relaxation. His learning was not, like that of so many classical scholars, confined to the minutiae of the Greek and Latin languages; indeed, in spite of his efforts he was not such a precise scholar nor brilliant writer as Keate and some earlier Headmasters. But he laid the foundation of a wide knowledge of literature, English and foreign (it showed itself later in his superb library of finely bound books) and he developed a cultivated taste which enabled him to hold his own as a gentleman in learning and habits. There is a pleasant tale of his being able to entertain important French and German visitors in their own languages—a feat beyond the capacity of the majority of Fellows themselves. All this went to build up an image of the Headmaster of Eton as a person of dignity and rank in his own right, not a mere employee of the reigning Provost and Fellow, which in the literal sense of the Statutes, he was.

This appreciation of a cultivated way of living was probably developed during the period following his Cambridge days. Unlike the majority of his predecessors, Hawtrey did not go straight back to Eton to teach. Perhaps there was no vacancy available, yet family reasons made it necessary for him to get a post at once. His father had died earlier and he had a mother and several sisters to support. It was said that this was the reason why Hawtrey remained unmarried all his life. Obviously in the later days, especially when he was Provost, economics were no bar; it is not difficult however to suppose that for feminine company his relative sufficed him.

On coming down from King's, then, he became for about three years a private tutor. For most of that time, his pupils were Lord Talbot's sons and perhaps his standards in politeness and culture were consolidated during that period. He came back to Eton in 1814 as an Assistant, later a College Tutor, under Keate, and worked on till he became Master of the Lower School. In 1834 he took up the Headship, intent on making some of the necessary reforms of which he had become very conscious. There was still the difficulty under which Keate had suffered; the Provost was the same Dr. Goodall (who had so much encouraged Hawtrey as a schoolboy, in his work) with the charming manner and the indolence which prevented him from being a reformer. As with Keate, he began by frustrating any attempt at the smallest alteration. But although the main reforms of rules and buildings had to wait, even Goodall could not ignore the rapidity with which the numbers of the schools were diminishing and he allowed some concessions.

One of these had to do with the work. Hawtrey managed to cut down the enormous divisions with which he had to cope. The Headmaster's Sixth was henceforth to consist of not more than 32 boys: "the first ten Collegers, the first ten Oppidans, and a part of the Fifth form." It had a room to itself—the Old Library of flogging fame. Hawtrey had this cleaned up and made attractive with panelling and pictures. As Master, employed to teach, Hawtrey was able to reduce the numbers which he himself took, but there were still four masters "teaching" in the one Schoolroom. He could not increase the size of rooms available nor, except in class, do much to help the Collegers, whose well-being rested with the Provost and Fellows.

Hawtrey as a person may have been obscured in that historians have, understandably, concentrated on what he did rather than what he was. His reforms were so important and long-needed that they overshadowed the man who had brought them about. And of course the relevant chapter on them in Hollis's book has to be headed "The new Brooms" (plural) because the work had to be shared with Provost Hodgson or it could not have been done at all. The reforms therefore had mostly to wait for six years, till Hodgson's arrival in 1840. For their importance and the difference they made to Eton, they deserve a long section to themselves; in fact some writers have gone so far as to say that had it not been for these reforms, Eton itself would hardly have survived as a school. But many of them are so "local", having reference to Eton abuses only, that here they need only be briefly touched on.

For instance—Long Chamber was partitioned up and other rooms used for scholars to sleep in, so that the boys had, in effect, private cubicles. (But at Rugby, they had had studies from days of Dr. James, while even at Uppingham small sheds existed as sanctuaries for boys quite early in the 19th century). It was arranged that a Master should have rooms in College; this had always been the founder's intention, but the duty of supervision had long been jettisoned by the Headmaster and Lower Master who removed to their own separate houses. The food was improved, but College feeding still remained deplorable in quality and arrangement—the Sixth form cut their own portions of the mutton, then the Fifth and so on down the scale, leaving little enough for the small boys. Boating became recognized and regularized with an organized swimming test; theatrical performance and other such activities were permitted, not merely winked at. (Keate had shown his knowledge of a disallowed production of *The Rivals* by referring to the boys under the names of the parts they were playing, especially "Lydia Languish" and other female parts.) Eton was not alone, surprisingly, in allowing an old and notorious Inn (The Christopher) to grow up on College property, but this had been for long a particular cause of scandal, a source of innumerable offences and the worst possible influence on the boys who passed it going to and fro, for instance to their Tutors' houses. Yet Hawtrey had to fight to prevent the lease of this being renewed by the Fellows (on profit-making grounds) though in the end it was made over for a boarding house. Finally a unique tradition was broken, with the abolition of Montem; an occasion of ancient ceremony but even more riot and expenditure, of which the official object was to supply the Captain of the School with a fund for his Cambridge career. With Hodgson's support, after trying for a year or two to reform this occasion, Hawtrey took the final and unpopular step of abolishing it, and compensated the next School Captain with £200 out of his own pocket. (For an account of Montem see Appendix A and chapter VIII, p.185)

Fortunately Headmaster Hawtrey and Provost Hodgson worked harmoniously together. (One remembers Hodgson's prayer on taking up his post; he had even more experience than Hawtrey of the evils that befell small Collegers.) When Hawtrey wrote suggesting some improvements, he got unqualified* support and a letter on "corporate reform" beginning: (The capitals perhaps show Hodgson's enthusiasm)

> I am delighted to find that in almost every Point which your Letter touches upon, we entirely agree. In many I have already anticipated your Views... Whatever become, I know that we have the same Object...

Certainly even after the efforts of Hawtrey and Hodgson there was plenty left to be reformed. The Clarendon Commission on Public Schools made a real occasion of the enquiry into Eton—in fact some Etonians have thought that the Commission was appointed chiefly to harry *them*. Whether this was true or not, the Commission lay nearly 20 years ahead. Meanwhile Hawtrey had rightly got credit for new buildings, new organisation and a new and gentler spirit, and it is on these that his reputation rests.

This is not to say that Hawtrey had not a personality of his own. He was the greatest contrast to Keate; the one thing they had in common was that both were ugly. But unlike Keate, Hawtrey was not comic, hardly caricaturable; he was probably, if the phrase can be used in the masculine—*un joli laid*. And his charm was such that in conversation his plainness was forgotten. He had something of interest to say, it seemed, on every subject of conversation—"Painting, Poetry, Paris, Politics, Pedigree, or anything else you please." His garb, again unlike that of Keate, was fashionable—and expensive; with his watch, signet, and other personal adornments, it was said he stood up in £700. He did not

---

* Unqualified save for one thing; Hawtrey would have liked to appoint masters from *outside* the circle of Eton-King's-Eton. This Hodgson refused to countenance, so the in-breeding went on, in general, for many years.

smoke—and declared that no gentleman ever did. But his tastes were extravagant, and together with his generosity (he added a widowed sister-in-law to the females he already supported) they outran his assets, and much of his lovely library had to be sold before his death. Hawtrey was unbusinesslike enough not to leave an available will, and his pecuniary affairs were often in confusion. Unfortunately this applied to some College affairs also; the accounts of the building of the Sanatorium were left in complete confusion for his successors to unravel. But all accounts of him lay stress (again by contrast with his predecessor) on his "refinement", pointing out that this was the quality outstandingly needed at the time. In the third year of Hawtrey's reign, "Sailor Billy" (who like his royal father was a great supporter of Eton) died, and it was his niece, Victoria, who succeeded him.

VI

THOMAS ARNOLD

In considering how Lawrence Sheriff's School changed from a small Grammar School into Rugby Public School, it was not necessary to mention Arnold because the change took place long before he appeared on the scene. But to deny Arnold his place in the roll-call of eminent headmasters would be to consider *Hamlet* without the Prince.

This was not so evident, except to Rugbeians, at the time. Samuel Butler, the least resentful or jealous of headmasters, said of the man whose school was to become an overpowering rival of his own: "I heard that after Dr. Arnold came to Rugby the numbers increased but have now fallen away again."

But after Arthur Stanley had written Arnold's life in 1844 (Arnold having then been dead two years) he was never out of the public eye. Since then, the amount of writing on Arnold, beginning with the publication quite early of his own sermons, scholarly work, and contributions to journals, must have filled several thousand pages yearly. But quite out of proportion even to this biographical literature are the references, daily uttered or written, to the man himself and even more to the aims and ideas he is supposed to have held. From the business correspondent of *The Times* to a minor speaker in a television interview—anyone may make allusion to Arnold in the belief that it will be accepted and understood. The references themselves often bear about as much relation to Dr. Arnold's own words as the notorious definition does to Plato: "Platonic is what you say when you don't want to get the woman into trouble."

Lives of Arnold have been continuously put out for over a century and the flow has not ceased, but much of the water has been used like the fountain's—over and over again. The effect of these and other representations has been to build up an image, to create a myth, to perpetuate a legend. Something was done half a century ago by Lytton Strachey to dispel the aura of reverence which such contemplation of The Doctor had produced. But the essay on him as an Eminent Victorian is remarkable rather for the snide chipping away at Arnold's personality than for any real re-estimation of his position in the educational world or the ultimate value of his work. Let it be clear that in trying to disentangle the actual person from the legendary figure, there need be no squalid disclosures. We may accept that Arnold had no sense of humour and was lacking in appreciation of Art and Music, possibly also of nature unless of natural scenery with human, moral, or historic associations. But if Arnold was a sadist, a secret drinker, a pervert or a homosexual, no sign of such delinquencies has been revealed. True, he has been found to have shown a ruthlessness of conduct as well as of temperament which seems at variance with the *Gentleman's Magazine*'s "mixture of fact and false praise":

> Dr. Arnold was remarkable for the uniform sweetness, the patience and the forbearing meekness of his disposition. He was an innate Christian; the bad passions might almost be said to have been omitted in his constitution.*

This is nonsense. He had this quality of ruthlessness, which was shown (as Mr. Bamford points out) in the Wratislaw controversy,† where he is seen getting rid of the youngest children, of whose presence at a Public School he disapproved altogether, by simple process of destroying the lowest form. But the legal evidence for this has always been available, so has another aspect of this ruthlessness which led him to expel or have removed the boys whom he thought detrimental to the good tone of the School. For example, he made clear that he would not tolerate a boy whose influence would tend to "a general idleness, when everyone did as little as he possibly could, and the whole tone of the school went to cry down any attempt on the part of one boy or more to show anything like diligence or a wish to improve himself." And it must be remembered that he seriously considers "sending away" Tom Brown and East whom their form master admits being "not hard workers and very thoughtless and full of spirits. . . " unless he sees them "gaining in character and manliness". This is not a liberty of fiction: Finlay quotes several examples where, without ill-will to the boy, Arnold simply refused to have him in the school any longer and made quite clear that the parent had no right to insist on his being retained there.

In a recent *Life,* Mr. Bamford devotes a chapter to *The Growth of the Arnold Legend.* Without exactly analysing this legend, he touches on some four causes of the extraordinary rise after his death of Arnold's reputation. Two of these might have been expected, two are fortuitous. First was the attitude of the Old Boys.† A man with the obvious charisma of Arnold was bound to impress himself deeply on

* T. W. Bamford, *Thomas Arnold,* p.173
† See p.223.

those with whom he came into contact (as well as more widely on those who were capable of being impressed by, say, his sermons); these were the Sixth Form, the young men who went to the Universities and likely to be the most articulate and enthusiastic of his pupils. If they met with opposition: "in self-defence his Old Boys stressed and over-stressed his virtues and genius".* "The Rugby contingents became closely knit groups at both universities and attracted sympathizers" (*op. cit.*, p.182). Their own variety resulted in their stressing quite different virtues and even doctrines; *The Doctor's Disciples* (F. J. Woodward) gives a most remarkable exposition of this variety. The Doctor's influence and his disciples' regard for him makes the extension of his reputation understandable. Following from the devotion of his Old Boys comes the work already referred to, that most famous, in its period, of biographies—Stanley's *Life of Arnold.* As Mr. Bamford truly says, much that was controversial was omitted (especially if not relevant to him as a schoolmaster) or smoothed over; "Stanley. . . had a case to make and when it is considered how passionately he felt, it is astonishing that the book is as wide as it is. . . He was more concerned with showing that side of the man not generally known."

This was in 1844. Twelve years later, "Arnold became a hero of fiction". But of what a fiction! It was Arnold's luck that he was embedded in the most popular of all school stories and that he was there embodied in a peculiarly acceptable form—clear in outline, resplendent in personality—and at exactly the right distance from Tom Brown and the reader. But this sublime figure was destined to eclipse for the general public any more subtle, more human characteristic belonging to the real Arnold, even though it was stated more than once by the author's contemporaries that this was an Arnold they did not know, a Rugby they did not recognize. The headmaster owes his widest fame to the novel and—ironically enough—to a subject in the novel with which he had no particular connection: Rugby Football. This link so brilliantly made by Mr. Bamford has been completely ignored when Arnold has been discussed. Yet the ever narrowing circles show how unpredictable are the relations between the public and subject: Football, Rugby, *Tom Brown's Schooldays,* Old Rugbeians, Stanley's *Life* and, hidden in the centre, Arnold himself.

So intently and so searchingly has the ground of Arnold's career been gone over that it is hardly necessary here to give even a biographical sketch. This is not to say that Arnold was like Thring in *having* practically no biography except his school, once he had found

---

* "The reputation of Arnold as a headmaster has arisen through the nostalgic loyalty of his staff, the enthusiasm of a handful of boys and a train of fortuitous circumstances" (Bamford, *op.cit.,* p.175).

his life's work. In all that Thring did, he had Uppingham at heart and though his reforms affected the whole of Public School life they radiated from his particular school-centred work and were only involuntarily conducted elsewhere.

Arnold's range was much wider. Certainly his school was what he regarded as his particular trust, but he saw this work in a wider context, religious and historical, though (I believe and hope to show) *not* sociological. But Arnold's relations with the other important figures of his time (Newman, Carlyle, Charles Kingsley and above all Dean Stanley), these have been often set down, together with his controversies over the Oxford Movement, his political radicalism, his religious tolerance and the works by which he hoped to be remembered—the *History of Rome,* the edition of Thucydides. His loss of a Chair of Divinity and possibly of a bishopric through his setting out his liberal opinions, his Professorship of History and the one set of lectures he delivered—all these make up a full and active life. To sum up, therefore, it may be accepted as known that he was born into a middle-class family, was educated at Winchester and Oriel College, Oxford where he became a Fellow, that he married and had a large family, that he spent ten years running a private tutoring establishment, refusing an offer to teach at Winchester, that before and after his appointment to Rugby he wrote assiduously and controversially, that he became Regius Professor of History at Oxford and that he died suddenly and unexpectedly in his 47th year.

But though all accounts of Arnold set down the facts of his life, and most of them say something of his activities in the world as well as in the school, only occasionally has a biographer made a real attempt to distinguish his work and its intention from the legend—i.e. to separate the person from the Image. To do this will be the chief aim of this chapter.

What are the chief points of the legend which should be examined? It is generally believed:

1. That Arnold made Rugby into a Public School—or, alternatively, delivered it from a condition almost beyond redemption.
2. That among the elements with which we generally associate Public Schools the compulsory playing of an accepted set of games is due to Arnold.
3. That he deliberately aimed at turning Rugby boys (and by implication Public School boys generally) into "leaders", prospective rulers, a national *élite.*
4. That he changed, according to a prophecy, "the face of the Public Schools".

To take these points one by one:

1. Rouse's classic *History of Rugby School* has the following dedication:

MANIBUS
HENRICI HOLYOAKE
THOMAE JAMES
THOMAE ARNOLD
hoc opusculum qualecunque, d.d.

Under three Heads, Rugby has had three revivals. Each was essential in its contribution to the school's growth. Holyoake first, after half a century of frustrated efforts, set up Lawrence Sheriff's school as an established Grammar School; Thomas James turned this Grammar School permanently into a Public School; Arnold gave Rugby a distinctive character which, because the image fitted the era about to be, enabled it to serve as a model. But it was the image rather than the school itself which became the model.

The fact that Rugby had been a Public School for nearly half a century before Arnold was appointed is more obvious to historians of the school than to biographers of Arnold. It is hoped, however, that after reading even such a slight sketch of its history as that in chapter III (Thomas James) little more evidence is needed on this point. Two more references may be made. One is from an account of Arnold's predecessor, written by a whole-hearted supporter of Arnold himself.* But in spite of his veneration for Dr. Arnold, Lt. Col. Sydney Selfe, writing in 1890, goes to great pains to establish that the "declension in which Arnold found the School was due to general causes affecting all Public Schools" rather than to the failure (or "failing powers") of the previous headmaster, Dr. Wooll. He emphasizes the great amount of rebuilding that took place in Wooll's time—the School House and "Old Schools", 1809-1813, and the Chapel, 1818-20, the erection of Great School and the extension of the Close, he also lists many distinguished Old Boys who had their schooling wholly or in part under Wooll—Roundell Palmer (Lord Chancellor) and his brother; Bishops; scholars; M.P.s and four Generals of the Crimean War. To this evidence of success he adds a minute of the Trustees clearing Dr. Wooll of blame for falling numbers, a document which they suggested he should circulate to parents, as he did.

---

* He regards Samuel ("Erewhon") Butler's slighting view of him as "rank heresy".

That the Trustees of Rugby School lamenting the Declension which has taken place on the number if Boys, have thought it incumbent on them to investigate the causes. They find no reason to complain of the want of ability in the Head Master and are convinced that no relaxation has taken place in his zeal and exertions. Nothing can exceed the tenderness and affectionate treatment which have always been shown to the Boys in sickness and in health. The general expenses of the Establishment appear to them to be kept within proper and moderate bounds and they cannot but hope that the prevailing unpopularity of the School, unjust as it is unfounded, will shortly subside.

Unfortunately it was the numbers which subsided still further under this "mild and forbearing" man (whom Macready the actor—a favourite pupil—calls "too indulgent") till Arnold found a school of but 123 boys on whom to exercise his stimulating power.

Clearly, Rugby was in a "trough", but no more so than other Public Schools were or had been, from which any reasonably good Head or a combination of circumstances might raise it.

For another witness we may again quote Mr. Bamford who refers us to the Act (58 Geo.III Cap. XCI, 1818) which set up the Charity Commissioners. Provision XII gives the exceptions to their powers of investigations which shall "not extend to the Universities of Oxford and Cambridge... nor to the Colleges of Westminster, Eton, Winchester, to the Charterhouse and to the Schools of Harrow or Rugby."

"Here then, we have Rugby grouped with that select band of exclusive schools and in 1818 at that, ten years before Arnold went there."

The gist of this statement may be found in histories of education and would not be worth repeating here were it not for the persistence with which it is in general talk implied that Arnold created Rugby as a Public School—or at the very least rescued it from worse than death. As to the latter, there is plenty of evidence to support W. C. Lake's assertion (he having been a pupil under Dr. Wooll and then Arnold): "It would be a mistake to suppose that (Arnold's) influence materially changed the character of school life in the ordinary school boy", i.e. that the actual conditions of living, eating, learning were immediately, if at all, altered by the new Headmaster.

The mistake lies in thinking that this was what he was trying to do. It is quite clear that what he set out to achieve and, to perhaps a great extent, did achieve, was to make it a school of Christian gentlemen. The accent was on both words, but the first definitely had priority in his mind. Indeed the main reason for Arnold's permanent achievement (if he did achieve this—and he himself always doubted it) was that this Christian ideal was just that which the British public in large measure was beginning to ask for, and it was on this tide that the school rose to prosperity.

To support this view one may quote Charles Wordsworth's *Annals of my Early Life 1806-46:*

> The truth is, there was a general awakening, which in many instances, as with us at Winchester, partook decidedly of a Church character, such as Arnold's teaching and example, however excellent, had little or no tendency to create.

This may be a natural denigration, but if the emphasis is wrong and Arnold was paramount among those engaged in this "awakening", it still brings out what was the *direction* of his effort, as perceived by his contemporaries. The famous letter to Dr. Moberly to Stanley (which will be quoted at greater length) has as its core the phrases "a most striking change . . . in respect of piety and reverence" due to his example and "influence for good which (for how many years I know not) had been absolutely unknown to our Public Schools."

2. As an example of what Arnold did *not* do to change the character and conditions of Rugby, we may deal with the more specific erroneous belief that he introduced compulsory games or encouraged this, later, important element in Public School life. This is, as a matter of fact, quite untrue. Even those who have quite a superficial knowledge of *Tom Brown's Schooldays* must have been aware that Tom and his friends were breaking no *school* rule or custom when they went rambling over the countryside on their half holidays; other boys may or may not have been playing games then. When they elect to go with about 50 others on "Big-side Hare and Hounds" paperchase, the whole thing is arranged by the boys themselves and quite unsupervised. The great match into which Tom literally falls on his first day is a traditional affair, and Arnold (in his actual sermons and no doubt personally also) does not hesitate to give his uncomplimentary opinion of schoolboy tradition: "At no place or time of life are people so much the slaves of custom as boys at school". Physical culture he does not disapprove of, but he ranks it low in the scale of good things to be sought after, less important than moral principles, right conduct and intellectual attainments.

That recognised games, and compulsion to play and even to watch, did become important in school life is undeniable. But it was not Arnold who encouraged this, and it did not come to Rugby in his time. Curiously enough we hear that at Harrow, at the time Arnold was at

Rugby, the large school game was "by a *lex non scripta* compulsory". A later Headmaster abolished the custom there.

It was not till the next generation of headmasters, many of whom certainly were "Arnold's men", that games were fully and formally introduced, but the disciples were definitely going beyond their master in this. There was however a reason for their policy, as we shall see.*

3. Arnold's connection—or lack of connection—with compulsory games can be easily disposed of, but a wider and more difficult question arises: how far was he responsible for the idea that boys should govern each other? Arnold's name has always been associated with "the prefect system" and it has been repeated *ad nauseam* that he prepared his boys for Leadership, groomed them for Government, trained an *élite,* or whatever phrase is current. It is most important to distinguish three questions: what did Arnold do with his prefects in the school, and why? what happened in other schools? did he look beyond school, and if so, to what?

On his appointment, Arnold records as one of his main feelings a dread of going where he would meet "so much wickedness". Historians are agreed (taking as evidence the amount of complaint in periodicals, articles and memoirs of the early nineteenth century) that much was wrong with the Public Schools. Curriculum apart, this was most evident in boarding schools or schools which had boarders (e.g. Westminster, Christ's Hospital) and it included very serious and horrible bullying. Arnold, we know, regarded boys as necessarily bad in a community because the majority of them were not yet capable of being fully Christian in character, but he regarded it as his task to fight this evil and create a good and Christian community. It is noticeable that he hardly ever talks of "sin" (which would have been the usual theological term) but in a sermon delivered after he had been at Rugby twelve years he analysed "evil", as it might corrupt a school, in words which his boys could understand—a procedure which amused Lytton Strachey but at least makes clear what Arnold was trying to change.

He begins with "sensual wickedness such as drunkenness. . . and other things forbidden in the scriptures." This is as near as Arnold gets to speaking of homosexuality. Whatever actually went on—and there are some few hints in *Tom Brown's Schooldays* and in reminiscences—the vice was not named. (Thring had the same inhibition; even in his diary he merely refers to "indecency".) When Arnold expands this heading, he refers simply to drinking which may lead "to actual drunkeness . . . to low and bad society and to dissipation."

"Falsehood systematically practised" is his second heading. He is not

---

* Appendix B.

unaware that schoolboys while prepared to lie to a master would have another standard among themselves. Arnold's standpoint is that lying is a sin against God.

To "cruelty" he roundly gives the school name of bullying, and hopes that at Rugby (this is 1840) it does not exist "in any very bad degree".

"Active disobedience" where authority was hated just because it *was* authority, and rules broken because they *were* rules, seems to be what we should now call "anarchy". Arnold hoped that they were free from this "very mischievous evil."

His case against "a general idleness" where everyone did as little as he could and the whole pressure of the school went to cry down any attempt to show diligence or improvement, is curiously modern. He explains it as "persecuting or annoying another because he does anything better than ourselves"—and presumably sends up the standard. Other unions besides those formed of schoolboys are capable of this.

He ends with a whole sermon on what he calls Combination or companionship. This takes a good deal of explaining because for actual friendship he has nothing but sympathy. It seems that by bad companionship he meant encouraging each other's worse (more frivolous?) qualities, and by "combination" he meant setting boys against masters. We might call this "lack of co-operation"; for Arnold it was "the feeling of one sympathy only. . . with one another, which is quite right and good, but it is the absence of sympathy with us, with whom you ought to feel it also, and with your parents, and above all with Christ and with God". This applies to the whole school: there is nothing to imply that the Sixth have a special responsibility about improving the co-operation. It is an individual matter.

Arnold's is not the language of to-day; many of his ideas are not to-day's either but it is impossible to estimate his work, influence or personality unless we make an effort to enter into these ideas, to see what he was trying to do. Quite simply as it appeared to him, and to his boys, he wanted to eradicate those things which (and he quotes the Rev. Dr. Bowdler, also to Lytton Strachey's amusement) made Public Schools "nurseries of vice" rather than Christian institutions, and temples of the Lord. Arnold knew that he could do something to defeat these evils and promote good by his preaching and by his talks* to individual boys and to the Sixth Form which he taught, and also by expelling those boys whose influence was hindering his ideals. But this was not enough; he needed helpers. So, as well as the staff, whom he picked with great care and on whom he had enormous influence, he

---

* This, unfortunately, as with all Heads, meant mostly when they were in some trouble!

relied for the Christianizing of the school on those boys whom he did teach and personally influenced. Here, as he put it to them, by setting an example and by embodying his principles and using his authority they had a chance, now, in school, of "doing good". He would give them every backing and they would be working with him, and with God, as partners in a great enterprise: to defeat evil. In the *Life*, Stanley puts it thus;

> While he made the Praepostors rely upon his support in all just use of their authority, as well as on his severe judgment of all abuse of it, he endeavoured also to make them feel that they were actually fellow-workers with him for the highest good of the school, upon the highest principles and motives—that they had, with him, a moral responsibility and a deep interest in the real welfare of the place. . . "I wish you to see fully how many and great are the opportunities offered to you here of doing good—and too, of lasting benefit to yourselves as well as to others. There is no place where you will find better opportunities for some time to come, and you will then have reason to look back to your life here with the greatest pleasure. . . "
>
> Exactly at a time when manly aspirations begin to expand, they found themselves invested with functions of government, great beyond their age, yet naturally growing out of their position; whilst the ground of their solemn responsibility on which they were constantly taught that their authority rested had a general . . . tendency to counteract any notions of mere personal self-importance.

This so far as one can judge from sermons, talks and the boys' reminiscences, is what he meant Praepostors to be and do; it was the function of the Sixth in the Christian community. But there was also another, the practical aspect to be considered.

Arnold's most direct statement of his ideas on the government of a school seems to have been written in 1835 as a "Letter" for the Journal of Education which he did not even sign but called himself A WYKEHAMIST which, of course, he was. It was an answer to an article on *Flogging and Fagging. . . at Winchester,* and is sandwiched between his reflections on those two. Briefly, he believes that in a boarding school of boys there must be a "government" (masters cannot form this; there will be too few of them; besides they have not a "natural bond" to enable them to govern directly) or else there will be "the lawless tyranny of physical strength." (He could hardly have envisaged Summerhill on the one hand nor *Lord of the Flies* on the other.) As government is needed, "the actual constitution of public schools places it in... those who have risen to the highest form in the school—that is to say, they will probably be at once the oldest, and the strongest, and the cleverest and, further... those who have made the best use of the opportunities which the school affords and are most capable of entering into its objects... And their business is to keep order amongst the boys; to put a stop to improprieties of conduct, especially to prevent oppression and ill-usage of the weaker boys by the stronger... For these purposes a general authority over the rest of the school is given them... This governing part of the school, thus invested with great responsibility, treated by the masters with great confidence and consideration, and *being constantly in direct communication with the headmaster and receiving their instruction almost exclusively from him,* * learn to feel a corresponding self-respect in the best sense of the term; they look upon themselves as answerable for the character of the school and by the natural effect of their position acquire a manliness† of mind and habits of conduct infinitely superior, generally speaking, to those of young men of the same age who have not enjoyed the same advantages."

This is Arnold's statement of his reasons and expectations regarding his prefects. How much more is there in it than a reversal of the common phrase to mean: "If you can't beat them, let them join *you*"? For him, the key sentence was that about being in direct communication with the Headmaster; the system would work for him because he was Arnold. What the system would become without the Rugby organization and without himself as Headmaster, he hardly seems to have considered.

Most people are aware that Praepostors, Prepositors, Prefects or Monitors, under various names existed in various forms at the various schools long before Arnold came to Rugby. In each school their position, responsibilities and privileges were different. At Eton, they collected the names of absentees and their excuses; they brought to the Headmaster the boys due for punishment and at certain times they read prayers. At Charterhouse they had authority, for example over boys

---

* My italics—A.C.P.

† It is important to note that "manliness" here, as often in Arnold, means "grown-up-ness" as opposed to "childishness", *not* as opposed to effeminacy. What he here sets out is something quite different from handing over the government of the school to a hierarchy of boys selected or elected. (If the Prefect system turned out something other than he envisaged, this should not be attributed to Arnold.)

who broke bounds, and at one period they were used like the monitors in the National Society's schools to teach smaller boys the lessons of the day. At Winchester, in College, they were responsible for keeping discipline in the bare comfortless hall in which scholars had to prepare their lesson; when as a boy W. G. Ward, backed by a set of prefects, intelligent but lacking in strength, tried to assert prefectorial authority, he was set on and beaten up. For this revolt six scholars were expelled. At Harrow the position was different again.

What Arnold had found at Rugby was much in line with Eton, having been introduced by Dr. James. The Sixth were *ipso facto* Praepostors but their authority in the school was largely formal; about the House prefects, we know very little. Arnold therefore had the machinery for delegating authority and he set himself to see that the material should be of the highest type that his personal influence could make it. In that way, both order might be kept and "a place of Christian education" might be reared. And when one reads the memoirs of Stanley, of A. H. Clough, or Vaughan, or William Arnold, or Lake and others from his Sixth Form, one realizes that they entirely accepted Arnold's view, that their office was a moral, or even spiritual, one.

All this, it may be said, is very unlike what the Prefect system became, and very far from self-government. Maybe, but this was Arnold's idea and on his own premises his theory and practice hung together. They were based on his belief in the need on the one hand for Christianity implied in the founder's prayer for "Godliness and Good Learning". Few boys, he thought, were capable of this but they must be made to turn their faces continually towards this ideal, and when they had passed through the neutral stage of boyhood (hurried on, he admits, by his teaching and exhortations) they would reach the threshold of manhood, when they might become capable of the good life. All this depended on the school's being a place of Christian education.

On the other hand, Arnold believed (no less than Spens and the other 20th century educators) in the School as a Society. Society must be subject to law; only thus could it survive. (An adult society could, progressively, alter its laws and he believed it should;* boy-society was not capable of this and must accept the laws made for it by the more experienced.) Acceptance of the framework of law was essential for

---

* Arnold was seriously behind much reformation needed in the country. He thought it should be begun by a survey of the population to discover in the homes and occupations how people lived, what they read, where they worshipped, how much they earned. But the day of the Webbs was not yet.

everyone living in the society and this, as Mr. Bamford points out,

> explains many peculiar happenings at Rugby. Without compunction and even without waiting for explanations, he expelled boys who resisted authority...who put schoolboy honour before duty—the duty of preserving the well-being of the school community, of upholding school authority. It explains the way he backed the Sixth at every point, since they by his own decree represented the law and could not be legally resisted or questioned. He expected boys to obey the school law in the same way as men obey the law of the land.*

Arnold's outlook being so very individual, it is remarkable that so much survived as did of his basis for the Prefect system. This was probably due to his personal influence on his own Sixth and his staff who themselves became so important in the academic and scholastic world. The number of Rugby men who took Headships is famous and it explains not only the spread of the system but the cohesive thought about it for a long time in a large number of schools. But as the following generation died out, so it seems did a part of Arnold's own mystique. The practical use of prefects in a school society remained and the practice of delegating authority continued, but the search for the Christian community—though no 19th century Public School Head would have wished to be considered as having abandoned it—appeared less urgent. The goodness, in Arnold's sense, and the Christian character of the Sixth was perhaps less valued than other qualities apparent in school and House. This is not the place to trace a change in ideals but to point out that what Arnold created and set up was one thing and what survived elsewhere (and no doubt at Rugby after Arnold had gone) was something far removed from this. The idea—or many ideas—which grew up about an ideal system of school government in very different contexts should not be thoughtlessly attributed to Arnold.

There remains the question of how far Arnold looked to his pupils to become a governing *élite* in the outer world. The answer, to judge from his own words and the early recollections of his closest friends and pupils, seems to be just—not at all. This bit of iconoclasm might be discussed at great length but it should be enough here to quote Stanley again, noting also that more than one Old Boy points out that Rugby under Arnold was *not* an aristocratic school in the usual sense, considerably less so than under Dr. James.

What were the permanent effects of this system (of praepostors) and

---

* T. W. Bamford, *Thomas Arnold*, p.150.

influence is a question which cannot yet admit of an adequate answer, least of all from his pupils. The mass of boys are, doubtless, like the mass of men, incapable of receiving a deep and lasting impression from any individual character, however remarkable; and it must also be borne in mind that *hardly any of his scholars were called by rank or station to take a leading place in English society,** where the effect of his teaching and character. . . would have been far more conspicuous to the world at large.

This, being written so soon after Arnold's death, almost certainly reflects the master's mind. He did *not* expect them to take high places as statesmen, captains of industry or Empire-builders; the main spheres in which he hoped they might do noble work (and here he would not have been disappointed) were the Church and the Universities, and, of course, the schools. True, two of his own sons were for rather short periods Directors of Education overseas, but though these (like Matthew Arnold's Inspectorship) were certainly administrative posts, they are not exactly what first springs to mind with the words "Government" or "Empire". And if Arnold thought of his prefect system as maturing a lad for a post say, in India, he was less likely to envisage a Viceroy than a missionary—or at best, a Bishop.

4. To come now to that famous prophecy of Dr. Hawkins, Provost of Oriel, at the time of his application for the headship of Rugby, that "if Arnold were elected, he would change the face of education all through the public schools of England". This sentence alone is quoted by Stanley, and the quotation has inevitably been repeated in *all* lives of Arnold and all histories of Education where he is mentioned. To challenge, or even investigate it seems as foolhardy as to query whether the Duke of Wellington said Waterloo was "a d- -d near thing" or Holmes exclaimed "Elementary, my dear Watson!", which to speak precisely they did not. But in fact it is almost as often mis-quoted; in any case, investigated it shall be, though what follows is but a personal opinion.

I am very doubtful, first, whether that particular sentence, embedded, surely, in a sheaf of laudatory letters, was of any real help to Arnold in getting his appointment. I cannot believe that Lord Howe and his fellow Trustees were greatly interested in change either of education in general or of the public schools at large. What they wanted was to get more boys for their own school. It is one of the clearest indications of how compelling Arnold's personality was, even at second hand, that they decided he was the man to get them.

Secondly, was Dr. Hawkins' prophecy really delivered with such

---

* My italics—A.C.P.

intent as we read into it? It does not sound like the portentous pronouncement that our hindsight has made it. Rather it seems to those of us who have written a considerable number of testimonials the kind of good-sounding sentiment that flows off the pen to support a fine candidate with just that kind of hyperbole that sounds impressive and means very little. For, had Dr. Hawkins really considered the meaning of what he said, he would have expressed himself much more precisely. As it is, almost every term needs clarifying.

Which did he mean by the public schools of England? Presumably he was referring to Brougham's seven? They were in fact the last to admit Arnold's influence. Dr. Butler of Shrewsbury was visited by Drury and Dr. Longley, then Headmaster of Harrow, because his teaching was regarded as so good that they (and it seems even the redoubtable Keate) wanted to see how he did it. It does not seem that such Headmasters visited Arnold. The famous letters from Dr. Moberly and from Christopher Wordsworth, quoted by Stanley, show that they appreciated Arnold's influence on his boys, but implicitly deny that they, the writers, followed him, even when their reforms ran parallel to his.

To the new Public Schools where Arnold's staff, such as Percival, Cotton and Jex-Blake, spread his ideas from the beginning, Dr. Hawkins could not have been referring:

> The Spanish fleet thou canst not see because —
> It is not yet in sight!

and Cheltenham, the earliest, would not be founded for another dozen years. He may have known of the founding of schools in connection with University College and King's College, but these were London Day Schools; he may have been aware of the stirrings of some of the ancient grammar schools which were to unite at the Headmasters' Conference—still 30 years ahead—to form one stream with the established and coming public schools. But in which of the public schools of England he expected the education to change, it is hard to see.

The misquotation, of course, is that implied above—that it was "the face of the public schools" themselves that Arnold is thought to have changed, rather than the "face of education"—whatever that means. If Dr. Hawkins meant the curriculum, again he was seriously at fault. None of the Great Schools really stirred in her Classical sleep when Arnold began his innovation of inspired teaching of history. This also was a personal matter; he believed in the importance of following European, as well as English, "modern" history, in addition to paying particular attention to the classical writers of history. But it was his only major change. Some other schools already had a rather wider curriculum than his; at Harrow they still had the course of 12 science lectures, with demonstrations, given by a peripatetic Dr. Walker, which Arnold had eliminated from Rugby. As to the manner of teaching, this continued to vary from school to school. Butler at Shrewsbury, Kennedy at Harrow and then Shrewsbury, made the classics live—and their pupils swept the board till Rugby gave them competition. At Christ's Hospital long before, Lamb had for ever portrayed the two types—Boyer, the beater who taught Coleridge with terrifying ferocity, and the amiable dilettante, Field, who taught Lamb nothing. The first real stirring up of the curriculum, and those who worked it, had to wait for the Clarendon Commission.

If in fact the tendency to eliminate the word "education" is justified, did Arnold really change "the face" of the public schools? For the actual "machinery" he did very little; we have plenty of testimony like Lake's (see p. 114) that it changed very little for the ordinary schoolboy. Perhaps the most important innovation was to substitute the Housemaster (now a well-paid member of a team of Assistant Masters) for the Dame, in those houses where the former system still remained. Physical conditions seem to have been little altered. Studies the boys already had, for the most part; given by Dr. James; perhaps the rise of Rugby spread the knowledge of these and helped other schools to set some value on privacy for a boy. (It seems to have depended on individual Heads, and the funds available, whether boys could have a sanctum; Uppingham already had these joys; at Eton Collegers had to hire a room out to get any kind of study; at Winchester it was such conditions that provoked a rebellion and some improvement.) Sanitary conditions Arnold might well have set about improving had he lived, but he came too early for even the rudimentary knowledge of "Drains" which so fortified Thring. Rugby already possessed good playing fields (which Arnold refrained from turning into the maximum number of football pitches); Wooll had forestalled him in this as with the Chapel, which he would certainly have built and did his best to "beautify". Arnold did get rid of the School's pack of "hounds" by setting out of bounds the cottages where they were kept. But, unlike Thring, he built no gymnasium, and no concert hall, had no Old Boys' Association and organized no School Mission. Neither to Rugby nor, by example, to any of the existing schools, does it appear that Arnold gave a face-lift.

It would be absurd, however, to let these things prevent one from acknowledging the great power and influence that Arnold possessed. It is just that he has been credited in the wrong column. Instead of observing the "face" of the public schools, we should have been thinking about the heart. For *this* was where Arnold was of major importance. It may be cracking the wind of poor phrase too far, to make this distinction, otherwise we might go further and say that Arnold put a heart into a system that was, as many thought, moribund. Fortunately, Arnold himself believed in it—just! He kept a sense of proportion and in the interesting article already quoted he ends with very definite allusions to education in a day-school, and implies that this life may allow for a more natural and wholesome development. But he agrees that as England *has* this system of boarding, it should be judiciously reformed to make use of "all that is excellent in it".

This could not be done merely on an intellectual or material basis. There must be a spiritual education and a consciousness of God throughout. On this task he concentrated, and though his mind was constantly applying itself to social, theological and political problems outside the school, his spirit rested in perfect confidence on the belief that he was called to the work, before anything else, of Christianizing his school.

Was it then enough to account for Arnold's success as a Headmaster that he knew exactly what he wanted for his school and was prepared, literally, to throw to the winds anything or anyone that might hinder his work? Perhaps "success" should be defined; briefly its criterion was filling the School. (But Arnold would only have filled it with "Christian gentlemen".) For this, one would have to convince boys and parents that what happened to those in the school profited or satisfied them—or both. And "profit" should not be regarded wholly in its material sense; the ability to get a living may have been paramount but the quality of after-school life—the code of living, the kind of friends, the ability to enjoy and appreciate, these things would have been part of what the school was supposed to give a boy. At least, so one would have thought—but the Victorian parent, or boy, whether at school or after, was singularly unlikely to express himself in these terms. It is rare to meet an analysis of intention even so explicit as the fictional Brown's. The boys simply accepted that it was a good thing for them (witness James Milnes Gaskell when miserable at Eton, or even his loutish contemporary who only wanted to have fun, not to learn). The parents sent them for reasons of prestige, convenience, "insurance for a living"—one does not know. But it would not have been surprising (so fundamentally was English society going to change between the 18th and 19th centuries) for a parent, if pushed, to express himself in much the same terms as Arnold and to say he wanted his boy brought up in a Christian society.

Of course he could have said this to the headmaster of any

school—and it is remarkable how if any Head preached good sermons (as Dr. Moberly) this was mentioned by the boys. But in Arnold, he would find a man genuine in his beliefs and clear and articulate about them. There was in the society from which boys were sent to Arnold a real awakening as well as a swing towards religion even though that might be mere lip-service. It was part of the age of reform, from Wilberforce's Anti-slavery campaign to the slum-curates inspired by Newman and Keble through the whole spectrum of religious influence. Arnold himself regarded Christianity as the foundation of social reform; but the religion must come first.

Later, this singleness of purpose, as found in Arnold, disintegrated. "The Doctor's Disciples" (as shown in the book of that title) represented Arnold's ideas each in his own way. Similarly, the masters working at Rugby under Arnold, so many of whom would themselves be Heads, would take into their new schools each some parts of Arnold's doctrine and practice, according to his own temperament or as the spirit of a later age affected him. And each would think, and say, that he was carrying on Arnold's work, as he had learnt it under the Doctor and would quite fairly acknowledge the influence of Arnold.

The truth is that Arnold had what is recognized as "star quality", added to a very sound intellect and a completely secure moral basis. To refer (for the last time) to Lytton Strachey—he made play of a "puzzled" expression on Arnold's pictured face and applied to his mind. But the expression is due to no more than the physical set of the eyebrows (as often happens; we might compare early pictures of the Duke of Windsor). There was seldom a man less puzzled than Arnold. True, he had had his doubts before ordination, but these attacks throughout the 19th century were as usual with thoughtful young men as measles. He assured Stanley—and in this he was transparently honest—that since 1820 he had no longer been troubled by them.

If then he had this basic security, this intellectual ability and the unaccountable quality of the "Star," it is no wonder that he was a charismatic leader. When someone like this is in step with the times instead of, as so often happens, compelled to revolt against them, the effect is tremendous. After him comes "flooding in, the main". This is why the myths grew up around him. The catchwords passed from mouth to mouth; they still pass from book to book, crediting him, as the century has worn on, with whatever has become fashionable or was thought estimable. The myths should be dispelled; there is plenty to see in Arnold without them.

Arnold came to Rugby two years before the death of George IV, nearly ten years before Victoria's reign began. The 19th century Christian revival, a real thing, from High Churchmen to Evangelicals in spite of their tangled disputations, was rightly timed for Arnold. In this he was fortunate. The old Public schools were not too far gone in their decline to be revivified. In this they were fortunate.

Arnold was great by reason of what he was as much as what he did. Just as it is rare that a Johnson finds a Boswell, it is even more rare that a schoolmaster has a poet for a son. There is really no need to say why Thomas Arnold was a great man; Matthew has told us. But it needs a poet, not a historian, to write "Rugby Chapel".

INTERLUDE.
SOME SCHOLASTIC FAMILIES

When Samuel ("Erewhon") Butler wrote his grandfather's life, he had the sense to see that the Headmaster of Shrewsbury might well be confused with the Butlers of another, quite different, family eminent in the scholastic world. He therefore wrote a note to this effect, distinguishing Samuel Butler of Shrewsbury from George Butler and Henry Montagu Butler (father and son) each of whom became a Headmaster of Harrow. This did not really go far enough for though the Shrewsbury Butlers died out with the Second Samuel, the Harrow Butlers thrived and proliferated. They produced three more well-known Headmasters in the nineteenth century and a crop of distinguished administrators and academics, culminating at the present day with Lord Butler of the Butler Act, Master (as his great uncle was before him) of Trinity College, Cambridge. A genealogical table here shows relationships in this family of Butlers (Table I), and also of the Shrewsbury Butlers (Table I (a)).

Although not so prolific in headmasters nor so persistent in production of notables, another family, that of Drury, merits sorting out for their contribution to Eton and Harrow. Table II shows their connection also with Heath and Merivale.

The family of Wordsworth also produced an extensive group related to the poet. Their careers were strictly speaking more often literary and episcopal than scholastic but the name occurs so frequently in any writing of history or memoirs of the 19th century that it may be a help to have their relationships laid out in a table (Table III).

Note: In all these tables, the surname, wherever it occurs, is written in capitals; it is added where this seems helpful, though not always necessary. It was a constant and confusing habit to give the surnames of one generation (especially the mother's maiden name) to another generation as a forename.

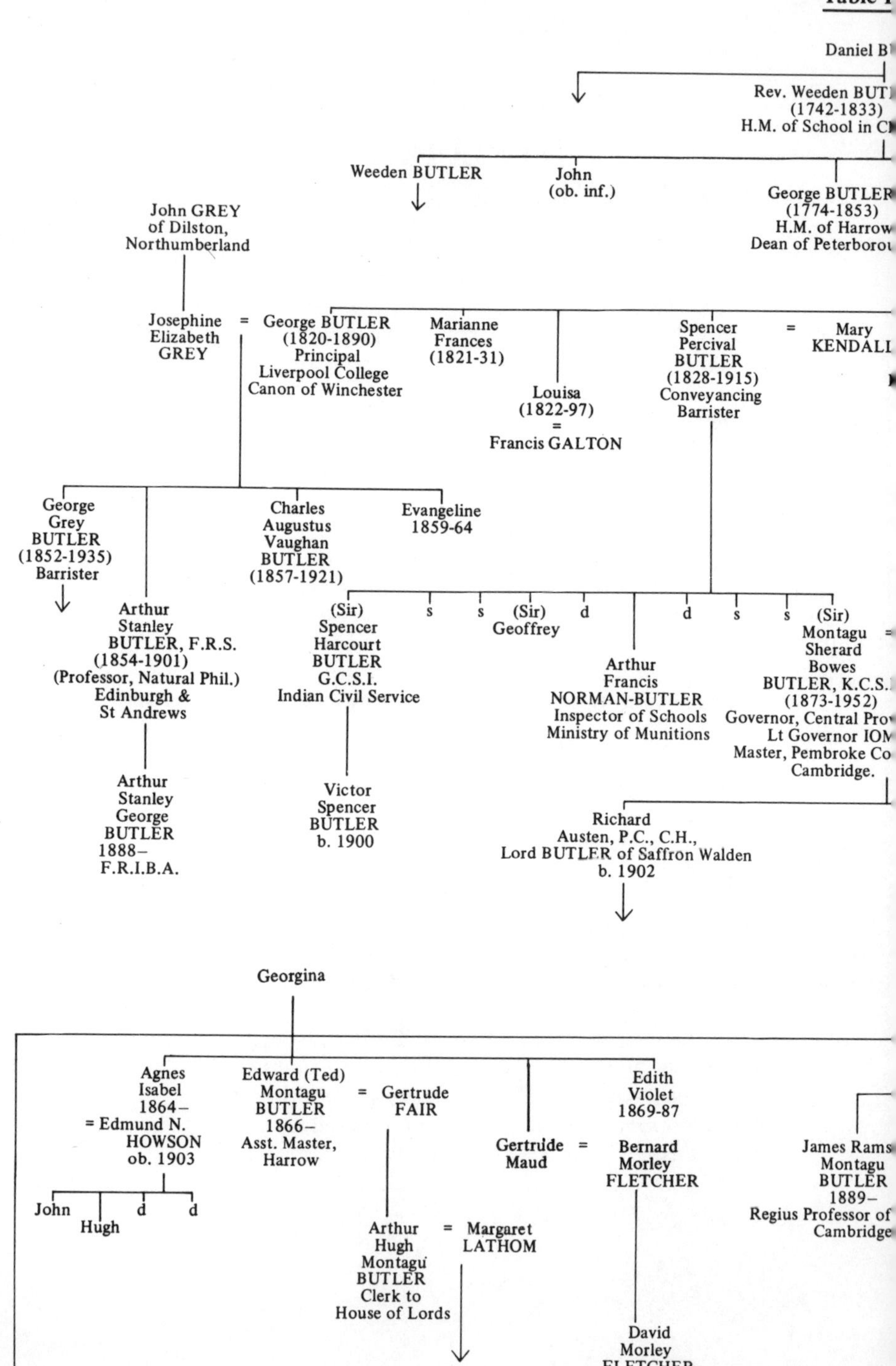

Daniel B[UTLER]

Rev. Weeden BUT[LER]
(1742-1833)
H.M. of School in C[helsea]

Weeden BUTLER
John
(ob. inf.)
George BUTLER
(1774-1853)
H.M. of Harrow
Dean of Peterborou[gh]

John GREY
of Dilston,
Northumberland

Josephine
Elizabeth
GREY
=
George BUTLER
(1820-1890)
Principal
Liverpool College
Canon of Winchester
Marianne
Frances
(1821-31)
Spencer
Percival
BUTLER
(1828-1915)
Conveyancing
Barrister
=
Mary
KENDALL

Louisa
(1822-97)
=
Francis GALTON

George
Grey
BUTLER
(1852-1935)
Barrister
Charles
Augustus
Vaughan
BUTLER
(1857-1921)
Evangeline
1859-64

Arthur
Stanley
BUTLER, F.R.S.
(1854-1901)
(Professor, Natural Phil.)
Edinburgh &
St Andrews

(Sir)
Spencer
Harcourt
BUTLER
G.C.S.I.
Indian Civil Service
s
s
(Sir)
Geoffrey
d
d
s
s
(Sir)
Montagu
Sherard
Bowes
BUTLER, K.C.S.[I]
(1873-1952)
Governor, Central Pro[vinces]
Lt Governor IOM
Master, Pembroke Co[llege]
Cambridge.
=

Arthur
Francis
NORMAN-BUTLER
Inspector of Schools
Ministry of Munitions

Arthur
Stanley
George
BUTLER
1888–
F.R.I.B.A.

Victor
Spencer
BUTLER
b. 1900

Richard
Austen, P.C., C.H.,
Lord BUTLER of Saffron Walden
b. 1902

Georgina

Agnes
Isabel
1864–
= Edmund N.
HOWSON
ob. 1903
Edward (Ted)
Montagu
BUTLER
1866–
Asst. Master,
Harrow
=
Gertrude
FAIR
Gertrude
Maud
=
Bernard
Morley
FLETCHER
Edith
Violet
1869-87
James Rams[ay]
Montagu
BUTLER
1889–
Regius Professor of [History]
Cambridge

John
Hugh
d
d

Arthur
Hugh
Montagu
BUTLER
Clerk to
House of Lords
=
Margaret
LATHOM

David
Morley
FLETCHER

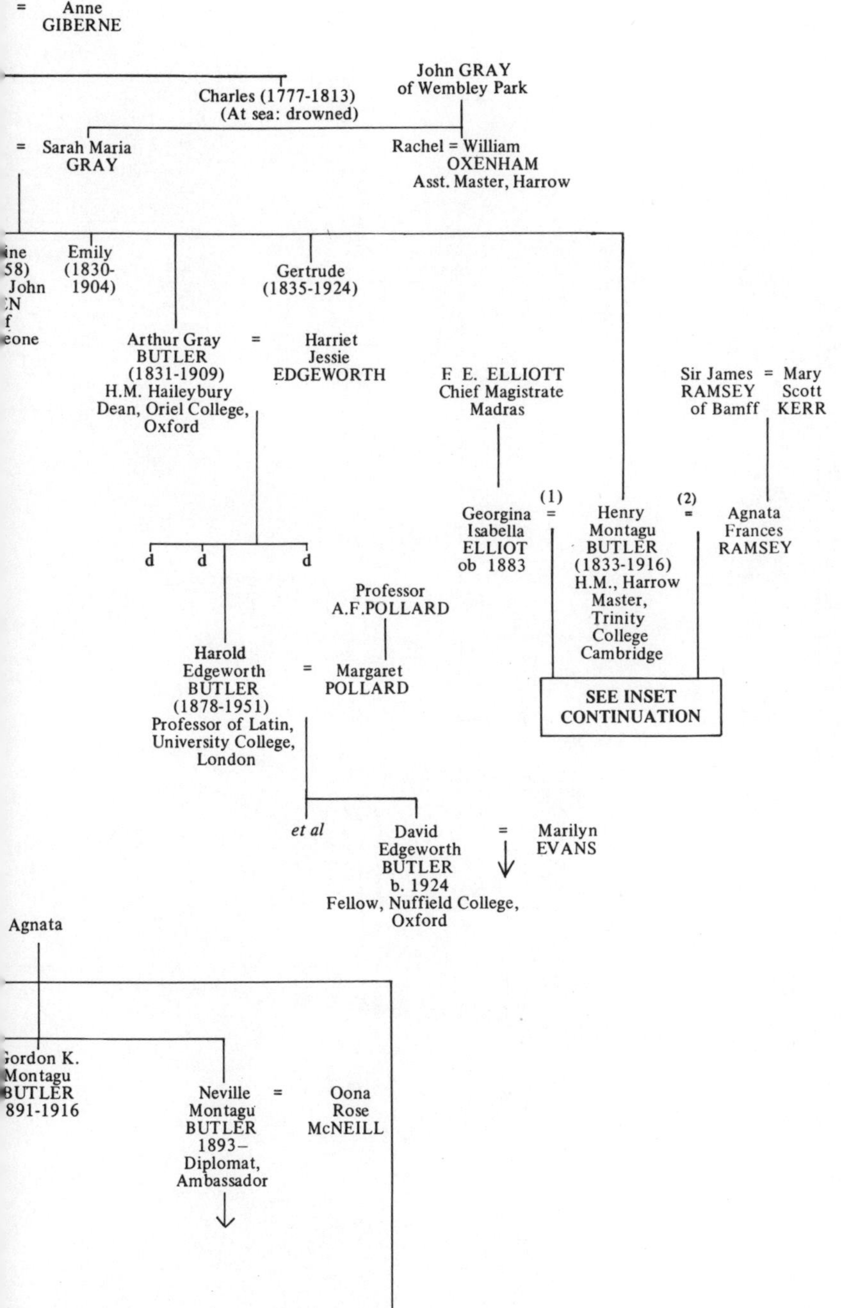
= Anne GIBERNE
Charles (1777-1813) (At sea: drowned)
John GRAY of Wembley Park
= Sarah Maria GRAY
Rachel = William OXENHAM Asst. Master, Harrow
ine 58) John N f eone
Emily (1830-1904)
Gertrude (1835-1924)
Arthur Gray BUTLER (1831-1909) H.M. Haileybury Dean, Oriel College, Oxford
= Harriet Jessie EDGEWORTH
F. E. ELLIOTT Chief Magistrate Madras
Sir James = Mary RAMSEY Scott of Bamff KERR
(1)
Georgina Isabella ELLIOT ob 1883
= Henry Montagu BUTLER (1833-1916) H.M., Harrow Master, Trinity College Cambridge
(2) = Agnata Frances RAMSEY
d   d   d
Professor A.F.POLLARD
Harold Edgeworth BUTLER (1878-1951) Professor of Latin, University College, London
= Margaret POLLARD
SEE INSET CONTINUATION
et al
David Edgeworth BUTLER b. 1924 Fellow, Nuffield College, Oxford
= Marilyn EVANS
Agnata
Gordon K. Montagu BUTLER 1891-1916
Neville Montagu BUTLER 1893– Diplomat, Ambassador
= Oona Rose McNEILL

Table II – The Families of Drury, Heath and Merivale

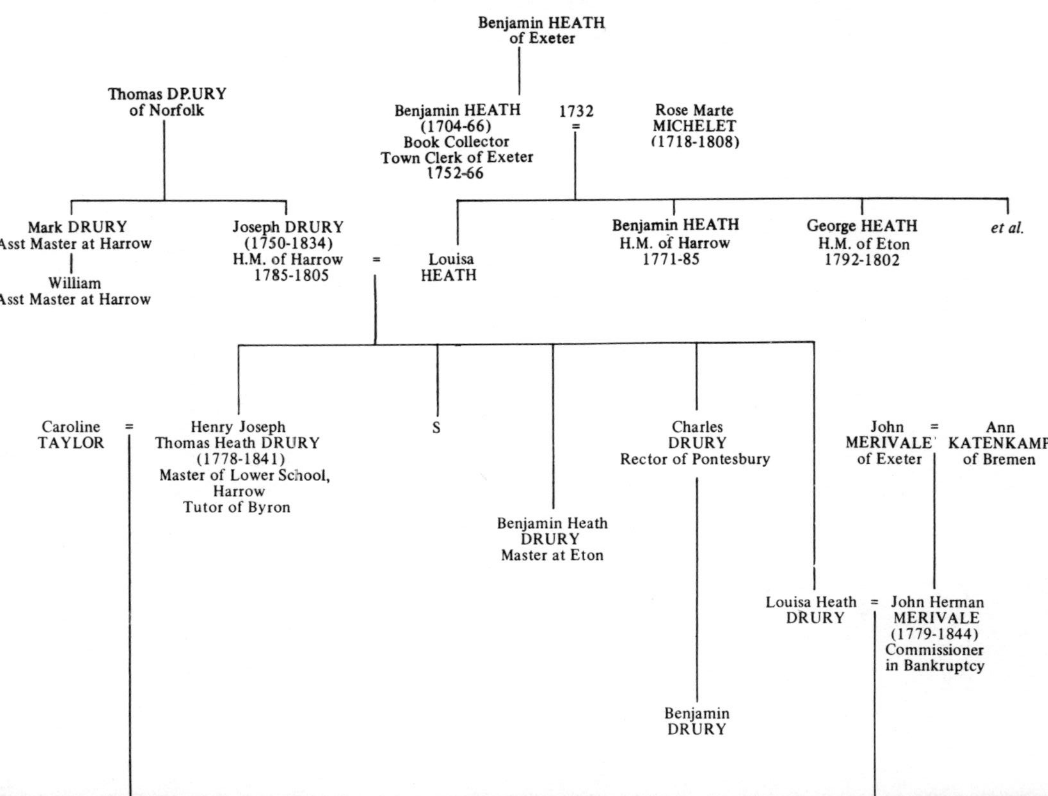

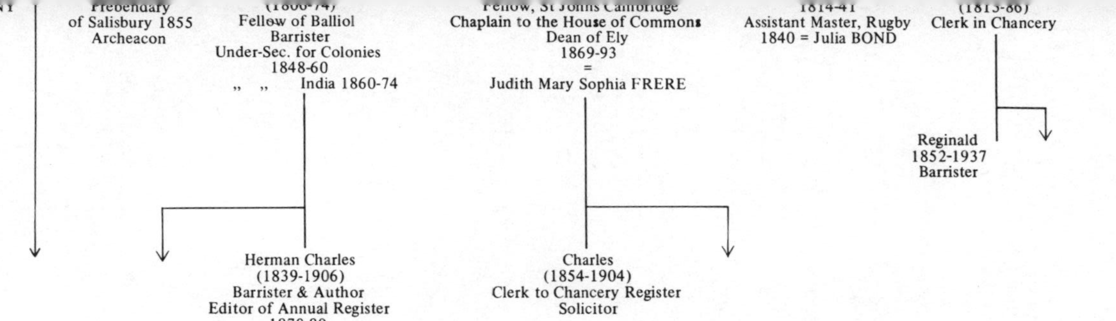

Table I(a) — The Butlers of Shrewsbury

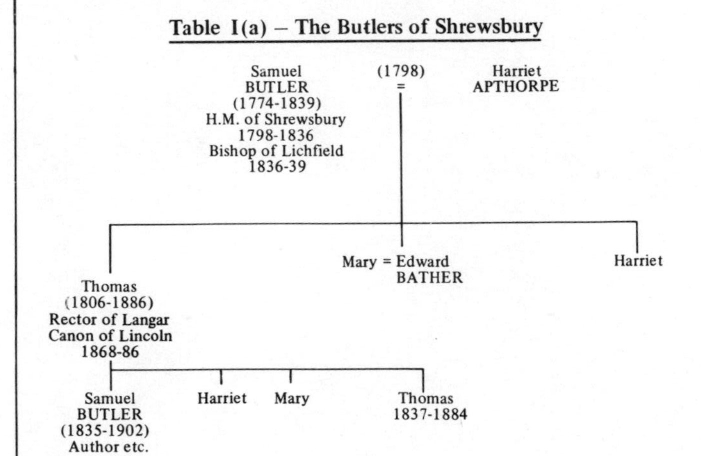

Table III – The Wordsworth Family

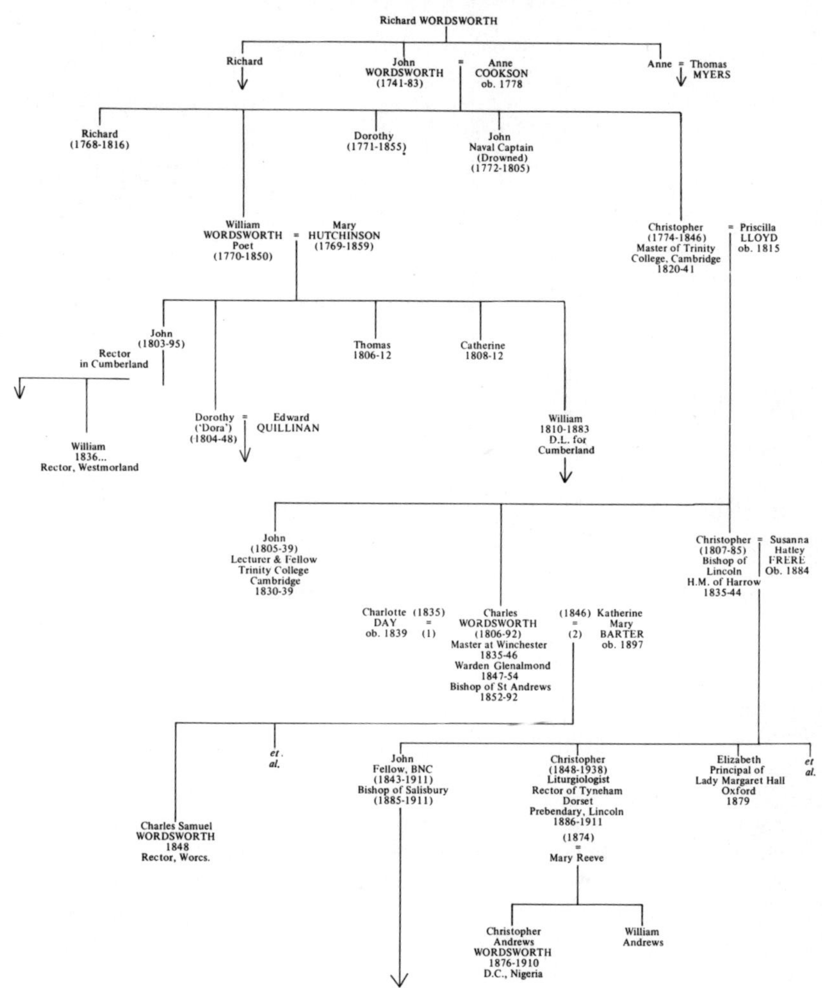

VII

ORDEAL BY COMMISSION

The Clarendon Commission on Public Schools:
Balston, Temple and others

In spite of the revival at Rugby and reforms at Eton, a storm was blowing up threatening it seemed the very existence of Public Schools. Its course has often been charted—there were letters in the *Quarterly Review* and an address to the Tiverton Athenaeum; Henry Reeve, Jacob Omnium, Paterfamilias—writers named, anonymous and pseudonymous—all rushed into print to complain of the discipline (or lack of it), the curriculum, the system of teaching, and to condemn the examples, especially Eton. The situation seemed to demand no less than a Royal Commission, such as had already been held on the Universities and on the Education of the Poorer Classes. (This latter is known from its chairman as the Newcastle Commission.) In 1861, another such Commission was appointed which would be known as the Clarendon Commission or, unofficially, the Public Schools Commission. Six Commissioners were nominated and a Secretary.

Lord Clarendon, the Chairman, was a politician and diplomat by career. He had never been to a Public School—or any school, it seems—but was early attached to the British Embassy in Moscow and afterwards in Spain, with later experience in Ireland. He had refused the Governor-generalship of Canada but had taken ministerial office under Melbourne and subsequent Liberal Governments, and later would again be Foreign Secretary. He was a correspondent of Henry Reeve whose article in the *Edinburgh Review* had helped to stir up the agitation following which the Commission had been set up, and he wrote to Reeve that he considered the article "unanswerable". It is not surprising that Etonian historians have considered him biased against the College.

William Reginald Courtenay, Earl of Devon, P.C.,D.C.L. ("our right trusty and well-beloved Cousin", reads the appointing preamble) had, as Hon. Colonel of the Devon Yeomanry, M.P. for South Devon, etc., done his duties in that state of life into which he had been born. Sir Stafford Northcote, also from the West Country, (later first Earl of Iddesleigh) had been at Eton but was "not a strenuous champion" and is stigmatized by the Etonian, Cust, as "a painstaking, not particularly brilliant politician and Devonshire squire." As the initiator and

135

hardworking architect of the scheme by which the Civil Service turned over from patronage to competitive entry and system, and as a politician who later became Chancellor of the Exchequer, this does him far less than justice, but in Gladstone's words he was "a man in whom it was the fixed habit of thought to put himself wholly out of view when he had before him the attainment of great public objects."

There was one other peer, Lord Lyttelton, 4th Baron, "straightlaced, even puritanical. . . having a high sense of moral and religious rectitude which made it impossible for him to tolerate abuses" (Cust). He was the other Old Etonian on the Commission and the fact that he produced a succession of Etonians in his own family gave him apparently no particular sympathy with the abuses there or in any other school. A man of great distinction, he knew well enough where the shoe pinched and could be trenchant in his remarks and questions. Equally "fastidious and merciless. . . when matters of scholarship or College administration were concerned" (Cust) was the Rev. William Hepworth Thompson, who later became Master of Trinity College, Cambridge.

The Hon. Edward Boyd Twistleton, M.A., was a Civil Service Commissioner; Henry Halford Vaughan, M.A. was a lawyer but also Professor of Modern History at Oxford. Finally, the Secretary was Bernard Mountague, B.C.L., Chichele Professor of International Law at Oxford.

Certainly the Commission was high-powered enough but it must be conceded that even at their fiercest the interlocutors were uniformly courteous. They themselves might indeed qualify as "Very Superior Men"; Thring unfortunately did not meet this lot but the next Commission, rather less grand. However, as this is a book not about Commissioners as such but about those whom they examined, their careers must not be further pursued. As a group they were well-chosen for carrying out their object, namely, "to investigate the Revenues and Management of Certain Colleges and Schools and the Studies pursued and Instruction given there." That they went rather beyond this is shown by their division of the field in their preliminary questionnaire which dealt not only with the finance and administration, and with the curriculum and methods of teaching but also with the minutiae of the boys' daily life and conditions, their class-rooms, bedrooms or studies, where they prepared their work; their diet ("some have meat once, others meat twice a day") and, being post-Arnold, with the discipline, the position, appointment and responsibility of monitors or prefects; the boys' religious life—both the sermons in chapel and facilities and atmosphere in which they said their private prayers.

The Commissioners were also extremely energetic. They had begun by sending round these detailed questionnaires, which went to the Head of each school, but which the Provost, Bursar, Assistant Masters and others were to have a chance of answering, in whole or in part. The return of these answers (which took up to nine months in some cases) was followed by visits, and in May and June of 1862, Commissioners went to each school. They spent three days at Rugby, the first they saw, two each at Shrewsbury, Winchester and Harrow, but confined their visit to the London Day Schools to one day each and even at Eton—of which two of them already had experience—a single day sufficed. They then called for verbal evidence and they interviewed 130 witnesses (three members of the Commission were allowed to form a Quorum but virtually always at least four were present, often the whole Commission). The witnesses naturally included all nine Headmasters but ranged also from the Dean of Christ Church and Professor Faraday to lads who had left their schools only two or three years before. Witnesses were classified into those who had at the time a connection with the schools (as Governors, Assistant Masters), those who had previously been so connected (as those recently at school) and persons, from Public Schools or not, eminent in science and literature. Perhaps in case they might suffer disparagement from having no scientific man on the Commission, they included as witnesses six Fellows of the Royal Society, two Doctors, a Professor of Chemistry as well as Max Müller the philologist and the Ven. Andrew Brown, examiner in Modern Languages. The Commissioners were interested enough to go beyond their brief and to look into four of the newly-founded schools; Marlborough, Wellington, Cheltenham and the City of London, also King's College School, Sandhurst and Woolwich, though the Heads of these institutions were not personally called. They also got, through Lord Clarendon's influence, a report on Higher Education in Prussia. In all they held 127 meetings and published their Report (with two volumes of Evidence and one of Appendices, including the answers to the questionnaire) in 1864, three years after their appointment.

This "brief", i.e. their terms of reference: to investigate "Certain Schools and Colleges", was deliberately non-committal, and the Commission themselves went to some pains to refute the idea that those they were investigating were "*The* Public Schools". They did not attempt to define these and neatly side-stepped individuals by speaking of "public school education, English style" as a phrase "which is popular and sufficiently intelligible." However, their circumspection proved in vain. The general opinion at the time and the trend of writers since has been to consider the Clarendon Nine (or Seven, if those which were virtually only Day Schools were eliminated) as comprising the lot. Certainly the Headmasters who were "in" regarded themselves as forming an exclusive group. One even considered the Commissioners had done them a very great favour by enumerating "nine schools as Public Schools. . . without any reflection on their brethren". Perhaps the general opinion was right, but the Commission was quite unwilling to say so.

The names and "styles" of those to be investigated here follow. They are as given in the Commission's Preamble, but after each (which is *not* in the Preamble) I have added the name of the Headmaster and the date of his appointment. The Commissioners generally brought out this last information somehow at the beginning of each Head's interview.

The College of the Blessed Mary of Eton, near Windsor (commonly called Eton College)	Edward Balston, February 25th, 1862
Saint Mary College, Winchester (commonly called Winchester College)	George Moberly, 1834
The Collegiate School of Saint Peter, Westminster	Charles B. Scott, 1855
The Hospital founded in Charterhouse in the County of Middlesex (commonly called Sutton's Hospital or the Charterhouse)	Richard Elwyn, 1856
St. Paul's School in the City of London	Herbert Kynaston, June 1838
The Merchant Taylors' School	J. A. Hessey, July 1838
The Free Grammar School of John Lyon at Harrow on the Hill, in the County of Middlesex	Henry Montagu Butler, November 1859
The School founded by Lawrence Sheriff at Rugby in the County of Warwick	Frederick Temple, November 1857
The Free Grammar School of King Edward the Sixth at Shrewsbury	Benjamin Hall Kennedy, February 1836

Of the nine Headmasters who walked up to the Commission's office in Victoria Street (that great thoroughfare which had but ten years before been ploughed through Westminster to connect the Abbey with the fine new station named after the Queen) some must have felt uncommonly nervous. Tall, handsome Dr. Balston might well be insecure—he had only taken up his post a few months before. Richard Elwyn was a good conscientious but worried little man who was to suffer a breakdown from overwork in the next year. The old established men were George Moberly of Winchester, desperately anxious to get across to the Commission that Wykehamists were not as other men are, and B. H. Kennedy of Shrewsbury, himself acknowledged as the greatest classical teacher of the age but deeply worried because his school was going down in numbers for reasons which he felt to be outside his control. Montagu Butler had held the headship of Harrow for three years only, but then his father had held it before him—and the family seemed to have had headships in the blood. The one man who must have approached the Commissioners with a completely easy mind was Frederick Temple of Rugby. There were several reasons why he could face them without dismay. It was not in his nature to be diffident and he had already given evidence before a Royal Commission, about the University of Oxford. Besides this, he must have known that for the men sitting there, Rugby still shone with the reflected glory of Dr. Arnold. In fact, since Stanley's *Life* had appeared, the public was beginning to focus on Thomas Arnold with such concentration that he would totally eclipse all other Headmasters in reputation, including those who were being interviewed that summer.

Yet of the nine there representing their schools, the majority were unusually well-known to their contemporaries, especially considering that the period was not long past in which Heads were virtually unrecognized outside their immediate surroundings. At Eton and Winchester they had but recently begun to rank alongside their respective Provosts/Wardens. But since the beginning of the century, those who were outstanding as scholars (Dr. Samuel Butler), as men of the world (Dr. Goodall), or university professors (as Dr. Arnold) were becoming more widely known. Of the men present, something was beginning to be known by others than their immediate pupils. They were at least *characters*. And it is rather remarkable that when F. D. How in 1923 wrote a book entitled *Six Great Schoolmasters,* four of his six were among those giving evidence in person to the Commission representing their Schools and one (Bradley) had given it in writing concerning Marlborough. Leaving aside Dr. Temple, who as a future Archbishop outclassed them all, and who was besides a Commission man *par excellence,* the interviewed headmasters showed great variety and some were in their own ways outstanding.

Dr. Edward Balston

Senior in his school, though latest in his tenure, was Dr. Edward Balston. His acceptance of his awkward position was rather to his credit, as he had taken it on in order to get Eton out of a very delicate situation. Dr. Hawtrey, the Provost, was still alive when the Commissioners' questionnaire was circulated, but he became ill before his answers could even be signed, and died at the end of January 1862. Dr. Goodford, the current Headmaster, was almost immediately nominated as Provost by the Queen, on the advice of Lord Palmerston who believed that this succession must take place as of right. This was not the case, but Goodford regarded the royal nomination as command. Strictly speaking too, the Headmaster should have given six months' notice to allow time for a successor to be appointed after due deliberation; Goodford gave a week. One other candidate besides Balston was generally admitted to be "of almost unsurpassed University distinction", though *The Times,* which had interested itself for ten days in the candidature, pointed out that "such attainments are perfectly compatible with a type of intellect and character wholly unsuited to the duties of so responsible a position." However, Dr. Balston, having (according to the minutes of the Fellows) been earnestly requested to undertake the office of Headmaster, rather reluctantly consented and was elected.

Edward Balston (1817-1891) seems to have grown into the image of Eton, and must for many people have typified all the qualities good and bad most associated with the place. Yet his was not an ancient family and had no previous Eton connections. He is another example of the unbelieved truth that Eton did not ever consist only of aristocratic traditional and outrageously wealthy people's sons. The Balstons (so it has been found; Edward simply ignored his ancestry) were farmers and rope-makers from Bridport near Dorchester (Forsyte country— "Superior Dosset"). Edward's grandfather came to London and set up a drapery business which eventually failed, and William his son, father of Edward and six other sons, was apprenticed to a paper-manufacturer. William succeeded first in getting a partnership in the Whatman paper mills, Kent, and then in setting up on his own. Two sons went into the mill, one to Rugby and one to Tonbridge. Edward was the fifth, and at the suggestion of a former teacher, was sent to Eton at 11½. As with so many boys, he was an Oppidan first, for four years, and his tutor, Edward Coleridge, wrote personal letters with excellent reports to his father prophesying distinction for him "if he will have the good sense not to be elated with self-conceit by early success." His temperament, and perhaps the atmosphere of the closely-knit family, kept him from this; the father and brothers corresponded continuously in very simple friendly terms.

Surprisingly, when at the age of 15 Edward became a Colleger, he appears to have been quite undismayed, though this was in Keate's day, long before Hodgson's reforms, when conditions could hardly have provided more cause for complaint. Balston wrote: "I am now very comfortably settled in College. I think I shall like it, if anything, better than as an Oppidan." Admittedly he was not in Long Chamber but in Carter's; moreover he was lucky enough to have a Sixth Form friend who allowed him the use of his study "where I can sap as I like." For the first term at least, he could say "Every day I seem to like it better"; unexpectedly he found "the mutton" gave him better dinners than at his Dame's. His later correspondence is unfortunately lost, but there is no record that he ceased to be happy in College. (It strikes one that once the plan was adopted of using College merely as a stepping stone to the privilege of entry into King's, and of not sending boys till they were within two or three years of leaving, the question of fagging and bullying *small* boys would simply not arise. A study of the age at which vacancies were taken up in College would be interesting. Can it be that the horrors, or at least the extent of them, have grown, myth-wise?) At any rate Balston flourished and ended his career as Newcastle Scholar and President of Pop. He also succeeded, though only just, in getting his vacancy at King's before his nineteenth (i.e. superannuation) birthday.

In addition to his scholastic record, Edward seems to have developed by the time he went to Cambridge (January 1837), a moral character which his friends respected, and principles which he sustained in the relaxed atmosphere of Etonian King's. Religious young men and moral reformers apparently were not *all* from Rugby, but Balston seems to have been that rare bird, an attractive one. The terms in which his friends wrote of him (and his obituary notices of 1891 were still a very long way off) are so strongly "Victorian" in style that to quote would be merely to obscure his character from us. One can only say that he did all the things a young man should, including winning University prizes and succeeding to a Fellowship (and in addition took a continental tour) and that after three years at King's he returned to be a master at Eton.

The closed circle for appointments (College, King's, Eton mastership) was still insisted on by Provost Hodgson, but there was a real difference between the "establishment" of the day, who in Okes' phrase determined "to wear the buckram" and the more relaxed, courteous and genial successors who as tutors and housemasters really wished to make some contact with their pupils and develop friendly, though still disciplined, relations with them. Edward was devoted to his, though there are hints that if they did not want to work he did not keep them up to the mark. He was an inspirer rather than a driver and at one time he clearly had too many. "His house was not a working house" said William Anson, a pupil who described him, with qualified respect, as "a finished scholar of the old school." He led this satisfying life for 20 years, during which he undertook the usual additions to a master's life, ordination and marriage. Through his wife, daughter of a Fellow, Carter, who became Vice Provost, Balston was accepted into the highest Etonian circle, so much so that he did actually put in for the Headship in 1853. When Goodford, an Assistant Master only five years senior to himself was elected, it looked as if there was something that Edward Balston would now never get, and he was in fact elected instead to a Fellowship in 1860 at the early age of 42. It was from this graceful semi-retirement (for he had not yet taken up a College living) that he was pulled out when the storm of public opinion broke over Eton and the Commission descended.

In the Examination (rightly described as a cross-examination rather than an examination in chief, but most urbanely conducted by the diplomatic Lord Clarendon) Dr. Balston could hardly shine. He did acquit himself rather better than the Provost, who must have been as new in *his* field as the Headmaster was in his and who was constantly having to confess that he did not know. To us, Dr. Goodford's complacency—or is it ineptitude?—is shattering. He is satisfied that though the system "may not have qualified each boy to enter at once on a profession. . . it has given him in most cases those habits and tone of mind which enable those who have to prepare him more immediately for his after course to deal with him more easily and to fit him for completely . . ." (And this was apparently all that Eton had done with five years of a boy's life.) And though he was forced to agree with the Commissioners that the scholarship of the Oppidans was getting worse, he considers "hardly any fundamental alteration of the system and course of education at Eton to be desirable."

Balston's attitude is not very different. He reveals not only an ignorance of detail remarkable for one who had taught there for 20 years but a lack of policy either specific or overall. As an example of such deficiency in a fundamental problem; arising out of the suggestion that science might be taught as an optional study (even this idea he looked on very coldly) he was asked what if a boy showed an inaptitude for Latin verses—could not his study of this be relaxed? His answer was: "This is a very difficult question. . . (which) I have not considered."

Understandably, he expanded and supported the function of the College Tutors, the construing and correcting of exercises in preparation for Division (i.e. the masters' classes), the "private business" which enabled them to enlarge the very restricted selection of classical texts studied, and the personal relations with each boy, which he considered the backbone of the system. (Of the *private* tutors he merely said they might enable some eccentric or temperamental boys to continue at school without constantly getting into scrapes.) The Fellows, he was forced to admit had in general no direct duties except their rota of preaching and he had nothing to say when Lord Clarendon asked whether the school would suffer, its utility and progress be injured, if there were no Fellows at all.

His unquestioning acceptance of tradition was laid bare again and again. On the question of appointing masters, for instance, he believed, but could give no reason, that the appointment of Kingsmen only was better on balance—and added the curious view that to get a master e.g. from Rugby would be "taking another man's servant."

When it came to curriculum, Edward Balston was of course not alone in believing that hardly an hour could be spared from the study of the classics nor a line cut off the weekly three to four hundred lines of Greek or Latin verse learnt by heart. (Revealingly, his comment on the latter was: "I value this as one of the most unfailing tests of the boys' industry. They cannot get this done for them at any rate.") The ancient languages were the only study to promote habits of hard work—no mention, of course, of their ever being enjoyed or used—so this linguistic study must be the main and, "distasteful to boys" as he admits it is, essential work. No room for "anything which interferes" with that. (In this narrowness of actual classical instruction, he and Eton in general were far behind the best type of teaching that was in fact being given at Shrewsbury, say, or Rugby.) If—as was put to him—a boy came knowing some French, it might be desirable to give him some opportunity to keep it up, even orally, but Dr. Balston had not worked out how that could be done. Indeed, he had no actual objection to boys learning French at school but only *before* a boy got into the Remove or *after* he reached the Upper Division—and the wholly classical period between would take about four years of his school life which should be devoted "almost entirely to Latin and Greek". When it was pointed out that in spite of this concentration, at Oxford "among those painfully deficient [in classical learning] Eton stands prominently first" he could only say "I am sorry for it" and fall back on the lame excuse that boys came badly prepared.

Dr. Balston must have had a miserable time, though occasionally he defended himself with spirit, for instance, over the Chapel sermons. When Lord Clarendon flung Arnold in his teeth, he spoke quite a piece beginning: "If I may be allowed to express an opinion." First, he said, Arnold was not an everyday man, so it was no use for other men to imitate his methods; secondly, was his preaching really so successful, or would the effect wear off? Balston boldly said he preferred the Eton system, presumably of listening to the Fellows, whom they could barely hear in the Chapel, (but Balston himself was an acknowledged and good preacher), as leading to freedom from the ostentation found at Rugby where "the teacher has seemed to have more influence than the truth he seeks to inculcate." When questioned as to his opportunity of knowing the Rugby system, he stated that he had had two brothers there and had known plenty of Rugbeians at Cambridge. In this matter, he really seems to have worked out his position and was no doubt sincere, though one cannot follow him all the way. He doubted whether a sermon by an Assistant master would be "very useful"—if the man had something he wished to get across, his senior should do it for him. At any rate when he was an Assistant, *he* never wanted to preach!

Perhaps the two least defensible positions he tries to defend are the Provost's veto, which he considers never interfered with anything important (others gave plenty of evidence to the contrary) and the Eton timetable, with its medley of Saints' Days and Eves and Royal holidays, each interfering with a whole week's timetable. He approves of its irregularity—"anything that breaks the routine of school work is very valuable". This is a typical outsider's *cliché*—and as to routine, Lord Clarendon confessed that the complexity of the timetable baffled him and he gave up trying to understand it.

After the departure of the Commission, Dr. Balston set himself to the rigours of his office and to the administration of the system he had been so busy defending. Accounts of his reign are mixed and it is difficult to get a clear picture of him but on the whole he was popular. He continued gently with a few of the most needed reforms—getting the staff accommodation improved, bolstering up the position of the Mathematical Master and doing away with some obsolescent rules and customs. But his popularity must have been due in great measure to personal qualities:

> Our boyish hero was the Head Master. He was a splendid figure; tall, handsome, stately, with great dark brown eyes, and a mellow ringing voice . . . I can still hear the noble cadence with which he called the names (at Absence)

This from Bernard, second Lord Coleridge and even in class at least his Sixth Form appreciated him: "His gracious kindliness won us all, and he made our work as interesting as was possible with the somewhat dry curriculum to which we were confined." He had his idiosyncratic form of speech too—always an endearing trait in a schoolmaster. His equivalent to Keate's "Go along, Sir" was "Run away, little boy, run away". Handed down also was his comment: "Telegrams, telegrams, Hasty things, hasty things."

On retiring he was re-elected to a Fellowship, and as a Fellow was at first kept busy working out the scheme to be presented under the Public Schools Act for the future government of the College. It was agreed that the majority of Fellows should take no part in the Governing body; he thus lopped off the branch he sat on, perhaps without too much sadness. For though he took a living in Derbyshire, he continued with his three months' turn of duty a year in residence at Eton, so was never quite removed from the place. He had no children but entertained nephews and nieces, and even the following generation, and he led the gently active life of a country parson till his seventy-fifth year. "Now, I am simply waiting", he wrote to a friend, and he passed away peacefully in his study after a Sunday morning service in his parish church, dying as gracefully as he had lived.

B. H. Kennedy

Balston was the first, and B. H. Kennedy of Shrewsbury (whose name has for nearly a century adorned the standard Latin primer for innumerable pupils in countless schools) brought up the rear, in the series of examinees. This place of Shrewsbury's was not fortuitous; the school which, however great in the day of its foundation, had not been even thought of for a century as other than local, had been pushed on to the Public band-wagon by the persistence and classical brilliance of Butler; Kennedy had held it there. Owing to its poor accommodation, its out-of-the way position and the parochial minds of its Governors, a constant effort was needed to keep up its numbers, and more than once in his evidence Kennedy pointedly alludes to what he regards as the unfair competition of other schools:

> I do not see how any of the old foundation schools, except the few which have fashion and great connections in their favour can hold their ground against the tide of Joint stock education.

These new schools, he thinks, because they have been founded by non-profit-making shareholders, are in a better position financially, and can also vary their curriculum, accommodating themselves to the parents who want modern studies and are prepared to pay for them. (Not, of course, that Kennedy would budge an inch in the importance of the classics; they were the breath of life to him.) No doubt the real competitor was Rugby which, had Arnold lived, might eventually have tackled Shrewsbury in her own field of scholarship; in this, however, Shrewsbury was still ahead though not unrivalled. But leaving Arnold aside (which Salopians, though not the Commissioners, tended to do) Rugby had the luck to be on a railway, which had not yet effectively helped Shrewsbury.

The Commissioners treated Kennedy with a special gentleness, not unmixed with a respected awe. Born in 1804, he had been teaching for 34 years in all, 26 of them as Headmaster of Shrewsbury, and his pupils' reverence for him was only just this side of idolatry. He was not yet sixty, but was beginning to feel himself growing old. When asked about his assistants, whom he still had to pay out of his own pocket, he said:

> I have been here 26 years and am not so strong as I was and if I

appoint new masters to give me a little relief, it is a matter for my own consideration...

His evidence is given like that of an old man; not at all wandering indeed, or lacking in grip, but simple and rather chatty. The assistants evidently came because it was an honour to teach under the grand old man, though hardly a financial advantage: "They have about the emolument of a moderate Fellowship", he said, "and they are looked upon by me as friends". Similarly he tells them about his relations with his elder boys; he believes that his confidence in the praepostors is "rarely abused".

Sometimes a compromise has been admitted but if the Head Master considers a certain course essential, he insists upon it, giving his reason and the praepostors, after consideration, have always yielded ground.

And he had a rather rambling tale of how he eventually allowed a "Hounds Dinner" but got it transferred from an Inn to a confectioners with beer not spirits as the drink. We might be happy, a hundred years after, if we could say our crises were resolved so amicably.

Kennedy's justification of his teaching methods is found not in his own evidence but in that of a pupil, C. E. Graves of St. John's, Cambridge who had just taken the second place in Classics (1st Division), which would not alone entitle him to be regarded as one of Shrewsbury's top fliers. Graves was asked for a list of his reading at school and began by saying modestly that he thought it very much the same as that at other schools. The Commissioners then asked whether he had read this and that author—he had, and told them exactly which books. After some twelve questions answered in this way, Mr. Thompson (future Master of Trinity, Cambridge) exclaimed: "You seem to have read about twice as much as boys from any other school!" and the young man quietly answered "I have been giving *all* I read in the course of five years" but goes on to say, "I have read some more but I cannot think of the names." But when prompted he continues for another five questions on Greek and twelve on Latin reading. The Commission were also glad to learn that he could read French easily enough ("novels" he added, diffidently), and that he had studied it for two or three hours (a day? a week?). Mathematics got only three hours a week, but he feels he had a grounding in Euclid, Algebra and trigonometry, and is taking up the mathematical side now that he has finished his classical course at Cambridge. While at school he considers that the boys read quite a lot of English, history and novels; they took papers and reviews, in their common room. They had about four hours leisure (a week?) and in the summer he spent most of his fishing.

There is a charming simplicity and matter-of-fact acceptance of this bumper programme without conceit, and of course his success is said to be due to Kennedy who taught him for four of his five years at the school. "You attribute your success mainly to the personal teaching of Dr. Kennedy?", they sum up, and he warmly agrees: "a consummate teacher".

This evidence, though only one example of the tributes he was constantly receiving, would have warmed Kennedy's heart, and it is worth while noting that it comes from a Town boy, not a boarder. Kennedy inherited the opprobrium and opposition that Dr. Butler always had to contend with, and certainly in his early days there was a good deal of fighting between the Head and the Burgesses. But the intransigence can never have extended to their sons. F. H. How (*Six Great Schoolmasters*, p.114) quotes a Shrewsbury boy who deplored his position as a non-boarder, but young Graves considers he was on a footing of perfect equality. Only, perhaps it was not so easy for him to get cricket—but anyway, he preferred fishing—and it was not the thing for Town boys to wear the cap outside school-times.*

What manner of man was this "greatest classical teacher" of the century, as the Commissioners had stated him to be? Benjamin Hall Kennedy was the son of a distinguished schoolmaster (Assistant at King Edward VI, Birmingham), of Scots origin, and had his middle name from his mother who was partly of Huguenot extraction. So there was a variety of strains in his make up. He was the eldest of four brothers all of whom became first class Classics, and had good careers, legal, scholastic and administrative. But Benjamin had a quite unusual brilliance in classical scholarship which not only developed early but continued in a life-pervasive way till his old age. A bunch of correspondence with Edward Baines, a friend of his very first schooldays, survives (dated 1873-82) in which classical, mainly Greek, quotations flow as easily to these ancients as ITMA catchwords did in

---

* Kennedy had introduced the school cap (there was no other uniform), and it was at first most unpopular. It was not the ordinary round cap with a peak, but a "mortar-board" as worn in the higher academic institutions; the boys called it a "tyle". One reason for its introduction was to help him get rid of drunkenness which he, no less than Arnold, found when he took over his Headship. There were no special licensing hours but Kennedy strongly disapproved of the boys' entering public houses and hoped that their being marked out by the academic headgear as schoolboys would prevent their being admitted. It would probably mark them out almost as clearly if they went bareheaded; we so often forget how constantly hats were worn up to this period.

war-time or the lyrics of the Beatles did among the young in the time of their popularity.

Kennedy, writing the preface to a memorial volume of Baines' sermons in 1882, says:

"I went to Shrewsbury School towards the end of January 1819, being then two months past the age of fourteen... Dr. Butler, after examination, placed me high in the upper remove of the fifth form, and a vacancy in the sixth form (or "the eighteen" as they were called) occurring at the Quarter, he took me up to fill it. Places were changed once a month, and at the close of my first half year I was raised to the ninth place, next the eight praepostors... In the August examination I became third boy in the school, and in that which followed I became second, Baines being head-boy. He went to Christ's College in October 1820 and I succeeded him in the headship, which I kept by examination for the rest of my schooltime, three years, going to College in October 1823."

It was partly these three years of Butler's teaching that enabled Kennedy to win the Porson Prize at Cambridge while still in his school Sixth form—an exploit which, like a similar Oxford success, in which Gladstone was defeated by a schoolboy, went down resoundingly in academic history. Kennedy goes on:

"When I went up as a Freshman to St. John's, Cambridge . . . I was heartily welcomed by Baines... and from that time to the end of his life we were close friends*...(I became) a member of the Conversazione Society, better known as "the Apostles", a soubriquet given because their number is twelve... Among our members were Frederick Maurice, John Sterling, Edward Romilly... R. C. Trench (the Archbishop)... We met every other Saturday evening to read essays and discuss their subjects... and for some years we published a magazine called the Metropolitan."

---

* In January 1882 he wrote to Baines: "What do you think I did in the summer? Persuaded by Jackson of Trin (?) I dined at (Brodmore?) with the Apostles!!! and had a seat of honour accorded me next to the Chairman, Lord Lyttelton, nor could I prevail on Lord Houghton to sit above me. We had a very pleasant evening—36 in number. None of our time (quoti enim supersunt?). Lord H., the only one near to it for he is not more than 3 or 4 years my junior—all the rest 'longo intervallo posteriores!' I took with me to the dinner a few copies of a translation newly made and not inappropriate to the lovely prospect which lay beneath us where we dined. I enclose you a copy—you promised us a great treat in saying that you will come to pay us a visit about April..."

He also joined the Cambridge Union, of which he became President in 1823. The long list of his classical distinctions and prizes might here follow, but it may be counted superfluous and even wearisome. They are of course all recorded on the Honours Boards at Shrewsbury and in the *Life* of Dr. Butler.

On leaving Cambridge, Kennedy put in a year as an Assistant Master at Shrewsbury which tided him over a period till he got his Fellowship at St. John's and at the same time enabled him to do Butler a service. His keeping the mastership for a year only filled up an interval while Tom Butler (later portrayed somewhat unfairly perhaps as "Ernest Pontifex") was taking his degree and could then be appointed to the place which Kennedy had kept warm, In 1827 Kennedy applied for the Headship of Rugby. It was not surprising that, at his youthful years, he did not get it and—somewhat unaccountably—the Trustees chose a last minute, private-school candidate, one Thomas Arnold. So Kennedy returned to Cambridge as a classical lecturer for two years and had as his pupils men who were afterwards distinguished·and not unprofitable acquaintances. They included William Cavendish who later, as Duke of Devonshire, became chancellor of Cambridge University. He then went as a master to Harrow, where he had already acted as an examiner, and from there, six years later, he came back to Shrewsbury to succeed his old headmaster. It would have been to his financial advantage to continue at Harrow where he might well have been appointed to the Headship in due course, and had he known the long and embarrassing years that were ahead of him at Shrewsbury, he might have hesitated. But he expressed himself to Butler unreservedly in favour of his old school:

> "Not only would I not be a candidate for Harrow, but I would not take it if offered me. I would rather have Shrewsbury, if after twenty years I could retire with £1,000 a year than Harrow with a prospect of a quintuple income. I am not fit for it nor it for me. Lucre cannot make me happy unless I feel myself to be doing good and see the good I do. I will take no school where fagging is a legalized system. Learning cannot flourish in it . . ."

Kennedy found his Headship no easy job and must have needed all his enthusiasm. True, Butler left him 228 pupils. (Where *did* he put them? There are stories of six beds i.e. 12 boys, in a very small room: the attics of Butler's school house can still be seen, but fortunately uninhabited by boys.) This number was a big decline from what had been near 300. In Butler's last days there had been a slackening both in teaching and in discipline. In work "boys were left in a great measure to themselves," and this was true also of games and in the House. They "managed their own affairs to an extent now hardly credible" (Oldham) and Kennedy, burdened as he immediately became, took steps to bring things under control.

His improvements—supervised preparation, better facilities for games and the reorganization of boating, for example—need not be examined in detail, but his actual teaching method is worth looking at. ("My Sixth Form is the hardest Sixth Form in England" he is reported as saying, "and I intend it to be so.") An account of his methods and Butler's can be found in an address given by Mr. D. S. Colman to the Classical Association in 1950. He quotes one pupil: "At first sight one would have said that Kennedy had no *method* at all. Indeed I do not think that he had ever formulated or worked out a method of teaching. But. . . his teaching sank in somehow. This was to a great extent owing to his astounding vigour and quickness. He was never tedious; a lesson . . . was got through at a terrific pace, and one wondered how on earth so much had been done in the time." There is a picture of him teaching: "His tall and striking figure never—or hardly ever—at rest, his bright, piercing eye, his mighty voice echoing among the rafters, all combined to fix attention."

The speed and freshness of the lessons were what attracted the boys and Mr. Colman comments, which may be a surprise to those who think primarily of Kennedy as the author of the familiar Latin Primer, that "there was very little reference to questions of formal grammar . . . There was a sort of assumption, quite unjustified, that a boy had all that at his fingers' ends by the time he reached the Sixth Form." If a boy had "no gift for verse composition, Kennedy did not harry him. But whether in verse or prose most of them could command languages in a way which few boys to-day can achieve. . . " Kennedy was clear about the one way in which a boy could become fluent in another tongue: "Think in Latin!" he would cry, "think in Greek!"

It is a curious thing that this emphasis was not immediately transferred to the teaching of modern languages, as soon as these were added or took the place of classics in the school curriculum; it would have formed the basis for speaking them.

To revert to his personal appearance—Dr. Kennedy was "a fine-looking man, with no claim to be considered handsome." "He was a heavily built man of square figure somewhere about 5ft. 10. . . in height. His 'springing step' was the result of his great vitality, for . . . he was clumsily formed about the feet and legs. He was clean-shaven, and his massive face lent itself to considerable play of feature. He could be bland and playful on occasion, but on the other hand he could terrify a small boy almost out of his wits by the ferocity of his expression." A rather comic example is given: a very small boy had been summoned to Dr. Kennedy's desk to be reprimanded. In a trembling voice the little fellow offered some excuse, on which the Doctor, rising from his seat and leaning his imposing form over the desk, roared out: "Do you want, Sir, to bully the Headmaster?"

A number of stories are quoted from Dr. Gifford who wrote for How his impressions of Kennedy in his early days as a Headmaster. One is too good to omit.

On the first of April a mischievous boy had put the clock forward and caused the bell for morning chapel to be rung an hour too soon. The delinquent was discovered, and much alarmed by an invitation to call on the Doctor a little before noon, at the usual place of execution. Swish! But strange to say, the culprit was untouched. Swish! as before. The boy was still trembling for the third stroke, when there came the words, "Go away, you April fool!"

Another anecdote, this time to exemplify his phenomenal memory (which was not confined, as here, to classical quotation):

A certain boy, who had to show up an original copy of verses, was so hard put to it that he searched out a certain rare and obscure classic, copied out a dozen or so lines and sent them up to the Doctor as his own. "Ah yes" said Kennedy, "beautiful verses! And if I remember right, they go on thus—" and he proceeded to quote the rest of the piece.

One more quotation shows the more serious and open aspect of Kennedy's relations with his boys and that Arnold was not the only Head to trust his Sixth:

He showed implicit trust in a boy's word. The sort of conversation that not infrequently occurred was this: "W—, I have sent for you on suspicion that you did such and such an act. The suspicion is so grave that I must ask you, did you or did you not?" "I did not, sir," "Very well, I believe you." And there the matter ended.

Legends certainly accumulated about Kennedy, and life under him though it may have been untranquil was certainly never dull. He would take up other enthusiasms besides the major ones of classics and school—croquet, riddles, a study of murder trials; his energy was bound to expend itself. He had married and reared a family; his Janet being by all accounts (including those of his old friends) most pleasant, hospitable and amiable, business-like also—the very wife to be the stabilising element in his life that she was for forty years.

The Commissioners' Report was congratulatory and favourable

(except for comments on the buildings) and recommended changes in delocalizing the school and moving it from its cramped quarters—suggestions generally in line with Kennedy's wishes. (They did not commit themselves, however, to his favourite piece of argument against the Burgesses,—that "Libera" in the school's original title did *not* mean "free" in the sense that they should have the special advantage of not-paying for their sons' education but a "chartered" institution subject to no "superiority" but that of the Crown.) Kennedy did not stay to see the most important of the Commissioners' recommendations turned into an Act of Parliament. He resigned, partly to give up the burden of his very heavy work and responsibility, and partly, he afterwards declared, to write that Latin Primer for which the Public School masters had so often asked, both in evidence before the Commission and in general demands made outside it.

He certainly did not rest entirely. Within a year of his resignation, the Regius Professorship in Greek was vacant at Cambridge; Kennedy was in the slightly embarrassing position of having no competitors but his own former pupils. All the same, he allowed himself to be elected, gaining with the post a canonry at Ely which was granted him for life with the right of dining in Trinity so that he remained there after his eventual retirement from work, in touch with his friends. A Professorship of Latin was founded, the two first occupants of which were his old pupils; Kennedy subscribed to the fund (which was largely raised in his honour on his leaving Shrewsbury) on condition that it should not be called after him; it now is. He continued to be a figure of respect both in the School and the world at large: his successor at Shrewsbury, H. W. Moss, had to carry through the move out from the town which Kennedy himself had never faced, nor perhaps entirely wanted to do. He wrote to Moss, however, of his "full conviction" of the truth and justice of his arguments—a letter which gave Moss no small pleasure and support. (Kennedy in fact expected all sorts of difficulties, but he was generous enough not to wish to add to those of Moss.) Except for the sadness of losing his wife 15 years before his own death, and the similar sorrow of seeing so many of his old pupils die before him, it must have been a happy old age. He continued to edit classical texts and revisions of his Grammar: "Yes, I am at work—always at work," he writes in 1879 "what else can I do" (but of course says it in Latin.) One pleasant glimpse survives of a reunion of old friends, in a letter from Gretton to Baines, November 6th, 1876:

> We was uncommon jolly wasn't we? I would not have missed going up for a good deal, and yet I was very unwilling to go—how laziness grows upon us with years. Not that years have much to do with you, except in counting of them up. . . . I heartily wish I could say the

same of our Host, it might be that he was below the mark as being
for the nonce not quite well; or it may be that the loss of his wife
(aei!) still hangs upon him; but I somehow missed his former energy
and go-ahead way. Yet it was very enjoyable in every way. "When
shall we three meet again?" I rather think that we *ex*stonished friend
Moss with our old time stories, he would hug himself in the belief
that he has nowadays no such rough spirit to keep in check. . .

"The chimes at midnight"? Echoes of another Ben?

Dr. George Moberly

George Moberly of Winchester appears in many writings but perhaps
the fundamental study is still his daughter's, *Dulce Domum.* This story
(her word) of the Moberly family is photographically convincing, with
much detail and quotation, though, in true Victorian style, it is too
long-drawn-out to make much real impact. The Moberlys, all seventeen
of them, established themselves so firmly as a family in College and
Cathedral that one simply had to accept them and naturally all these
young lives and interests were centred on their father.

Dr. Moberly met with a good deal of controversy in his life—as his
reputation has since. A fairly recent attack on the conventional picture
of a "pompous, dogmatic and pedantic" Victorian worthy was made by
Mrs. Iremonger in her book, *The Ghosts of Versailles,* a discussion of
the veracity of his daughter Annie who with Miss Eleanor Jourdain
wrote *An Adventure,* a book which caused no small stir in about 1908.
The ghosts, including that of Marie Antoinette, were those which these
ladies believed themselves to have seen. Mrs. Iremonger, discrediting the
daughter, Annie, begins with the family; the Headmaster was queer
(*not,* of course, in a modern sense); his family lived in Russia where
they were merchants; he married a Scot brought up in Italy who could
never bear to call him by his Christian name; the couple saw a
"portent" of coffins; he kept a diary in Latin. (Any 19th century
classicist might have done this without being thought peculiar; to go
from Latin to the vernacular would have been quite effortless to
Moberly.) Mrs. Iremonger considers him a jealous, disappointed man
who waited too long for episcopal preferment; he had 31 years as
Headmaster of Winchester and rather less than 15 as Bishop of
Salisbury. (Poor Samuel Butler enjoyed his well-earned episcopate for
only *three* years.) Her implication is that he felt himself inferior (the
term "complex" is hardly needed) to those around him; for example to
his second master, Charles Wordsworth who early became Bishop of St.
Andrews, and to the widely beloved John Keble. From their

correspondence one would think that Keble, who lived a few miles out of Winchester, and Dr. Moberly were great friends; they were in continual deep and earnest discussion over the state of the Church, its doctrines and the events of the day. One has no real understanding of the minds of intellectual and responsible men of the 19th century if one fails to appreciate the reality and importance that Church questions had for them; for decades these problems really engaged them, as talk of race relations or space travel was to do for a later age. The Church was simply of enormous importance in their lives, every element was hammered out, and a man's acceptance or non-acceptance determined after long consideration. It is doubtful whether Dr. Moberly would have supported his daughter's idea of *The Adventure;* his religion was of a sober, orthodox, type, and he rather disapproved of the Society for Psychical Research which he called "The Ghost Society".

Dr. Moberly in his controversies was not without principles and courage; he once registered his vote against the Archbishop's resolution in a minority of one, though unlike some of his contemporaries, he was not a fighter by temperament. (As a boy he had been very delicate and walked for a time with a crutch; he had been at Winchester, but it is said he made no mark till he reached Oxford.) He had had to struggle already against a Royal Commission; one had been enquiring into Oxford University when, oddly enough, Winchester and Eton were included, dragged in under the investigation of New College and Christ Church respectively. Now he had to face the "Inquiry" into his school itself.

In *Dr. Moberly's Mint-Mark* Mr. Christopher Dilke follows in some detail his interview with the Commissioners, the Chairman, Lord Clarendon, taking the major part. The Headmaster's main points were two—character and the classics. It is from a phrase in one of his answers that the title of Mr. Dilke's book is taken:

> Every school of this size has a definite character and gives a peculiar stamp to its pupils; and I could with more or less distinction characterize the pupils of the Public Schools of England by the particular *stamp or mint-mark they bear**. That which distinguishes our Winchester boys is ... of a very distinct and valuable kind. I consider that those boys who issue from the top of the school carry with them into life a stamp not of a very showy kind but distinguished by a self-reliance, a modesty, a practical good sense and a strong religious feeling; that religious feeling being of a very moderate, traditional and sober kind which, in my judgment, is beyond all price.

---

* My italics—A.C.P.

Moberly defined it, Winchester produced it, but examples of what he meant were perhaps best revealed in the work of that Victorian bestseller, Charlotte M. Yonge. Miss Yonge was a lifelong friend of the Moberly family, and her many books, originally intended for girls and the school room, were amazingly widely read. Her young heroes, especially *The Heir of Redclyffe,* held the admiration of Professors, undergraduates and Crimean officers, even of an Archbishop, and their blend of self-reliance, modesty and strong religious feeling of a sober traditional type (an appreciation, if not achievement, of classical learning might be taken for granted) was not at all unlike Dr. Moberly's Wykehamist. It may be added that, as Dr. Moberly said of his boys, they tended to be sons of clergy or at least of professional men. What a study his characterization of varied Public School types would have made! But Dr. Moberly never, to my knowledge, undertook it.

Of course in his other point, the unrivalled importance of the classics, Dr. Moberly was not alone among Public School Headmasters. But perhaps he was more single-minded. He had stated his views already in a pamphlet and in letters to Sir William Heathcote; they were repeated to the Commissioners, but need not be detailed here. Suffice to say, he regarded them as all-important to education.

One of the earlier Commission's recommendations (on the University of Oxford) had been that some kind of science should be allowed into the curriculum. (French was there, but as the Commissioners elicited from him, a boy's progress in this made no difference to the important matter of his position in the school.) The school, it was believed, had accepted this recommendation, but Moberly (with the backing of the Warden and Fellows) had substituted a set of lectures, reduced from 12 to "not so many as ten" a year, frankly considering that "physical science in the way we can give it, is worthless." He had a fairly good argument; that the kind of man who was prepared to come to Winchester and to give a set of lectures over and over again would be "a very inferior person". He would be doing no research and have no scientific society. It sounded plausible, and Moberly had other arguments against doing what the Commissioners wanted, but at the bottom is a kind of obstinate myopia; he wasn't going to have it.

Dr. Moberly was a good disputant; he was also an effective disciplinarian (though he made, perhaps, too much use of sarcasm), a bright and interesting teacher, but above all, he was a preserver of things as he found them. He saw well enough, for instance, the faults of the system of dual control between himself and the Warden (but he was fortunate in having at first someone who was exceptionally wise and cooperative, Warden Barter, and after him, someone he could manage). He did not try to justify the system to the Commissioners, but neither did he suggest to them that it should be altered. He was not, however, quite as naif as Warden Lee who had taken everything so much for granted that he could only answer: "I never thought about it"—a fairly typical reply of his. Moberly's epitaph among Wykehamists when he died at the age of 80 (as Bishop of Salisbury) was "Look back on him gratefully and respectfully for what he was, without asking what he was not."

Perhaps one's deepest suspicions are roused not by anything he said or did but by his portraits. They agree well enough in showing his delicacy (which went with his well-modulated tones and silver-tongued voice often referred to) his intelligence, his firmness, even fanaticism. But there is a curious look in the eye—a dark piercing eye over which the brows crook low, leaving a great expanse of forehead running up. Here is evidently a very remarkable man but it leaves one with some uncertainty—saint or serpent?

Charles Scott

The rest of the headmasters of the "certain Schools" need not detain us so long, worthy men as some of them were. The Headmaster of Harrow has been noted in the outstanding Butler dynasty; the Heads of the four London day-schools—Westminster, St. Paul's, Charterhouse and Merchant Taylors—were each in his own way working for improvement but without any great achievement.

One thing which really paralysed the efforts of these schools was the uncertainty of their physical future; should they—*could* they—move, or was it better to stay and concentrate on improvement? Feeling was strongly divided in all but perhaps specially at Westminster, where there was such a weight of old tradition and historic association in favour of staying where they were, to set against the desire for "country air" and the very pressing fear of ill-health and the dangers of city life. A bad outbreak of scarlet fever in 1853 had led to renewed agitation to move.

One of the opponents of the move was a former headmaster, Dr. Liddell, now Dean of Christ Church, Oxford. He was an influential man with a powerful personality and two other claims to fame which have survived him. He compiled the ever-useful Greek Lexicon, "Liddell and Scott" (about which it must be conceded a tag was current: "Scott did write it and Liddell did *not*"), and he was the father of the three little girls whom a young mathematics don took on a river party when Alice first followed the White Rabbit into Wonderland. Liddell told the Commissioners that the decline in numbers at Westminster had begun 40 years before, and though he agreed that the prevalence of fever might have had something to do with it, he was, on "sentimental" grounds in favour of not moving but staying and pressing on with reforms. But he was very critical of the teaching and, being now at the receiving end for scholars, complained that in spite of valuable studentships (i.e. Fellowships) fewer boys were being sent up to Christ Church (which had a connection with Westminster parallel to that of Winchester and New College) and that those who came were of poor quality.

Charles Scott, the current Headmaster (no relation of Liddell's collaborator) was a reformer, who had begun by favouring the move but had been converted to the policy of remaining and improving conditions. He had arrived in 1855, in time to celebrate the peace after the Crimean War. In 1860, the school celebrated its tercentenary and the Old Westminsters appointed a Committee to confer with the Dean and Chapter as to the state and condition of the School with a view to improving the present site and ascertaining a fit and proper site elsewhere.

Scott could hardly hope to raise the school again to the position it had enjoyed in the days of Dr. Busby, nor even to the time when Dr. Thomas Spratt thanked God that, *though* no Westminster, he was Bishop—that one school having occupied so large a proportion of the Bench. One must remember that the Dean and Chapter brooded over the Headmaster and staff as Resident Governors, much as the Provost and Fellows of Eton or the Warden and Fellows at Winchester; however, the Headmaster managed, at least in theory, to retain control over internal matters. Scott's main cry was for better accommodation. He was quite prepared to unburden himself to the Commissioners (the Westminster examination took up more pages than any except that of Eton) and had committed himself fully to paper ". . . because I wish to tell the Commissioners everything". He complained to them particularly of the state of the school's finances (again the scandal was implicit of a Governing body which had power and financial precedence over the school in any improvement of revenues). Certainly some extension of class-room space had lately been granted but Scott held strong views about the obligation of the Dean and Chapter towards the school, and he was prepared to state them. He did not hesitate, in general, to attack what he considered abuses; unfortunately he failed to get the Governors to see his point of view.

The Commissioners' Report supported a good many of Scott's contentions and when in 1868 an Act was passed, giving the school a greatly altered Governing Body, Scott, it has been said, had some of the qualities by which the promise (of the Act) might be realized. His courage rose in the face of opposition. He hung on to see a number of improvements carried out and particularly to see the school's finances on a better footing. By the time he resigned in 1883, his energy had done much for Westminster.

Dr. Kynaston

Herbert Kynaston of St. Paul's pointed out at once that the title used in his school was *High Master*. He said he had a good standing vis-à-vis his Governors who were a "Court" of the Mercers' Company. They would summon him to their Standing Committee and showed great willingness to carry out improvements though they did not initiate any. All he complained of was that the High Master was "indifferently paid"—his salary had, in fact been increased from the £600 of Sleath, his distinguished predecessor, to £1,000. However, Kynaston did not wish to supplement his income, as his predecessors had done, by taking boarders; they required too much looking after. Even the eight he had found could not, he thought, be adequately supervised.

The Commissioners give the impression that they did not take to Dr. Kynaston, though he had made some changes which might be considered improvements. He had abolished boarding houses in connection with the school and merely referred parents to "respectable men who would take boys from the country." He raised the entrance age so that no boy was admitted under nine years old. He got the class-room space slightly extended. There were games (unsupervised) at Kennington Oval; the monitors saw to them. He had reduced punishment, which now meant caning on the hand only, and there was much less of it than there used to be. (A comment, not made to the Commissioners, has survived that he abolished the birch but did not replace it by discipline, which he was unable to maintain.) The curriculum was unusually narrow even for the time and type of school; no music, no drawing, little mathematics teaching (though he claimed to have "remodelled" this); four hours' French, taught by an Italian: it came out later that his classes were "a bear-garden". The standard even of his classical boys was dropping; young Mr. Spurling still at College admitted that it was "not a very hardworking school" and the Commissioners found that boys going up to the Universities had read less than the average.

Kynaston's own scholarship was not in question but he made a point of telling the Commissioners that his own Latin verses were recited at the Tercentenary celebration (1859) and no doubt at "Apposition" (the equivalent of Speech Day) at which Royalty was often present. He had longings for recognition of his English achievements also and had been a candidate for the Professorship of Poetry at Oxford. He evidently had a great sense of his own dignity; for example when the question was raised of what happened to the boys at mid-day and whether it would not be possible to run dinners and let the boys know these were available, his reaction was sharp: "It would not accord with my ideas of the dignity of a Master; I do not press and scarcely even mention it."

He was pretty well satisfied with his school as it was and did not suggest any improvements that the Commission should advocate. On the great controversy of moving, he would have liked to see the school expand beyond the 153 boys that Colet (and the Dean is constantly referred to by all witnesses) had laid down, with reference to John XXI: 11. These, he sensibly suggested should remain foundationers but others should be allowed as paying pupils. But the school should not go too far out because of the day-boys, many of whom had already long distances to travel.

There is a handsome portrait of Dr. Herbert Kynaston and one gains the impression that he thought himself a very superior man. He was from Winchester and Christ Church, had been High Master since 1838, and had another 12 years to run. What Thring would have thought of him had he arrived at the Headmasters' Conference it is interesting to speculate; in fact St. Paul's was not represented there till Kynaston retired. Two comments complementary to each other may be quoted from the historians:

> Though he cannot be ranked among the great High Masters, he had a remarkable gift of inspiring a love of scholarship in a select number of his pupils, while neglecting the educational needs of the rest.
>
> (Macdonall)

and

> A more polished scholar and a worse disciplinarian there could not well be. (E. L. Tew)

Richard Elwyn

A very different character was Richard Elwyn, Headmaster of Charterhouse school, whose position must be distinguished from that of The Master of the Charterhouse, in charge of the whole double foundation of Pensioners and boys. (The most famous fictional Pensioner is Thackeray's Colonel Newcome who makes friends with the little gownboy i.e. scholar, and dies so movingly at the "Adsum".)

Elwyn had been a Carthusian and a very brilliant boy, then a scholar prizewinner and finally a Fellow of Trinity College, Cambridge. Though a senior Classic, he afterwards studied law but eventually returned to the Charterhouse as the Usher. (The Foundation provided four posts: Master, Preacher, School Master and Usher.) Unfortunately the Head (school) Master, Dr. Elder, a great man whom we shall meet as the inspirer of Dr. Mitchinson, and who had lately come from Durham with a following of his boys, fell sick. He was "much absent through illness" during the next three years and eventually died at the age of 42. Elwyn, during that period, had the Headmaster's burden on his shoulders as well as his own work. The difficulties of the school were very great, owing principally to lack of space in the historic but cramped buildings, and to the general troubles bound to beset a school in that crowded city area, but also to the complex interlocking of the Head's and the Master's authority. The latter was responsible for the "economic government of the whole household," including the diet and clothing of the scholars, and the arrangement of the house where they lived.

Elwyn suffered some frustration from this but he does not complain much. What shows clearly is his great knowledge and understanding of the boys and his interest in their wants. He knows their origins, professionals and tradesmen; the relation of boarders to day-boys—there used to be ill feeling but is no longer; the position of the Gownboys who are highly thought of—"it is a greater honour to be head monitor of the Gownboys than head of the school". This man was living among them in every sense, so much so that when the boys were locked in at night and any needed to be let out for illness or natural purposes, they would call out and he would unlock, wait up for some minutes and turn the key again. (Imagine Keate attending to his scholars' night wants!)

He had done his best with the curriculum. Mathematics was compulsory throughout the school, singing was voluntary (the great John Hullar came to teach them), and the boys could take either drawing or chemistry. A course on electricity put on out of school time drew 40 volunteers out of 120 boys. French was taught in sets. It was not compulsory but *not* to learn was exceptional; it depended on the wish of the parent. Even German could be added to the curriculum in the Sixth, but this was not paid for by the School. Two things, casually said, indicate the forward look and the unselfishness of this admirable Headmaster. If, after he reached 15 years, a boy had no aptitude for Greek, he could be excused "at my discretion" and the time given to other things. And even more unusual, he mentions that he allows a young man fresh from the University to teach the Sixth instead of continuing to take them himself, because it will be an advantage for them to have the benefit of the new man's knowledge and attainments. Elwyn shows his integrity also in his disapproval of the idea of putting boys on to the foundation simply that they may compete for the exhibitions; this he considers would be an evasion of the founder's intention. With regard to the intention that the school was founded to educate poor children, he honestly says that their foundationers are "a different class from those. . . originally looked on as poor children" but adds that many of the boys who are nominated are certainly really in need of help to ensure their getting a good education.

The important question of moving, he had studied carefully. There was, he said, even among Old Boys, a strong feeling against London and though he realizes the difficulties and expense, he thinks it would be most beneficial. (In this he differed from the Master, who disapproved.) But Elwyn does not think it should be necessary for the Pensioners to move out also; theirs is a separate organization. In the long run, of course, that was what happened, but Elwyn never carried out the move; that was the work of his mighty successor, Haig Brown, who arrived in 1863 and got the school to Godalming after a struggle of nearly ten years.

For during the time of his very arduous task, as Usher and then as Head, Elwyn's hard and consistent work told severely on his health and in 1863 there was evidently a breakdown and he resigned. Fortunately a year or so of rest put him on his feet again, after which he became Head of St. Peter's, York, where he stayed eight years. Eventually he became the Vicar of Ramsgate and a Canon, chosen by the Archbishop himself for his labour and character.

The number of boys at the Charterhouse had gone down during Elder's illness and had not yet pulled up; they began to do so later under Haig Brown. But it must have pleased Canon Elwyn that his reign produced two outstanding classicists, R. C. Jebb and Henry Nettleship.

Richard Elwyn rates only four lines in the short school history by Tod and the period is summed up thus: "Under Dr. Saunders, Dr. Elder and Canon Elwyn,. . . the school went on quietly."

Dr. Hessey

The last of the four London Day Schools was the Merchant Taylors' Company's, then still placed near Cannon Street in the City. The Headmaster was James Augustus Hessey (whose father had been in the firm that published Keats' works). He himself was an old Merchant Taylor boy, had gone on to St. John's College, Oxford, with which the Merchant Taylors' Company had close financial links, though the former Royal Commission, on the Universities, had, to the Company's disgust, brought about a rearrangement which opened the Fellowships and reduced the number of closed scholarships. Hessey had taken a double first in 1836 and had gone on to become a Fellow and eventually Dean of the College. He came to the school without any experience of teaching school boys (not at that time so very unusual) but he immediately set about some reforms which were so necessary that it would have been wrong to wait on the distant prospect of removing the school before attempting them.

They were mostly reforms of a practical type. For example, he found that in their dinner hour the boys either went to public houses or confectioners, or rambled about the streets because no place was available for them in the school. He saw to it that a place was provided where they could go at mid-day, eat what they brought and not have to range around. So far as possible, he was a civilizing influence and induced them to give up what he termed "rough sports." Another practical improvement was to persuade the Company to introduce gas light into the terribly dark little rooms which, besides the main hall, served as class-rooms.

The organizing of the school forms was early taken in hand; Hessey arranged for the boys to be divided into ten of these. Unfortunately there were but five masters, so each had to take two forms. He complains bitterly to the Commission of the inconvenience and lack of space, of the noise of traffic, the dark in winter and the heat in summer. This was almost his chief theme and clearly the circumstances in which the 270 boys had to be taught were so bad that a move of some kind was almost inevitable. He himself found conditions so unbearable that he asked to become non-resident. This was allowed on condition that he gave up his boarders and went to the suburbs. He then pointed out that the School would need a resident porter; the conditions under which this fellow and *his* family were to live did not, apparently, trouble anyone.

The Company who provided the school out, of income (i.e. it had never been endowed, neither at its foundation nor since) did not perhaps appreciate the Headmaster's difficulties. He complained also that he needed assistance for his correspondence and for keeping accounts and made a revealing remark to the Commissioners: "I should not then have to occupy the time of my Monitors . . . in assisting me nearly as much as at present." Another sentence throws light on conditions: "A few of the elder boys for a small fee assist in the work of the school." When asked about the boys' recreation, he said there was little to be done; those who came from a distance had no time; those who were at hand, no space. "London", he remarked "in this district especially, is much changed for the worse."

In spite of the difficulties, Hessey claimed "At the Universities we gain more credit each year." This, of course, would be for his classical teaching, though he pressed the claims of science, German and drawing, as he wanted to foster the School's connection with St. Thomas's Hospital and with the R.M.A. at Woolwich for those boys who would not be going to the University. For those who did go, he insisted on teaching the Thirty-Nine Articles, because he found that so many of them became clergy later, when they found the Articles much more difficult to learn. At any rate he had improved on the beginning of the century when nothing was taught but Latin, Greek, Hebrew (in the Sixth) and a little Divinity on Saturdays.

In connection with his classical teaching, he had a curious little passage with one of the Commissioners on the subject of reading the Odes of Catullus (selected). He was asked whether he did not find a difficulty with the "objectionable parts" and took a robust view of this, pointing out that the same difficulty would arise in studying English, e.g. the works of Swift. "I do not think they are very injurious" he said of the Odes, "I think the boys are disgusted with filthiness; they don't read the worst parts", and follows this up with the sensible statement that contamination is thrown off; if not a boy will pick it up quite independently of school sources. A refreshing view for a mid-Victorian Head.

Dr. Hessey gained great fame as a preacher; he preached at Gray's Inn Chapel for their Tercentenary and was thus described:

> Dr. Hessey... (is) a man of middle size and about 45 years of age. He is not handsome, not a man to run after; there is no exhibition of a white hand, or pretty ring or a noble forehead; he is a man, not an exhibition. Still, call him plain if you like—there is a pleasing almost a winning expression on his countenance at times. But you have not found out the cause of his great popularity until he begins to preach. His voice is the great charm and his delivery is perfect. The one is melodious and well-modulated, the other quietly sober and earnest, his graces are natural.

With this tribute we may leave the good Doctor.

Note on the Day-Schools. The Commissioners did in fact give a recommendation on the question of removal from London of each of the London Day Schools. They suggested that St. Paul's and Westminster should move into "the country" i.e. about a mile and a half out of London. The Charterhouse and Merchant Taylors', they thought, should rebuild, expand, and stay in the City. They should confine themselves to being Day Schools, whereas the other two should have boarding houses. Of course it was part of the foundation at Westminster that accommodation and board as well as teaching should be supplied for the King's Scholars and there were already houses either kept by masters or by (in effect) Dames, to which a master was attached. Probably the Commissioners envisaged a kind of revised Eton for Westminster, once it was transported from the slums, bad air and temptations of its present locality.

In the event things turned out quite otherwise. Westminster stayed; St. Paul's moved to Hammersmith; out of London certainly but not in the country. The Charterhouse made a move of more than 30 miles into the country near Godalming where it became entirely boarding, indistinguishable from other Public Schools, new or old, except that there was even less pressure than in most towns to accommodate local pupils as the population was so sparse. Merchant Taylors' took advantage of the departure of the School section of the Charterhouse (the Pensioners have stayed in the City ever since) to move into their buildings near Smithfield; the comparative sizes of the two schools made this a great improvement for the Merchant Taylors'. However, they have now moved to Northfield, and St. Paul's is busy settling down from its second uprooting, extending itself in Barnes. The Commissioners were less prescient than usual in their forecasts.

It may strike one as a remarkable thing that the schools investigated were Nine, not Ten; what of the Blue Coat School, Christ's Hospital? Undoubtedly it ranked, or had ranked academically, with the other London Day Schools in scholarship and fame; it was equally a charitable foundation—and Lamb's well-known essays had made it as familiar to the general public as any of the others. Presumably it was excluded because of its system of recruitment, which was by nomination exclusively (though this was true of the Charterhouse Gownboys not long before). But it must have been difficult to draw the line; what, for instance, would be the place of Alleyn's College of God's Gift at Dulwich? The commissioners were wise indeed when they underlined the word "certain" (schools) in their terms of reference.

Frederick Temple

The appearance of Frederick Temple before the Clarendon Commission was only one of his many engagements with such bodies, either as witness or as Commissioner. As any history of English education shows, the last half of the nineteenth century was an era when the country became aware of the need to examine education at every level, so from 1850 onwards Royal Commissions were appointed to poke the fingers of enquiry ("Inquiry" it was spelt) everywhere from Oxford University to the smallest Charity or Elementary school—though these had already been subjected to investigation by the Charity Commissioners with disquieting results. Secondary Education in its several forms was so subjected on two or three occasions, before the great Act of 1902. With more than half a dozen of these major investigations was Temple concerned, giving evidence, written or verbal, to those on Oxford, Public Schools, Popular (i.e. elementary) Education, Secondary Education, and himself sitting on that most far-reaching Schools Inquiry Commission, often known as the Taunton

Commission and on the Cross Commission of 1888, on Elementary Education. An important chapter, No. VII, of the Taunton Report was written entirely by Temple.

Yet Commission work, important as this turned out to be for the whole history of this country's education, was only one of Temple's very many activities. His career itself was of remarkable diversity. After a short period as an Oxford College Tutor, he worked under the Privy Council's Committee on Education (the earliest form of what has most recently become the Department of Education and Science) as an Examiner, then Inspector, and head of a Training College for Poor Law Schoolteachers. From this he went to Rugby as Headmaster from 1858 to 1869 and then to the bishoprics first of Exeter and then of London. He was well into his seventies when he became Archbishop of Canterbury and he died, almost literally on his feet, speaking in the House of Lords in favour of Balfour's Education Bill of 1902.

Temple's origins and upbringing also were unusual, quite out of the Eton-King's tradition of the past or the Rugby nursery of future Heads. He was perhaps alone among important headmasters but for Thring (who incidentally shared with Temple the quality of directness, even brusqueness in speech) in being a real countryman; a west countryman, though without Thring's deep-rooted family background of Squire and Parson. Temple's father was a soldier serving overseas (which accounts for Frederick's being born in the Ionian Islands, as he was, in November 1821), but his mother—by far the most important influence in his life—was Cornish by descent. Major Temple on retiring had tried unsuccessfully to farm in Devon, went out as Lieutenant-Governor to Sierra Leone and died there when Frederick, youngest survivor of a large family, was about 13. He was still living with his mother, and she was his only teacher, till he went to the small market town of Tiverton, to Blundell's well-established school. Two examples illustrate her extraordinary way of educating the child; when hearing his propositions in geometry (of which she herself understood nothing) she firmly refused to let him substitute one set of letters for another, when he came to see the point of principle involved, but made him learn it by heart and say it "precisely as it is here." Similarly with reading, it was: "Freddy, don't argue; do your work." That he got over the difficulties of such stultifying teaching seems to us the best proof of his extraordinary brilliant and perceptive mind. The same influence would, one might have expected, have produced a limited, strait-laced intolerance morally and intellectually, which was in fact the exact opposite of the future Archbishop's attitude. There is a very revealing passage in his contribution to that much-disputed collection: *Essays and Studies* where he traces the human being's development from childhood to youth ("adolescence" is our jargon-word) seeing a child as wholly restricted with all his life planned for him by "a careful mother," which restrictions he compares in the history of man's moral development to the Mosaic Law. From this, he says, man must progress by the help of living examples and the free spirit within him, through the bright period of friendship and happiness to a life based on principles which he found and worked out by his own conscience.

Two experiences unusual in headmasters (though possibly less so than is conventionally taken for granted) came to Temple, physical labour and very straitened circumstances. He *knew* working men in his after life, because as a boy he did work—ploughing and threshing. He knew poverty and, even when he had won a scholarship to Balliol, would sometimes be unable to afford a fire, have to economise on light, feed cheaply and, what distressed him more, wear patched clothes and shoes. These things did not sour or inhibit him. The "Old Master" of Balliol, Dr. Jenkyns, was prejudiced against Blundell men because theirs was a closed scholarship and told Temple: "You Blundell Scholars have certainly very great advantages; coming up as you do very *inferior* men into the society of *very superior* men; some of you are improved by it, and some are not." (Dr. Jenkyns admitted to Balliol as commoners almost solely Etonians, Harrovians and Rugbeians; the admission of Jowett from St. Paul's had also been by Scholarship.) Temple's comment was "I really ... was very near laughing in his face". However, when Jenkyns realized the kind of scholar he had got, he called up Temple to his room. "Young man," he said, "I wish to be regarded as a father by all the undergraduates and I wish so to be regarded by you; and you must let me give you that"—and put a £10 note into the lad's hands. Temple afterwards says he was ashamed to take it, but he was big enough to keep both the note and his self-respect.

The boy had considered himself well taught and kindly treated at Blundell's but the life at Balliol must have been a revelation—he found in fact the most brilliant group of men in England at the time. Jowett became and remained one of his firmest friends; he found also A. H. Clough, Lake and Arthur (later Dean) Stanley—"the Doctor's Disciples" from Rugby; Goulburn whom he later suceeded there; Northcote, whom he was meeting again on the Clarendon Commission; Tait, his predecessor as Archbishop. W. G. Ward* (prominent in the Oxford Movement and later as a Roman Catholic convert) was Temple's tutor

---

* Temple, later, was one of the few who voted against the censure on Ward who was disowned by the University for his Romeward-looking book: an early example of Temple's religious tolerance.

in mathematics, which was the subject Temple himself was to teach when a Fellow; Matthew Arnold came later and was a pupil of Temple's own.

No serious-minded young man of the time failed to be involved in and to take sides over the great religious issues of doctrine and practices raised at Oxford chiefly by Newman and the Tractarians; they were to undergraduates and Fellows what ideologies and power-centres or questions of discipline became in recent times. But nothing shows that Temple's part in controversy particularly struck his friends, and he made no great mark at the time as a Churchman in any party, though Wilberforce, the Bishop who ordained him "remarked him as a man of special promise". As a *person* indeed, he was well-remembered; his integrity, strength, directness and rough humour marked him out in a brilliant society as an unforgettable individual.

Indeed, all his life, Frederick Temple was a man who attracted the attribution of anecdotes and remarks; some now ascribed to other persons, Headmasters included, seem to have originated with him. To anticipate; he is the original of "a beast, but a just beast" of the schoolboy's letter. He also it was who made the reply when a boy rashly called out to a fellow: "Oh yes, I'm entered for the Confirmation stakes"—"Well, you're scratched now". Equally decisive, after a bit of impertinence from one of the Sixth form, misled by their new Head's easy manner and uncoventional dress, was his—"Conduct like that will alter the relations between us." More characteristic, even, was his remark *à propos* the local examinations brought about in Devon by Acland and himself, "What does it matter who does a good thing so long as it is done?" Also his answer when consulted about a change of bishopric by Bishop Walsham How: "I do not see that you could do better work there". This was his own criterion for a new job—would it give a chance for better work than he at present had? On this ground he himself refused a deanery at the end of his 11 years at Rugby—though he went to Exeter shortly after as Bishop, in a storm of controversy.

It was probably this same idea that led him to refuse the offer made by Tait, newly appointed Head, of an Assistant Mastership at Rugby soon after he had taken his degree and Fellowship at Balliol. Having got a double First in Mathematics, he had in 1842 already been elected to the Fellowship and considered he should spend some time as a tutor there. After this, however, his first educational post was not in the Public School world but with the Committee of (the Privy) Council on Education—the forerunner of all administration of our national education. In 1850 he became, under the Committee, the first Principal of a new venture, training young men to be teachers for the Workhouse Schools.

The College was housed in Kneller Hall, Twickenham—an early example of a stately home being used for such an institution. Temple presided here for five years during which time the number of students rose from 5 to about 48, but in the end the venture was given up by the Government. Its lack of success was due to the Workhouse system itself; it had been hoped that Schools for the Poor Law children could be set up centrally for an area (and that eventually these children would attend the ordinary schools in the locality) but each Board of Guardians tended to keep its children in its own schools and the trained teachers were employed on duties quite unexpected by them. Temple reported:

> . . . the master has to discharge duties which properly belong to the parents . . . e.g. to see them washed and combed, to attend them at meals, to see them go to bed and get up, to teach the boys bed-making and scrubbing and to assist them in the operations. . . Men who have never had to do these things find themselves much at a loss, and what is still worse, look upon such occupations as menial (for with that rank custom is everything) and feel degraded.

Their training also had suffered from lack of practical experience in actual class management. The inadequacy of a small school attached to the College must have become clear as the teachers tended to out-number the children there, a state of things that helped them little for their subsequent careers. In some ways, however, the curriculum was wide and practical; the students' own training included rural studies in a really down-to-earth way. This gave rise to a tale about Temple which underlines the meaning of the last remark quoted above. Temple, no more than George Herbert, found any service degrading, and was prepared (and able) to do anything his students had to do. One young man protested at having to muck out a pig-sty. "Am I forced to do such dirty work?" "I suppose not," said Temple; "give me that broom". He took off his coat and, to the student's new protest, answered "Some one must do it" and set to work in an experienced way. One thing which made Temple so formidable was that he did seem to know about everything, from Horace to elm-disease; he could hold his own in any conversation, and woe betide anyone who made any pretentions he could not support. Temple, as Archbishop, Bishop, Headmaster, no less than as agricultural instructor, would pulverise him with one laconic sentence. (It was said that not being thin-skinned himself, he did not always know what effect his words had.) His motto might well have been that of Dr. Johnson: "Clear your mind of cant" and like the earlier Doctor he had the knowledge and verbal capacity to help bring this operation about. One of his Kneller Hall students long after gave what seems a shrewd comment—and not as denigratory as it sounds at first:

> I am indisposed to believe that Mr. Temple was by nature a kind-hearted man. My own theory. . . is that he compelled himself to do the many kindly actions which indicated sympathy. It seemed to me. . . that there were two spirits striving within him for mastery, a naturally domineering spirit, and a determination to act in a just and kindly manner.

In 1855 he returned to the administrative side of educational work but two years later was a candidate for the Headmastership of Rugby. His supporters, ignoring his lack of teaching experience in this type, or indeed any sort, of school believed implicitly in the power of his personality. They continued to feel this about him. Arthur Stanley considered him "the best Head Master in England", even Matthew Arnold said that Temple resembled "more than any other man I have known. . . my late father", than which, clearly, there was no more acceptable tribute. It was also said in his testimonial that "the appointment of Mr. Temple would make an epoch in the Public Education of this country not less notable than that which followed the appointment of Dr. Arnold."

This, really, is only appropriate if the meaning given to the word "Public" is nearer the American sense than the exclusive English one. It does indicate however one thing very clearly; up to the end of his headship of Rugby, he had shown small sign of becoming a Bishop. Rugbeians would have thought of this destiny as a far more likely one for his predecessor, the "saintly-minded" Dean Goulburn.

Certainly the testimonials he received at the outset of his Headship show well enough what course he was supposed to be pursuing. He may certainly be counted a success at Rugby but though he altered things and tried experiments and was by his force of personality a powerful influence, his term of office brought about no far-reaching changes at Rugby, nor, directly, at any other school. He was perhaps remembered as a teacher, certainly as a person in himself—exciting, inspiring, respected by all, loved by some and of immense personal influence on boys. Witness the boy who wrote home in reply about Temple's unorthodox religious views, at the time of his contribution to *Essays and Reviews*; "Dear Mother—Temple's all right but if he turns Mahometan, all the school will turn too." Temple was particularly anxious that boys should not take part in controversy and never introduced such beliefs into their school instructions; ethical, emotional, and practical teaching, not unlike that of Arnold, was his aim. His influence sprang from his transparent integrity and single-minded faith, shown especially in his well-prepared, finely thought out sermons, and in the Saturday evening voluntary and quite informal services which he held to prepare for Holy Communion.

His own class teaching did not result in a great crop of classical scholars of the kind which gave University renown to the school though at the time of the Clarendon Commission Rugby was second (to Marlborough!) of all Public Schools in the number of scholarships obtained at Oxbridge. (But not so high in proportion to its numbers; it was still a big school in comparison with, say, Winchester.) Temple was not himself a scholar of the Shrewsbury type; both his temperament and his early unbringing were against this. What seems to have impressed boys was the vividness of his teaching, the pace at which he went, and the "lay-out"; his analysis of a whole situation or complex of ideas and his ability to leave the detail to the tutors working with him and to give a general comprehension of a whole work, whether in Greek, Latin, French or English.

This clarity of mind is shown in his answers before the Clarendon Commission; as a rule he expressed himself shortly, if not abruptly. "No." "Yes." "Decidedly." "I prefer our way." Yet when he wanted to put over a point he would do so at some length. One such answer is in support of the merit of a classical education over a mathematical one; this would not be so remarkable but for the fact that it was Mathematics that Temple had taught as a College Tutor. His reason was the humanizing power of the former—he would extend this to a literary education in itself.

Another long answer set out with clarity the relations Temple wanted to see between the Headmaster and the Trustees/Governors. An extract exemplifies his pithy and logic-pursuing style; on the knife-edge between directness and offensiveness, but not (here) going over, even when he disagrees:

If. . . the Headmaster is not capable . . .the worst that can happen is that the school will languish a little and that improvements will be delayed until the time comes for electing another Headmaster. But this is a very minor evil in comparison with hampering all Headmasters by subjecting them to constant interference. For this reason I cannot concur in the recommendation to elect four trustees eminent for literature and science. This recommendation seems to me to rest on an entirely mistaken supposition in regard to the true nature of the services which the Trustees can render to the school. What the school needs in the Trustess is good sen: e and knowledge of the world. The four gentlemen elected for their eminence in literature or science would be perpetually tempted to justify their election by doing what the Headmaster ought to do and, if he is fit for his post, can do better than anyone else. . .

One thing more which he put before the Commissioners was a project for solving the problem of relations with the townsfolk, who in Rugby as elsewhere considered themselves defrauded by the non-local nature of their school—a characteristic which the Commissioners were going to encourage and extend. Temple proposed the founding of a second School in which the curriculum and cost should be geared to the wants of the Rugby townspeople. It would be run by the Lawrence Sheriff Trustees on the same financial foundation as Rugby. Temple had the details worked out; they need not be given here but the plan was in the long run accepted and the school is the present Lawrence Sheriff school which inherits the founder's name and shares his bequest.*

Even when he was Headmaster, the education of the nation as a whole must have taken precedence in Temple's mind over education in the Public Schools. He had already thought out his ideas on Elementary Education and given them both before the Commission on Popular Education (Newcastle Commission) and in an *Essay on National Education*. As one example of his power of foresight (or was it his influence which helped to bring it about?) he recommended that Rate aid should be combined with Government grants for the founding and upkeep of elementary schools. He went into the financial questions practically and into the immensely complicated religion issue, including the insertion of a Conscience Clause authorising the withdrawing of a child for religious instruction.

One more Commission—though it was by no means the last with which he would have to deal—must be mentioned if only to show the immense labour of which Temple was capable. It was the Taunton (Schools Inquiry) Commission which looked into all the schools ("endowed") which had not been covered either by the Popular Education (Newcastle) Commission nor by the Public Schools (Clarendon) Commission, already discussed. This time Temple was on the other side of the table; he was a Commissioner along with Lord Lyttelton, Lord Stanley, Northcote, W. A. Forster (of the 1870 Act), Acland (of the "Local" examinations) the Chief Charity Commissioner;

---

* Temple's evidence was given not only to the Royal Commission under Lord Clarendon but to a Select Committee of the House of Lords appointed two years later, also under the chairmanship of Clarendon, to which the Public Schools Bill had been referred. As Temple's views remained the same, if anything strengthened by his experience at Rugby, it is not worth distinguishing the separate occasions of his evidence.

all persons who had been or were to be significant in education. The Secretary of the Committee, H. J. Roby (who should know) stated later that Temple was the leading spirit. The result of the Commission's work (it sat from 1864 and reported in 1868) is found in 22 thick volumes. Their Report runs to seven chapters; of these the seventh, which gives their recommendations, was drafted by Temple and passed with very little discussion by the rest. He also wrote a part of another chapter, to help out the over-worked Secretary. All this (including the taking of evidence, verbal and written, and the sifting of the accounts sent in by the Assistant Commissioners who visited over 700 schools) was done while Temple was still Head of Rugby and apparently without diminishing in the least his care for and availability in the school. It makes one stare amazed at the physical and mental stamina of the man.

He left Rugby after nearly twelve years amid great emotional scenes (Temple himself was by no means inhibited from emotional display—we hear more than once of the tears glistening on his cheek) for the bishopric of Exeter. He arrived to a cry of protest. His *Essay on National Education,* though it could hardly be found controversial in itself, had been published in the same volume as others by such controversial figures as Jowett. Temple characteristically would not budge nor offer a word of explanation until he had been accepted; after that he withdrew the Essay.

Into his life as Bishop, first of Exeter and then of London, and finally as Archbishop, it will not be necessary to go far though he did not lose his concern for education at any level when he moved to the episcopate. But the ecclesiastical controversies and the many causes with which he engaged himself, from Temperance to support for the Blind, do not bear directly on education; besides, he has received the customary two-volume memorial accorded to good and great Victorians. It is remarkable that it takes seven writers, ecclesiastical and lay, not to mention some hundreds of letters and reminiscences, to cover this long (1821–1902) and full life.

With all his activities, ecclesiastical, educational, administrative and theological (he gave the Bampton Lectures at Oxford in 1884) any account of his domestic life fares but slimly in the Reminiscences. Undoubtedly till she died, while living with him at Rugby, in 1866, his mother was by far the strongest influence on him; to turn that influence into an affectionate but not guiding relationship shows an extraordinary strength of character on his side (or hers?). Like Mrs. Ruskin, she came to live at Oxford when he was there,—but not until he had done his course and won his Fellowship. At Rugby, it was his sister, Jennetta, evidently remarkable like himself in temperament and outlook, who ran his house. When, after three years at Exeter her health broke down and she was preparing to go abroad, she was happy to be able to write to Dr. E. W. Benson, later Archbishop, that he was "engaged to be married to Beatrice Lascelles and is very happy" She had only seen her future sister-in-law once but loyally called her "a true, sweet woman with a most pleasant voice and charming simple manners." One cannot help feeling that there was little time for home life but it satisfied him and he wrote of "a wonderful wife and two perfect boys." The elder boy became an engineer, but William the younger followed his father in brilliant scholarship, school headship, University Fellowship, ecclesiastical office up to his sadly brief Archbishopric.

It is curious that Frederick Temple has never, like Gladstone, Florence Nightingale or even Ruskin, become a nationally known 19th century figure. Probably the very diversity of his work into so many fields has hindered this. Commissioners are notoriously anonymous, except for the Chairman, and the specific posts which Temple was holding on all occasions when a Commission was appointed would have made him ineligible for such a full-time responsibility. In his headship of Rugby, he had to compete in reputation with the very greatest—one outstanding and several notable holders of that high-lighted post. As a bishop, he was liable to be involved both as a controversialist and also as an administrator, at a time when the more famous holders of such offices were theologians and devotionalists. And as Archbishop, which he was for seven years only, he is perhaps eclipsed for the present generation by (if not confused with) his son. One biographer of William Temple entitled his book "The People's Archbishop". William Temple certainly deserved the appellation. But it might with equal truth have been applied to his father.

Frederick Temple would not have cared. "What does it matter who does a good thing as long as it is done?" He was a good man and he did good things.

Note. In one particular aspect of the investigation, the Schools defeated the Commissioners, that of actually holding an examination of the boys. The incident is found in Appendix B, Vol. II of the Report. The Commissioners wanted to get some ideas of the teaching given to the average and under average boys,—those whom they would *not* find at the Universities. "We proposed", they wrote ingenuously, "to institute an examination of a certain proportion of the boys actually receiving education there . . . of a simple kind and conducted by examiners of acknowledged competency". About one-fifth of each school should be so examined, and they proposed to cover, as well as translation of Greek and Latin, French and German translation, ancient and English history, arithmetic, algebra, and Geometry, physical science and the Greek Testament. All this, they thought would take six days, or more.

The proposal must have created consternation at some schools. The Commission had blandly, or innocently, pointed out that they would need the willing co-operation of the Head Master in each school and this, in no uncertain terms, was withheld. In all but two schools the very idea was anathema: "I strongly deprecate any such measure", answered Dr. Moberly of Winchester; it was "so strongly objectionable that I decline to entertain the proposal" (Scott of Westminster), "unsatisfactory" (Eton), "Unnecessary... injurious" (Merchant Taylors'), and so on.

The objections put forward were that the schools were already examined and that an "extrinsic authority would cause confusion". (What, as they did *not* say, if he should take a less favourable view than that to which they were accustomed?) It would interrupt their studies and discipline to have "unsympathetic" strangers around. Worst of all, it would "undermine the Head's authority" and interfere with his responsibility—how, exactly, is not specified. Only two schools would even contemplate it; Rugby and, naturally, Shrewsbury. Even they, though having no "abstract" objection, found fault with details; the timing suggested by the Commissioners would not suit them.

The Commissioners, confronted with this digging in of heels, knew themselves defeated, and withdrew. "We found ourselves," they recorded, "unable to obtain this general concurrence, two Head Masters· only (of Rugby and Shrewsbury) having signified to us, and that with some reluctance, their assent." They abandoned their suggestion, but no doubt they drew from the incident their own unfavourable conclusions. As the Headmaster of Charterhouse had the grace to acknowledge "It would practically be an examination of schoolmasters rather than of boys," and these one and all respectfully declined—even Kennedy, who suspected he was past his prime. But one curious thing emerges from a phrase dropped by the High Master of St. Paul's: *"In common with most of my brother Headmasters*, I consider the scheme objectionable because it is an infringement of our own independent rights. . . " Evidently the Headmasters as a group had so far let their anxiety and alarm overcome their habit of isolation and their self-importance sufficiently to arrange to meet and talk over the matters the Commission might raise or perhaps had raised. This hint is confirmed by a reference of Moberly's to their having met in London, though it is clear that nothing like a common policy was agreed on, except in this one matter. In this it would seem from a comparison of ideas and even phrases common to all their letters, "ordeal by Commission" resulted in their uniting—but it was not to be a permanent unity, rather a ganging-up for defensive action against a common enemy. Yet Moberly (was it he who had drawn the meeting together? One cannot tell for certain.), had said that the enumeration of the Nine schools had enabled the Masters of those nine to meet together without any reflection on the other heads, and he at least had contemplated their going "to take counsel together upon matters. . . relating to us all in common", and he instances the need for one Grammar book (which Kennedy was eventually to supply)–a suggestion he would like the Commissioners to make.

But once the danger was passed, nothing further followed in the way of meetings. Any opposition to the Bill was staged by individuals, and the schemes were in any case individual to each school. It took a greater Headmaster than any there to see the full possibilities of an Association of Schools and a more powerful personality to found it. Before that, another and more wide-reaching Royal Commission had to be established.

VIII

THRING OF UPPINGHAM

Howard Staunton in *The Great Schools of England (1877)* lists: The Ten Great Endowed Schools (i.e. the Clarendon Nine plus Christ's Hospital); The Proprietory Schools of Cheltenham, Marlborough, Rossall and Wellington; Dulwich College, and in an Appendix, Endowed Grammar Schools of England and Wales. Among these last is placed Uppingham.

This school was the scene for the work of Edward Thring, regarded as second only to Arnold in the order of 19th century headmasters and by some as having had a greater influence on schools themselves.

When, soon after the middle of the century, both the Clarendon and Taunton Commissions were past, it looked as if the lists had been closed. Two or three "traditional" foundations might be claiming (as Shrewsbury had done earlier) that they had been wrongly overlooked; a few more new institutions would discard the term "Proprietory" (as being confusable with "Private") and travel along with the Nine on the ground that they had always been designed for Public Schools; see the list above for examples. But up and down the country, among the old endowed schools which the Taunton Commission had been investigating, were some hundred (rather more than one eighth of the total founded) which could still be regarded as "Classical". Of these, Archdeacon Johnson's Schools at Oakham and Uppingham were two quite ordinary ones. It was chiefly owing to the Headmaster of one of these that not only his own school but a sizeable proportion of that Classical hundred, and almost as many others, have now entered the greatly enlarged circle of those claiming the title "Public".

The foundation of Uppingham school originated neither, as at Rugby, with a member of a City Company, nor, as at Shrewsbury, with Royalty petitioned by local burgesses, but with the son of a merchant (of Stamford, not of Uppingham), Robert Johnson. He eventually became Archdeacon of Leicester, and it will be easiest to refer to him throughout by his clerical dignity as he had acquired this by the time he founded his Charity. An account of him written by his son, in the course of an application for a grant of arms, formed the basis of a pamphlet (*Our Founder*, by C. R. Bingham) issued for the school's tercentenary, 1884. (This included some discussion as to which of various Robert Johnsons the founder can be identified with; the most likely is here, arbitrarily, assumed.)

The Archdeacon lived from about 1540 to 1625, so that his life stretched over the reigns of six sovereigns, four Tudors and (just) two Stuarts. Apart from some ecclesiastical censure, he seems to have been remarkably free from political trouble. He was fairly well connected by birth and family friendships; his father (who had been a Merchant of the Staple and three times Alderman of Stamford) was one of the two M.P.s of that town, his co-Burgess in 1525 being David Cecil, father to Queen Elizabeth's Secretary and Councillor. Robert used on at least one occasion "the intervention of William Lord Burghley, his noble Friend and Patrone."

Robert's elder brother who went to St. John's College, Cambridge, there became "a zealous supporter of the Reformation" in accordance with the character of that College, and the home may also have been Puritan. But when Robert was only 11, his father died and the boy was brought up by a relative, (possibly a godfather) Robert Smith of Standground near Peterborough. After going to Clare Hall as a Sizar and then for three years abroad probably to study languages, Robert Johnson became Chaplain to Sir Nicholas Bacon, the Lord Keeper, who had recently finished his new and beautiful house with private chapel at Gorhambury. Johnson may also have held a preaching post at St. Albans; he certainly became a Canon of Peterborough, of Norwich, and of Rochester. In 1571 he had to answer not so much for his pluralities (which apparently troubled him not at all) but for some scruples expressed about the Prayer Book and usages of the Church of England. His Puritan leanings were not so strong as to prevent his eventually accepting the Prayer Book as "not defective or expressly contrary to the Word of God" and he agreed that its imperfections might "for unity and charity-sake. . . be suffered." He managed, in spite of its being "offensive" to Archbishop Parker to hold on to his three prebends, and his Archdeaconry followed in 1591.

In 1574, probably on leaving Gorhambury, he had been installed at North Luffenham not far from Uppingham, where he remained as Rector for nearly 50 years. He had acquired a sufficient income to live comfortably and to leave a considerable estate when he died, and meanwhile to found "as many Free Schools in Rutland as there were Market Towns therein, one at Oakham, another at Uppingham, well faced with buildings and lined with endowments." (Fuller, quoted by Bingham.) His Charity, like so many others, coupled as works of mercy the care of the old with the education of the young. The inscription for his tomb records that he founded "a faire Free Grammar Schoole" in both towns and appointed to each school a School-master and an Usher; that "he erected also a Hospitalle of Christ" (Almshouses) in each and arranged for an endowment which included lands bought from Queen Elizabeth. The Queen, who had given her own gift to the Charity, granted a Charter and, to hold the property, there were set up "The Governors of the Goods, Possessions, and Revenues of the Free Grammar Schools of Robert Johnson, Clerke."

The Schools profited greatly from having been set up in the founder's life-time, with so much settled financially and administratively. There was no delay either in having them built; the "School room" at Uppingham (which still survives) was in the churchyard, adjoining the parish Church. The administration ran on under his eye until, just before his death (and this is a much more typical Tudor timing) the Archdeacon laid down a group of ordinances for the governance of both schools and "hospitals" under which they continued to function tranquilly for many years. One example will do of the clarity and precision with which the statutes were drawn up: those relating to the appointment of the School Master (who was also Warden of the Almshouse).

> He... shall be at the time of his election, and so continue, an honest and discreet man, master of arts, and diligent in his place, painful in the educating of children in good learning and religion, such as can make a Greek and Latin verse... If he shall prove to be negligent in his place and of lewd conversation, the major part of the Governors in the diocese of Peterborough shall admonish him thrice, either *viva voce* or under their hands set in one paper; and if he do not reform himself, the major part of the Governors aforesaid shall deprive him of the place and choose another in his stead. But otherwise if my Schoolmasters be painful and careful in their places, I desire and hope that the governors will encourage them and mend their stipends, if they can conveniently.

This is very well-stated; Johnson also defines the Usher's place. *He* has to be able to make "true Latin"—Greek is not required.

> He shall carry himself reverently towards the Schoolmaster and be ruled by him in his discipline and for the matter and manner of teaching whom and when. He shall not disgrace the schoolmaster or animate the scholars in undutifulness towards him, or seek to withdraw their or their parents' affections from him, but shall be diligent in his school.

Johnson may sound hard and authoritarian in so clearly laying down the relations between the two men, but this is far better than leaving room for misunderstanding. It sounds as if the Archdeacon had had some experience of divided authority or "party-making". One thinks of Samuel Butler's years of misery with Jeudwine; Johnson's Head could propose his own Usher and on his instance after two warnings, the Governors should dismiss him.

The first two Heads (with salaries of £24 each, + £6 for the Wardenship of the Almshouses) had already been confirmed some two months before his death:-

John Clarke, My* Schoolmaster of Uppingham
Jeremy Whitaker, My* Schoolmaster of Oakham.

The Schoolmasters are included in the list of Governors; they may have been laymen, and the founder's two grandsons were so (also, usually, their successors), but the rest were all clerics. There were twenty-four in all, but as the list starts off with "the Reverend Fathers in God, the now Lord Bishop of London, and the now Lord Bishop of Peterborough, the now Archdeacon of Northampton, the now Master of Trinity College Cambridge and the now Master of St. John's . . ." and these worthies may vote by proxy for the Master's appointment, it seems (rightly as it turned out) that he did not expect them to come very often to the meetings. The rest were local parsons, with the exception of the ex-officio members and the Patron who was to be one of his own family "in perpetuity" (and so continued till the 19th century), and they were a self-electing, self-perpetuating body. They were not likely to be very progressive but for some two hundred and twenty years they kept the schools on the even tenor of their way.

The schools were, rather remarkably, "double-twinned"; the almshouse connection was of course very familiar but for two schools like Oakham and Uppingham to share Governors and endowments was not common. There must have been a certain amount of rivalry between them; as the reputation of the one went up the other tended to be depressed:

> "Oakham up; Uppingham down;
> Oakham down; Uppingham up"

it was said locally. The towns are six miles apart and the same agricultural population and land-owning farmers and gentlemen formed the background of both. Oakham being the county town probably had a slight advantage in prestige.

---

* Even an ecclesiastic cannot, it seems, forbear that word so characteristic of the 16th century founder, or is it a temptation common to all benefactors always to insert the possessive ("My Hospitals, my Schools") in Wills etc.? It is a small touch of vanity in a very worthy and competent benefactor.

The Archdeacon seems to have provided for all contingencies, though the Schools were rather low on exhibitions to the Universities—but the number of boys in each school competent to take them up was also, as a rule, low. One cannot deny that the annals of the two centuries following his death were (as shown in the Trustees' minutes) "chronicles of small beer." A very few references will illustrate the progress of Uppingham.

The effect of the Civil War (as at Shrewsbury) was to hamper the collection of revenue, which seems to have got £250 behind in 1643, but a few years later an exceptionally good financier was found among the Governors. He became the "Receiver", for whom the Archdeacon had made provision in his Will. There seems to have been no dispossessing of the schoolmaster, though a Royalist-minded governor was extruded. The usual church-going to the parish Church was the rule and in 1723 it is noted that the Usher is to "sit with ye scholars on the scaffold"; one imagines this to be the very usual Gallery. School equipment had to be provided at intervals, and in 1772 twelve-inch Globes were purchased both for Oakham and for Uppingham. Table, benches and even lockers are mentioned at various times, but a considerable innovation was made by Master John Butt, who had "Studies" built for the boys against the wall in the school yard. (They had got away from the churchyard by this time.) To do this, he advanced money himself, which the Governors afterwards repaid. (This common but deplorable custom continued much longer than one might expect.) These small boxes of rooms, though without heat and almost without light, must have appeared as great prizes to their early owners. They remained *in situ* till the mid-twentieth century.

One important non-development is implied in a pronouncement made in 1716; to teach the boys English, it was stated, was against the statutes, "the Institution being ordered by the Founder for Latin, Greek and Hebrew." This period marks one of the first sharp declines in the number of boys. This could be attributed to the Headmaster for there was no comparable decline at Oakham where presumably the curriculum was the same, but it is just possible that the local landowners and farmers were beginning to think that English was more needful to a country gentleman than a great quantity of written Latin, let alone Greek or Hebrew.

By 1806 the numbers seem to have risen again, as John Clayton, son of the Town Clerk of Newcastle-on-Tyne was writing home that there were 50 boarders in the Headmaster's house; they must have been seriously cramped. This young man from the Border was taught "Accounts", but no doubt his father paid extra for him to be taught this on half-holidays.

But by 1811 a second decline was setting in; there were 30 boarders and only a few day-boys, and it became sufficiently marked for the Governors to minute that "note should be taken" of it. One cause may well have been the conditions. The Governors seem to have had no objection to the Head's taking as many boarders as he wished but they did nothing to help him accomodate them. Boys were sleeping two or three in a bed, and there were protests about the food.

The state of the town itself was also uninviting; "Ill lit, ill paved, some of the houses presenting a very tumbled-down appearance, roads unfenced and rubbish placed in unsavoury heaps."—this is how it was described in 1853 and probably it had been like that for a long time. A weekly market was held in the Square; the names "Beast Hill", "Hog-Hill", and "Horn Lane" testify to the kind of place, agriculture predominating. There were a few small industries, such as rope-making, quarrying, and tailoring, and the number of public houses was put as 20. Perhaps these hostelries had grown up because of the coaching roads that crossed in the town, but by the middle of the 19th century these would be declining in importance, and the railway came not near.

Under the Rev. H. Holden (1845) the school seemed to be pulling up. The masters had been increased to four and the salaries increased to £150 for the Head and £130 for the Second Master. In five years there were 63 boys and four masters, besides the Master to teach Writing and Arithmetic. There had been an earlier attempt to introduce "the Eton plan" but this probably only meant teaching from the Eton Grammar book. It was left to Dr. Holden to organize the school into six forms.

Uppingham boys continued to take up the exhibitions to the Universities and the School could look back on a fair number of old scholars who had become Fellows of their Colleges, military men or Divines of some note. There was a Bell Medallist and a 9th Wrangler in 1820—just before these university distinctions had begun to seem the prerogative of Butler's Shrewsbury. The majority of the earlier Exhibitioners became parsons, but some entered other professions. A Bishop (of Tasmania) and the Principal of the London College of Divinity showed that even when the School was numerically at its lowest, it was possible for a boy coming from it to do well for himself.

Yet, all in all, it was by the mid-nineteenth century rather an undistinguished little Grammar School in a sleepy market town, overshadowed by its neighbour and paralleled by scores of others. There was absolutely nothing outstanding about it. When Dr. Holden left for Durham after eight years (taking with him 11 out of the school's 36 boys) his successor saw much that wanted change, though he believed the foundations to be sound. Probably not even he realized how much, during his tenure of office, *would* be changed. Hoyland's title for his life of Thring—*The Man who made a School*—was not quite accurate, but there is no doubt that Thring *re*-made it. Uppingham after he had established himself was a different place.

Thring was born in 1821 and died in 1887 but in one sense there is no biography to record after 1853. There is simply the story of Thring, Headmaster. Not that this absorption made him in any way less impressive as a person—as a friend, a father, or a Christian; nor did he live any less fully and vividly. But these "personae" were swallowed up in the work from the moment he undertook it. Earlier, his prayer had been: "Work till the end of my life, and life till the end of my work." From his first look at Uppingham, he knew one part of the answer had come: "I think I have found my life-work to-day." By this he meant simply Education, and this, as he interpreted it, was the widest of assignments, ranging from publishing books on Grammar at one end to presiding over the Headmistresses' Conference at the other. But the *personally* wide interests of Samuel Butler, even the little quirks that peep out from Thomas James' scanty records are entirely absent from Thring. His was an active, many-sided personality devoted to one end only—or, as his friends more bluntly put it: "In conversation, he had but one horse to ride, and its name was 'Uppingham'."

Edward Thring's parsonage home and West Country childhood were certainly reflected in his later personality, but the strongest influence on his early days was undoubtedly his mother. She was a very remarkable woman with scholarly connections in her own family, her brother being Dr. Jenkyns, for so long "The Old Master" of Balliol, but her outstanding qualities were her affection and her firm sense of duty. Edward's charm and openness of manner and the real interest he took in individual people must have come from her, to judge from accounts of her own easy uninhibited manner. It did not come from his father. Biographies of Edward Thring say little about the Rev. John Thring, who was clearly an autocrat in his family life; *this* trait may also have had its effect on his son. No doubt he ruled with equal domination the Somerset parish of which he was Rector and later, Squire. Edward grew up "under the mingled influence of what was at once an affluent English country house and a strictly managed English rectory." His later difficulty in ever making economies stemmed partly from the open-handedness of a well-off "Squarson's" household. This is the view of Parkin, author of the customary two volume "Life" (with Diary-extracts and Letters) which was Thring's only full nineteenth century biography. He personally knew Thring who probably gave him the account of his life before he found his work at Uppingham.

His first school—a private preparatory one at Ilminster—he hated. It left an impression of great severity and constriction. The "high walls with which the playground was surrounded" were symbols of the restraint and suspicion with which the boys were treated—methods which he condemned as "dreadfully mistaken." He and his brothers got through without any open rebellion and went on to Eton, ruled at the time by Keate.

Thring, like so many boys of the period, began as an Oppidan and later became a Colleger. For his first years he was in Chapman's house, where his Tutor and Housemaster took a real interest in him both as a pupil and as a developing boy. The letters Chapman wrote to his father about "little Edward" and his brother show what Thring called later "the idea of doing something for every boy" even in the "most impossible circumstances" of Eton. He set the standard in Thring's mind of what a Housemaster *should* be.

Thring was then in College for six years, ending up as Captain of the Collegers and therefore head of the School. He had learnt to accept its conditions, including flogging and the material circumstances of Long Chamber—"One ill-paid servant to seventy boys". He seems to have complained most about the lack of privacy to get on with his work, but he held his own against bullying. When a Headmaster, he was not inhibited about beating but he saw to it that the conditions in which he had to do it seldom arose. Even in his schooldays he was critical of the numbers in classes and the lack of supervision in College which to a great extent were responsible for the indiscipline. The contrast of the strictly supervised preparatory school and the *laissez faire* of College, with the efficient but humanized discipline of his Eton House—this underlay much in Thring's subsequent dealing with his own boys and the "machinery" at Uppingham. His account of "this wild college life" (often quoted) is not wholly disapproving, "for freedom is better than slavery", but he deplored "the wretchedness and coarseness and idleness at the time, which is brought on the majority of those cast into its whirl." (Never at any time did he wish to see Eton reproduced in his own school.) He himself, accustomed to severity in the home and a rough outdoor country life with its pursuits requiring strength and energy, triumphed over harsh conditions of living and working. The two environments may have combined to develop in him the unyielding and aggressive characteristics of which so many examples appear later. But he had brought from his country vicarage more than a sound body. One of his friends sums him up with:

The epithet which I would apply to him is "sturdy"—sturdy in build, in mind, in principle, in fidelity, in antagonism to all that was wrong and false.

Thring passed through Eton, even in his last year as Captain of Montem experiencing the uproar and temptations of that traditional festival,* without being brutalized, perverted, or having his head turned. His place at Cambridge was assured by the regular Eton-King's arrangement for the top Colleger, and he went up in the autumn of 1841.

The system still held whereby King's men took their degrees without undergoing any University examination; this favoured the weak or idle but hid the merit of a scholar like Thring, whose place in the Tripos would probably have been high. He did have the triumph of winning the University's Porson Prize for Greek Verse and various College prizes. It is worth mentioning these proofs of his scholarship because it always appeared that he set so little store by this, but it was only by contrast with his major aims that he *seemed* to underrate scholastic achievement. When his boys began to prove themselves in the Universities, he showed in his letters and diary how much this meant to him. His correspondence with R. L. Nettleship, the Platonic scholar and Tutor at Balliol, is a case in point.

Looking back, Thring considered he spent "a very quiet powerful three years at Cambridge", though a friend, junior to him at Eton, remembers him more characteristically as active and athletic (an especially good fives player) and full of energy in everything he undertook; "I was rather afraid of him while I admired him." He eventually made up his mind to be a clergyman and was ordained in 1847, going as a curate to St. James' parish in Gloucester. Here the chief influence on him was the Vicar, the Rev. Thomas Hedley. It seems to have been this man's idea of pastoral care that Thring accepted without reserve and carried over into his work as a headmaster. He could never have made any real difference between the parson and the teacher. Hedley also helped to deepen his religious belief and

---

* There is a long and vivid account in Thring's Life of this occasion, giving all the bills kept by him. The nominal reason for the whole show was to make a collection of money ("salt") to be given to the Captain for his University career, i.e. the balance after he had paid all the enormous expenses. But it was really the supreme occasion for display, fancy dress, marching, music, riot and festivity. Even Royalty attended, but in 1841 the extension of the railway to Slough brought so many undesirable characters for the day that it "made Eton on Montem day little better than Greenwich Fair", according to Dr. Hawtrey. As explained in the account of Eton, one of Provost Hodgson's reforms, after "an attempt to mitigate its evils". was to get it abolished altogether in 1844. See Appendix A and p.107.

experiences; "the vivid conceptions of personal relations to God and the consecration of all his powers to God's service" (Parkin, probably from Thring himself).

This afterwards became the ruling motive of his life, and the ground of innumerable talks and sermons; it also perhaps gave him a special Miltonic feeling of his own place as a servant of God. It was in the active rather than in the contemplative life that he found satisfaction. *Solvitur ambulando* was the motto he would use at the start of the Headmasters' Conference.*

In a Presidential Address to the Education Society in 1888, Thring said that everything he most valued of teaching thought and experience came from the teaching he did as a curate in the National Schools. ("National", as used in the 19th century in connection with "School", *never* meant "State School" but always one set up by the National Society. In 1850 they were entirely the responsibility of the Church of England.) This shows that even in the earliest days he was getting down to the principles of "educating" or "training" rather than of teaching, or instructing. For there can have been little in common in the techniques of actual teaching between having, as he says, "to get at the minds of these little labourers' sons, with their unfurnished heads and no time to give" in order to impart to them the rudiments of English, and the enlightening of the country gentlemen's sons, confronted with years of study in Latin and Greek of an extremely conventional pattern. The main truth, which Thring from then-onwards accepted was that what counts is not how much the teacher hammers into his pupils' heads, whether they repudiate or reproduce it, but how far he has communicated with them. It is largely due to Thring that this fundamental principle was re-discovered, or at least republished. But Thring always had the actual class-room in mind, not a theory or principle; that is why he *had* to teach before he knew that he wanted to, or could. It is in this way that the National Schools were the start of his career.

It was not an auspicious beginning. After a short time his work as a curate (into which he threw himself with all energy of a young parson confronted with a mean, red-brick suburban parish of artisans and. labourers) resulted in a break-down, and incidentally in that most common trial of the untrained teacher, a throat weakness. He was still four years away from Uppingham; he rested, took another curacy, and travelled abroad. It was this travel which, indirectly, led him back to teaching. In 1852, in Rome, he met his future wife and, with marriage

---

* He took it also in a literal manner; Conference moved to a different school each year. *(Translated:* We solve it by going on. *Literally:* it is loosed by walking.)

in mind, he hurried back to begin seeking a Headship. During the summer of 1853 there was a vacancy for a Headmaster at the Cathedral School at Durham. The successful candidate was Dr. Holden of Uppingham. Thring was the runner-up and no sooner was the result known than he applied for the post left vacant by Holden. He was appointed at the end of August, and on September 10th at the age of 31 he "commenced Headmaster". Henceforward Thring's life is bound up with the school's and to tell briefly of its progress is to deal with all that was of most importance to him.

To look at numbers first. In a year, these grew from 28, on the boarding side, to 46. Growth was at first not spectacular but steady; later it shot ahead. In 1861 there were 171 boarders and 4 day-boys; two years later, when Thring had been ten years Headmaster, there were 200 in all. Boarders continued to form the great majority; indeed, local boys may well have tended to stay away as Uppingham changed in character, and to betake themselves to Oakham, only a few miles away, which remained the same kind of school as they were used to. In 1865, the 300 mark was reached. A Lower School grew up and by 1868 there were 45 in it and 310 in the School proper. Thenceforth it was a question of refusing boys. Thring set his face against a "large school" in which the Headmaster could not know each individual boy. He stated his reasons:

> A Headmaster is only the Headmaster of the boys he knows. If he does not know the boys, the master who does is their Headmaster—and his also.*

Specifically, when a question arises of punishing a boy whom he does not personally know, the Head, if he cannot tell whether punishment is deserved, is doing no more than acting as the Housemaster's (or Form-master's) policeman.

With the School's expansion came the need for more masters and new buildings. Thring was an indefatigable raiser of bricks and mortar, but human beings came first. His staff had to be won over to what he called his "system", i.e. his point of view, but he always let people know exactly where they stood with him. "In the early days, as Mr. William Earle knows, the giving up of his curacy was the condition of working under me on my system." When additional staff were needed, Thring had a short way with the problem. He made his principles quite clear and demanded unquestioning obedience to them:

---

* G. R. Parkin, (ed.) *Diary, Life and Letters of Edward Thring,* Vol. II, p.142. These reasons seem to me never to have been superseded by *any* argument in favour of the large school.

My own beliefs are decided Church, but I am *broad* towards other people who are religious, but no irreligious man can be appointed by me. Again, I am very strong on the matter of *teaching,* by which I mean applying knowledge to the individual boy, however stupid he may be. I consider it a great science of infinite interest. You will have to take a low class if you come, and unless you take that view your place is not here. . .

I lay great stress on the diet and living of the boys, as I consider it belongs to moral training, and I require your house in this respect, more especially in the matter of beer, to be kept up to the standard of my own house.* I also wish you to employ Mr. Bell as the doctor for your boys. Of course our school laws and system must be yours also; I believe there is no other point to mention, unless perhaps to state that I wish the extra masters (*non-classical?*–A.C.P.) who are thoroughly superior men, to be supported.

Thring would then offer the post, and if the salary was insufficient would guarantee an addition to it out of his own resources. Thus, not surprisingly, he early saddled himself with large debts, nearly £3,000 in the first five years and later up to £3,600.

Thring's attitude to the growth of Houses and to Housemasters is shown in his diary:

I have written to Mr. C. telling him my terms if he stays here, and laying down very strongly that if he builds a house here, he does it because he trusts the system and trusts my management, not that I sell any fraction of my management to him or any one else.

This is characteristic of the procedure of both the Headmaster and the Housemasters at Uppingham. As a rule, those who could, laid down the money to build (sometimes buy) their own Houses, regarding them as an investment, so great was their faith in Thring's ultimate success. Sometimes, however, Thring helped a Housemaster with an advance for his House, which he would pay back from the profits; these, however, under Thring's system were never large. (Thring's own debts included money advanced as mortgage for land and premises which he thought the school ought to have. These were sometimes repaid by funds raised as subscriptions, but Thring never made money.) As the curriculum was reorganized and widened, more staff were needed, and Thring could

---

* It is interesting to note that the issue of beer, on a parent's demand, continued till about 1900. The house formula then was that it was not to be *stronger* than School House beer. (Personal information).

pick his men—who were likely to be well-off, though he would never have picked them for this—but he ruled them all the time.

As to school buildings, Thring was unswerving in his determination that the visible signs of the school's transformation should match its internal growth, and he constantly stirred up all connected with the school to bring this about. He had hard work, for the Governors and parents in those days were not so well trained as later in putting their hands into their own pockets to supply what the school accounted necessary and could/would not pay for. But to Thring's first "fund"—for the Chapel—parents did contribute, though a great part was met by Old Boys and an even larger share by the masters. Thring's own friends and family also rallied to his support.

The need for a Chapel he realized almost at once. Of all people Thring would need to be master in his own house, spiritually as well as physically. He quite simply would not delegate this spiritual direction of his boys to the parish clergyman. (The actual incumbent was a school Governor, and no great supporter of Thring's. It would be natural for him to be a bit jealous of the great dynamo of spiritual power which had planted itself alongside him.) The idea of a School Chapel was brought forward in 1858 though to raise one that Thring considered worthy took many years. There was an appeal for funds which came in gradually, and there were consultations about an architect. The Governors wrangled; they suggested an architect to report. Thring's diary:

> I sent back that I was sure the masters would not take Mr. — who is no man for that style, but if they would send down Street, or Scott or Woodyer or Butterfield or any man of proved renown—we would consider his opinion on the site and building conclusive.

Street was finally chosen*—"that style" being, of course, Victorian Gothic, of which the present chapel is a notable and characteristic example. Street was a man after Thring's own heart in his "daring to speak so plainly." The occasion of this commendation was the architect's very significant remark that the Governors did not approve of the change in Uppingham and wished it to remain in its old state.

This comment of Street's was very shrewd. It was solely due to Thring that, for better or worse, Uppingham *was* going to change irrecoverably and moreover that many of the changes introduced (the building of a School Chapel is as good an example as any) were going to

---

* The Chapel was not consecrated till 1865, by which time the new Schoolroom, which Thring had asked for in 1860, had also been built (by Street) and the first sermon preached in it.

be adopted throughout the rising group of Public Schools to be. Not all these schools modelled themselves on Uppingham (but see p.207 on Mitchinson) indeed, it becomes clear that until the Conference became established, Headmasters often did not know what other Heads and their schools were like. But to Thring, the need for each innovation became clear *as* he worked (*solvitur ambulando,* again) and as he saw each need he worked for it and fought and shook up people until he got his way.

In looking at his relations with individuals, one becomes aware of his great strength and of his emotional appeal—this was in tune with a time when such a type of appeal met with enormous response. But it must have been successful also because Thring had in a high degree that quality which his own century might have described as "magnetic" and a later age "charismatic". It is rare; perhaps one has known two or three people who have had this quality in greater or less degree; so far no explanation has been given of it. But (like Housman with poetry) we *know* it by the symptoms it raises in us. One effect is beautifully described by Sartre in *Les Mains Sales:* "When I am with him, all storms cease." This comes over in numberless accounts of him; the quality is indefinable. On analysis three aspects are mentioned (by Rawnsley, *Early days at Uppingham*):

> His energy was infectious, whatever he took in hand, he went at it with such a will. . . but what to us boys seemed his greatest attribute, next to his absolute fairness, was his dauntless courage.

For, unlike some of his predecessors who had re-created schools, each in his own way, Thring was by temperament a fighter, not that he went out looking for worlds to conquer, but he was a pioneer and he was unyielding. He had the missionary, with a touch of the fanatical, temperament of a Livingstone or a Gordon. "He seemed to see God with his eye—watching over all his work at Uppingham." (J. Lovedale, 1888, letter after Thring's death.) During the long years of his headship, he was at different times at conflict with the Governors (frequently), the Education Commissioners (fundamentally), the Town Authorities (critically), the Parents (occasionally), the Masters (understandably), and even with his own creation, the Headmasters' Conference. This last happened once only; his threat to resign defeated them. From this list, boys have been omitted. He was not without some disciplinary troubles, and, when he felt the cause warranted it, he could be fierce enough in word and deed—particularly the former as he was very ready to improve the occasion with a general talk or "one of Teddy's paternal's" addressed to the individual boy. But (and this one can see from his diary) he was never haunted by a feeling that the *School* was against him. In all his other conflicts his words, especially in the later part of his life, reveal a touch of persecution mania. It sprang from his sense of mission; he is doing the Lord's work and the enemies of the Lord are round about him. But more and more his comments on the boys and the School itself end: "*Laus Deo*".

It would be tedious to take his tussles much in detail; they are evident in all accounts of Thring or of Uppingham. The Governors, for instance, dragged their feet every step of the way, Thring tugging them forward by his own straining initiative. The great Borth experiment was undertaken independently by Thring and his staff. The Governors had insisted on closing the school during a typhoid epidemic, and when Thring established it in a Hydro in Wales they stated they could take no cognizance of it until it returned to Uppingham. (He did manage to get them to pay the masters' salaries.) They certainly never came to see him during his evacuation, and the experiment must have confirmed his belief that he could get along well enough without them. The same occasion illustrated his struggle with the Town which was on a matter he considered vital—health. (Any opposition to his own and his Doctor's methods for achieving this he dismissed as BOSH! Modern thinking might regard this as an over-simplification but the obverse of Thring's demand for absolute loyalty from the staff was that he would back them all the way.) After he had found the premises, the evacuation was carried out in a fortnight and "Uppingham by the Sea" survived for a year. In the meantime, the town was under a miasmic cloud; the typhoid continued, trade languished and the name of Uppingham became notorious. And, though he never triumphs, Thring must have seen it as the finger of God that the Chairman of the Sanitary Committee, one of his most determined opponents, himself died as a result of the fever. In May 1877 when the school returned to a purified and repentant city, the position of the Headmaster was entirely altered. He was received with enthusiastic demonstrations and his victory was complete. Thring was magnanimous enough (and busy enough) to dismiss his enemies entirely from his mind, though the School preserved a day of rejoicing for several years.

Parents as a rule gave him their loyal backing. It was only in his last year—a mark perhaps of faltering mental balance?—that he attacked, and then only in his diary, the two men who had been exceptionally helpful throughout, and combative on his behalf. Earlier, "the Jackson affair" which got into the papers had assumed for him "gigantic proportions." It was the occasion when two boys returned late from leave and were beaten for this. Their father protested. There were articles in *Punch* and in *The Saturday Review,* and some wag quipped: "Mr. Thring may not train their minds, but he makes them mind their trains." For that season the entries were affected, but within two years the School was full, so the results cannot have been very harmful.

Thring's staff were carefully chosen but they were not "yes-men" and within the fairly close limits of his system he gave them plenty of scope, especially if they were Housemasters. Staff meetings must have been quite lively; the questions of argument which Thring records are usually about punishment or money. (A different complaint shows Thring's difficulties as an innovator; "T...blurted out that 'fellows were doing music when they ought to be doing mathematics'.") Perhaps unconsciously Thring felt that as he himself made so little money out of the School, and for many years actually lost it, there was no reason why those who were working under him should look to make large profits. His policy of the small House left a problem for Housemasters present and future, for the smaller the House, the greater the difficulty of making ends meet. Thring considered he had done all that was needed by warning those whom he proposed to appoint about what he would not allow. He had two main prohibitions; one was against taking on extraneous paid duties, even those of a clergyman; the other was against taking more in a House than about 30 boys. He made 33 an absolute limit (allowing for brothers) on the ground that a Housemaster could not give proper pastoral care to any more. As to discipline and punishment, Thring managed to walk the tight-rope without losing the respect of boys or masters or incurring the charge of injustice and weakness. He was at heart—and this shows again and again in his diary—"on the boys' side" but his loyalty to his staff would prevent his letting down a master by not punishing a boy who had been sent to him for a specific fault. He might give his views fiercely enough to the individual master or very convincingly in the masters' meetings.

Thring's staff were part of his creation of Uppingham and though he was prepared to clash with them occasionally, he recognized that they were trying to work what he oddly called "his system"—or they would not have been there at all. But of his differences with the Education Commissioners the same cannot be said for he based his stand against them on one of his Principles, from which there was no budging him. This was, that the running of a school should be left to the "experts", i.e. the Head and other Masters, not to the "amateurs" i.e. Governors, Inspectors, Schools Inquiry Commissioners and such like!

Thring's dislike of "amateur meddling" showed most clearly in his attitude to the Commissioners, both those of the Schools Inquiry (Taunton) Commission and the Education Commissioners in London who succeeded them. It was, however, his least successful struggle. He was able to obtain some modification of their scheme for Uppingham but times were too strong for him. (For example, his argument that

Uppingham ought to be treated as a Church school on account of its Founder could not be accepted.) Even though many of his contemporaries would have agreed in their hearts: "I see how impossible it is for a Government like ours to promote good except by stopping evil. How dangerous it is to meddle with liberty and work!"—these were the sentiments of John Stuart Mill and little more than lip-service was being paid to them. The days of *laissez faire* were passing.

Apart then, from the Headmasters' Conference, Thring's chief educational significance appears to lie in what he did for his own school, both in his ideas and in the ways in which he saw that they should be carried out. He did not care whether these ideas spread; in fact he makes a point over and over again, that Uppingham is *different.* One of many examples is found in the sharp strong blast with which he attacked what might have been thought a venial evil among schoolboys—cheating at work. After some plain speaking—"you who do it are liars and cheats"—he goes on:

> Oh yes, I know the mean things that you say to yourselves, some of you, in your mean hearts, about its being natural for boys, and "they do it in other schools." There have been times, and I knew them well enough, when schools were like prisons, and there was some wretched kind of excuse for cheating your gaolers. But you don't live in a prison here. We make your life free and pleasant, we trust you. . . Now, which you will! The prison, if you prefer; bolts and bars (I could make a prison if I chose) or the free life of a true society . . . Remember, in other things other schools will be your equals and superiors; in things which are their glory they will beat you; yes, they will beat you as far as numbers and social reputation, and intellect-power goes. Our glory will be to show the world that in a school there can be true life. There you can be first. Win that. That is what you can do from the oldest to the least, for the name of Uppingham.

If Thring's "system", as he always called his methods of education and discipline together with the "machinery" he devised to make it work, was taken over into the Public School image, this was to Thring quite beside the point. He was creating the here-and-now School of Uppingham as much as if he had founded his own school, yet never regarding it as Private, to himself, but simply as an example of what the Good Life for boys should be. He was hardly conscious that the country as a whole would regard the characteristics of his school as inherent in a type to be generally recognized.

In one respect Thring *was* characteristic of his time; in the emotional side of his appeal as exemplified in the quotation above. But he also had a very practical way of fostering loyalty to the school in every boy. It was simple enough once it had been thought out—namely to make him feel that there was something he could do that was appreciated by the school. And this was by no means all moral idealism; it was activity. Thring wanted to provide a chance for every boy, and he insisted that· masters—housemasters particularly—should help him in this. Naturally, all good schoolmasters had tried to do this—Thring may have learnt it from his own Eton housemaster. Butler for instance had done what he could for the "non-reading" boys; but no-one had been so active about it as Thring. It followed that—in the modern phrase—"opportunities for self-development must be provided". (One glance at any school prospectus will show how deeply Thring's idea has penetrated.) Hence came those additions to school building and equipment which in the small grammar schools, such as Uppingham, had been hardly even contemplated. Thring is always complaining that the Governors do not see the need for this or that. These opportunities were infrequent enough in many of the Public Schools; in Private Schools, which could be more experimental, they might sometimes be found—if the money would allow. But so much of what is now taken for granted was pioneered by Thring; the gymnasium, the athletics field, the fives court, the carpentry shop, the school gardens, the swimming bath, and the Concert Hall. (Not that Thring was in the least musical; it was a measure of his wide view that this should make no difference to his insistence on getting the best man he could for music and giving him the greatest support.)

Thring was a born group-leader—of the personal kind; he knew instinctively how a large number of adolescents (but never a "mass"; his was always an organized group or society) want to be treated. He even had the skill to gather up what was most idealistic in such a group and turn it outwards. Hence, not only did Uppingham have collections at an early stage for a Mission school in India, and Church work in Brisbane (on both of which the boys were addressed by people who were at work there) but they started what was probably the first school-supported mission at home. One of the Old Boys took charge of this and eventually the club and church in North Woolwich developed all the characteristics of reciprocal visiting and of personal and financial help from the school which are now taken for granted in the work of a School or College for the "under-privileged".

Thring encouraged this extensive variety of activities because he saw life as a whole. Studying the Classics, competitions for jumping gates, wood-carving, visiting the School Mission, swimming, Scripture at First School (with the Head)—all were manifestations of the full, the good life. Thring taught that whatever a boy did up to his own highest standard, which gave him confidence and self-respect and which enabled him to go on to do or learn something else was—for that boy—Education. Educators accept this easily enough now, in theory at least, following Rousseau, Dewey and Whitehead among others. But a hundred years ago or more, when Thring thought it out, the doctrine was not merely unacceptable; it was incomprehensible. It seemed totally irrelevant to schooling, because it combined ideas which the parents did not think of as having any connection with each other. Fathers when they sent away their sons to school paid their money for them to be taught the recognized curriculum which—heaven and the pedagogues knew why; *they* didn't—made him an educated man and, if this was what was wanted, took him to the University. Or else, like Tom Brown's father they sent him to acquire from his fellows and through the school discipline a code and habits of living.* These things were beginning to come together (see *Godliness and Good Learning,* Newsome), and Arnold, recognizing that both the learning and the code of behaviour were based on Christianity, produced his famous trilogy:

First, religious and moral principles,
Secondly, gentlemanly conduct,
Thirdly, intellectual ability†

If this was to be successfully realized in a boy, Arnold brought it about by his own teaching and personality; Thring believed that his aim would be achieved by working on educational principles or "system".

To impress a principle on the scholastic world, one has to be something of a fanatic, and a glance at the piercing blue eyes of Thring's portrait would tell us this truth about him, even if we knew no more. Yet the most distinctive feature in his face is the mouth—a generous, gentle, sympathetic mouth—but one that could on occasions (and there were plenty of such occasions) tighten up like a rat-trap and confront an opponent with all the obstinacy in the world. This

---

* Squire Brown's monologue is often quoted: Tom's own views not so often. When pushed to it he answers embarrassedly: "I want to be A1 at cricket and football and all the other games and to make my hands keep my head against any fellow, lout or gentleman. I want to get into the sixth before I leave, and to please the Doctor; and I want to carry away just as much Latin and Greek as will take me through Oxford respectably. . . I want to leave behind me the name of a fellow who never bullied a little boy, or turned his back on a big one."

† A. P. Stanley, *Life of Thomas Arnold, D.D.,* p.86.

aggressiveness was easily roused, and both tenderness and aggression could produce some curious, even laughable manifestations.

There was the occasion when Thring was playing fives, mis-hit a ball, and slammed it against his partner's cheek. No apology—he merely snapped: "Why don't you keep your head out of the light?" A similar fierce indictment of what seemed to him mere stupidity occurred when a boy was playing some party-game which involved a bag of flour. The boy was subject to asthma and the effort brought on one of his attacks. All Thring said by way of sympathy was: "What do you mean by attempting the game if you knew you were liable to fits?" The comment is said, rather improbably, to have cured the boy of his complaint.

Though rough in speech he would never knock the boys about nor have this done; there are letters threatening with dismissal a master who did this. "I never struck a boy and I will never permit a boy to be struck", he said, and when once, towards the end of his life, he did hit a boy who was breaking a rule, he was much distressed about it. His generosity was open-handed. If a boy came up to see him in his house at tea-time, he would not only cut off a large chunk of cake for him but if the lad shared a study with a friend would cut another chunk "for the bosom." A few months before his death he was deeply touched when two small boys, new that term, whose father was in India, came to his door and were shown into his study where they pulled out a letter from their father which they could not understand and asked him to read it to them.

Yet his very way of recording this and of writing on for nearly a dozen lines about it as "the most honourable, touching and prettiest thing, I believe, that ever happened to me" stresses the difference between the emotional climate of his day and a century later. In his time the blown-up emotion was accepted; the appeals to feeling, to ideals, to open sentiment were effective and, apparently, not resented nor ridiculed. (Yet it was not more than 12 years or so after Thring's death that the boys of Stalky's school were addressed in the emotional flag-wagging strain that produced such dire results and Kipling wrote the paragraph beginning: "Now the reserve of a boy is tenfold deeper than the reserve of a maid . . .")

Not that Thring's approach could be called "sloppy-sentimental"; he was much too genuine a character for that. Besides, when the logic of a situation demanded severity, Thring was not afraid to act severely. His expulsions were very few compared to Arnold's but he could write:

> I am extremely grieved at having been obliged to pass such a sentence. But in a Public School, apart from any other knowledge, I

deem the getting out at night a crime never to be pardoned. . . In any case, it is known to be expulsion.

Not only did he know every pupil so well (no mother could ever have felt for a moment that he was confusing her son with some other boy) but he was always prepared to explain himself. He wrote long and widely, and though old pupils rather than parents got the full flower of his thought and warmth of his heart, he never shirked an explanation nor failed to put an issue clearly—sometimes with almost brutal clearness.

Canon Skrine put the difference between Thring and Arnold, on the matter of expulsion, in religious terms: "Arnold discovered that a Public school was a Christian society; Thring discovered that every boy has a soul to be saved." But there was remarkably little of the "Search your soul, Eric" type of religion about him. To bring a boy's mind in touch with the thoughts of great men, of Biblical and Classical heroes, the humble as well as the great; to give him something to do with his head, his hands, his feet, eyes, ears and his whole body in which he could feel he was serving God, and by success grow in self-respect—these were Thring's ways of reaching each pupil. This, with his corresponding idea of trusting boys, giving them all the freedom and responsibility they could manage, he was for ever trying to get over to his staff, to parents, and to educators generally. In the long run—and by no means in boys' Public Schools only—he was remarkably successful.

Yet perhaps of all his actual works, that for which he is best known is the calling of the Headmasters' Conference. And this is ironic, because not only did he *not* call the first meeting of Headmasters, but he very nearly did not go to it at all. Even when, at the second meeting, he offered an invitation to the Heads already gathered (and later sent out to others) to meet at his school in the Christmas holidays, it is doubtful whether he was sure that a permanent body could be established. Equally ironic and untrue is the common notion that a Conference was held by the Heads of the Great Public Schools with the idea of deciding which should be admitted to their group and which should be excluded; had it been so, Thring would not have been there. Dr. Moberly's tentative idea of a small exclusive body meeting periodically came to nothing once the threat of the Clarendon Commission was past. The body that was to become the Headmasters' Conference did indeed meet to combat, as they thought, a Government threat but it was the result of the later Schools' Inquiry (Taunton) Commission—of which more hereafter—which produced their meeting. And, as by definition the schools affected were the Endowed Schools—Grammar Schools like Uppingham—those conferring were

Heads of schools *not* then generally regarded as Public Schools. The Clarendon Nine were by this fact excluded. No Headmaster had been asked from Eton or Rugby, nor even from the newly-founded schools such as Cheltenham or Clifton. None of these were at the first gathering and many did not join the Conference for two or three years after Thring's venture started.

For, though Thring did not call the first gathering, popular opinion is right to associate the Conference with his name. He did write the invitation to those who had already met and he wondered (with good reason) how many of those whom he had asked would accept. "I am not thin-skinned about it," he wrote in his diary, "If they won't combine, they won't. If they will, my position as the leading school under this bill makes me the fittest person to send out such a summons." Uppingham had in fact no distinctive position under the Bill. Yet Mitchinson and Harper, the men who, one by his initiative and the other by his organization, had made the first gathering possible, without hesitation yielded place to Thring. Looking at the variety and individuality of the Heads who had attended the first meetings of the group, it must have been clear to them that only a very exceptional man would be able to get and to hold them together. It could only be Thring.

IX

THE CONFERENCE-CALLERS

Mitchinson, Harper and others

The First Conference

Thring, then, did not call that first meeting of Headmaster which
eventually became the Headmasters' Conference. But who did? Why?
Where? and who came? Oddly enough there is no complete answer to
this last question. The meeting was quite informal, no minutes seem to
have been taken: and though there must have been a list of those who
attended and were called to a second meeting it has disappeared. The
Heads concerned, some 26, met on 2 March 1869 at the Freemasons'
Tavern in Great Queen Street, London, and the meeting was called to
consider a policy of defence against a Government Bill.

A look at chronology will help pull together the references which
have so far been made to the Government's dealing with Headmasters.

After the investigations by the Charity Commission, the Clarendon
(Public Schools) Commission, the Newcastle (Education of the Poorer
Classes) Commission, there was still room (in fact, need) for another on
schools. This was to deal with those which had been founded and
endowed as Grammar Schools. It was set up under the chairmanship of
Lord Taunton (Frederick Temple was among the Commissioners, see
p.171) at the end of 1864, and it was "to inquire" (in the spelling of
the day) into the schools which had not been comprised within the
terms of reference of the other Commissions. It is commonly known as
the Taunton or Schools Inquiry Commission (S.I.C.) In its report it
recommended a great deal of reform and reconstruction and this led to
the Endowed Schools Bill of 1869. It was to consider their attitudes
towards this Bill that the Headmasters, whose schools the Taunton
Commission had investigated, met, nine months before the Christmas
Conference at Uppingham. It is hardly necessary now to study the
details of the meetings that preceded the Conference, but it must be
stressed that Thring was not the originator of these. ("I laid the egg",
commented Mitchinson of Canterbury later, "Thring hatched it.") In
fact, Thring only accepted the invitation with great reluctance and
anxiety and under pressure from his friend Harper of Sherborne.
However, when he got there, he was greatly cheered by finding himself

199

among very "superior" men with whose general appearance and behaviour he was much struck. He noted that there were some 26 present and the next day (March 4th) mentioned in a letter to Mitchinson his idea that Headmasters might combine and have an annual meeting at Christmas. This he put forward at the second meeting which was held to receive the report of a deputation that had gone to W. E. Forster, the Government official in charge of the Bill. The deputation had been courteously received, and Thring then made the suggestion that the contact thus begun should be continued between them and offered his own hospitality at Christmas. The proposal had been acclaimed and unanimously accepted but no sooner had the Heads dispersed than at least half began to make excuses. Perhaps some felt they had successfully put their case in the cause for which they had been called together and this was enough.

The subsequent Act (embodying the first part of the Bill which had so much agitated the Headmasters) set up Education Commissioners with power to receive, suggest, or in the last resort compulsorily apply, a scheme of reform to any one of the many Grammar Schools which had been the subject of the original Taunton "Inquiry". For John Lyon, Lawrence Sheriff, Archdeacon Johnson and the Burgesses of Shrewsbury represented only a tiny fraction of the number who had founded and endowed Grammar Schools in the 15th and early 16th centuries. (Anyone who has lived in an old market or county town can bear this out by quoting some such school called after a Tudor sovereign or, more often, a worthy citizen—"local-boy-makes-good" type.) There had been some 800 of these for the Commission to investigate, but the three to four hundred years since their foundation had taken their toll. The Commission's report had uncovered a positive graveyard of decayed institutions and frustrated plans; only about one in eight was still flourishing to the extent of fulfilling their original purpose—to supply an education which would fit boys for the University. (This surviving group the Commission had termed "Classical"; the rest were "semi-classical", "non-classical", "elementary"—and in some cases, non-existent.) It was from this remnant that the majority of the Heads had come to the meeting, for the few schools which had kept on or been revived had in recent years soared into educational distinction—like the schools of Dr. Thomas James and Dr. Samuel Butler—but not by any means into Public School status. A few (like the King's School, Canterbury) were of very old foundation; two (Lancing and Liverpool College) were quite new, but otherwise the schools from which these Heads came were Grammar School foundations, or re-foundations, of the Tudor and Stuart period. They were not at the time thought of as among "The Great Schools of

England" (see p.177) and even to-day their names do not mostly leap to the mind immediately Public Schools are mentioned. Their head-masters' names have not (except Thring's) become household words, even among educationists. Yet this was a group of men outstanding both for their individual, even idiosyncratic, characters and for the extraordinarily successful work which each was doing—or had already done. The majority of those at Uppingham had performed a remarkable rescue operation on a school which had become a decaying local institution, perhaps even a semi-private venture grafted on to a financially moribund foundation; at best a small country grammar school catering only for its own sparsely populated neighbourhood. A glance at the rise in numbers under a few of these headmasters shows something of their success; numbers do not mean everything but in fact their standards and reputations had risen likewise.

Highgate under Dyne increased from	19 to 200
Tunbridge (sic) under Welldon	43 to 235
Sherborne under Harper	40 to 282
Repton under Pears	50 to 250 (approx.)
Richmond (Yorks) under Stokoe	15 to 150

Thring himself, the first host of the *permanent* Conference, had raised Uppingham from 25 to 320, the figure he himself had set as a limit.

The invitations from the beginning had been issued not to schools but to persons. There were individual members of the Conference, not delegates nor representatives. (They still are, for this principle has been strictly followed through the life of the Headmasters' Conference). Thring set down in his diary the names (*followed*, be it noted, by their schools) of those who were coming (December 18th, 1869). The list of those who had been *asked* is lost to us; it is surprising how sparse are the records of those early Conferences. It must be admitted that to-day those names have been generally forgotten except in their own schools, where the nomenclature of a House or of some school building often commemorates them. Here is the list, as Thring gives it:

Harper	—	Sherborne
Pears	—	Repton
Welldon	—	Tunbridge [sic]
G. Butler	—	Liverpool College
Wratislaw	—	Bury [St. Edmunds, Suffolk]
Stokoe	—	Richmond [Yorks]
Blore	—	Bromsgrove
Wood	—	Oakham
Mitchinson	—	Canterbury
Grignon	—	Felsted

Sanderson	—	Lancing [School omitted by Thring. N.B. *Not* the later H.M. of Oundle.]
Dyne	—	Highgate
Jessopp	—	Norwich
Carver	—	Dulwich

[Notes in square brackets by A.C.P.]

"These", wrote Thring, "will actually appear unless something unforeseen happens". (Something, apparently, did, to Dyne and Carver, but Dyne made an attendance on the second day.) Eighteen years later, when he recounted the story to the first meeting of *Headmistresses*, also at Uppingham, Thring positively gloried in the fact that "only twelve came". For these dozen were the hard-core, amounting to less than half of the original meeting. Thring declares that he sent out between 60 and 70 invitations, but this may possibly refer to the circular which it was decided to send for the next Conference—when 26 came.

No account has ever been written of this Agincourt-like band of brothers, except in so far as each will have been mentioned in his own school's history. But it was a group of quite remarkable and very dissimilar men, varying in temperament, circumstances and destiny, alike only in that each did a great work for his school (or schools). No wonder Thring (whose own power must have been evident in his dealing with this very diverse group) was "well-satisfied", as he continued to note at the second meeting a year later, with "the superior style" of those present. If only briefly, their lives and characters are worth studying.

John Mitchinson

Of all those gathered at the first (i.e. London) meeting of headmasters, Thring excepted, the most extraordinary was its convener, John Mitchinson, instigator of the whole enterprise. By 1869 he had already made a mark on his own school, King's School, Canterbury, but he was little known outside it. He was to have a remarkable career, comprising three (even four) completely different lives, starting with no social advantages and reaching a peak of educational eminence. (His life has never been written in full, though he left some early reminiscences, published in the school magazine, *The Cantuarian*, many years after his death.*) He became in turn a Headmaster, a Colonial Bishop, a Coadjutor Bishop at home, a Master of an Oxford College, and Canon of an English Cathedral.

His character was complex and ambiguous; he was fearless, yet sensitive; affectionate, yet inhibited; generous, yet fierce. He has been

---

* *The Cantuarian*, 1946—47.

charged with sadism, but this does not appear from his autobiographical fragment. He was an ardent reformer, over-zealous and quite aware of this. But of all his characteristics, what stands out is his energy, showing itself in his tremendous drives to accomplish what he thought necessary. And this was so much.

In his early life in the north he must have known poverty. The only son of a Merchant sea-captain who died shortly after John's birth, the boy was brought up by a severe mother and aunt. Mrs. Mitchinson kept a girls' school to support the family, and she helped her son with his studies. He later deplored the "detrimental feminine influence" of his up-bringing, not that he was mollycoddled but because, he said, the want of a father "put me out of touch and sympathy with what appeals so largely to the interests of the young." (His great contemporary, Dorothea Beale, likewise recognized that it was a loss in her that she "never knew how to play".) He was a "duffer" at games and did not play but he took to boating and paper-chases, the latter he introduced afterwards at Canterbury.

At nine years old, as "a wee shrimp", he went to the Cathedral School at Durham, a hard place physically, of which he has left a critical and in some ways horrifying account. But the teaching was good, and the Headmaster, Edward Elder,* was a man of outstanding personality on whom Mitchinson looked back with great affection and whose influence on him was life-long. Another legacy of these days remained with him all his life—his north-country speech—"the sharp voice with its Durham accent", was how one pupil remembered it. The same authority calls his face "the plainest imaginable" and though this matured and softened with age, "plain" was always the right word. He had not even a pleasing ugliness, but seems in face and physique to have been sheerly unattractive.

Mitchinson describes fully the excitement of winning a scholarship at Pembroke College, Oxford, showing how much this meant to him, and from this time onwards his academic success was assured. He took Firsts in both Classics and Natural Philosophy (science), and proceeded to a Fellowship at his College. (Later in life he became a D.D. and D.C.L.) After two years' tutoring he left Oxford—why, he does not tell; family stringency, perhaps?—to go as Assistant to the Headmaster of the Merchant Taylors' School, then in cramped quarters in the City. This was an equivocal and unsatisfactory post, as he was not strictly on the staff and therefore subject to snubs like being omitted from the invitation to dine at the Company's Hall on Doctors' Day. But he won the support and goodwill of his colleagues in the Common Room (to

---

* See p.159.

which he was admitted "by courtesy only."). With the boys too he seems to have got on well in spite of sharp ways (as Assistant, he could not "carry the cane") and he records taking groups out into Epping Forest in search of flowers and fossils; clearly he extended the boys' horizon both physically and mentally.

He got to know London, perhaps including the Freemasons' Tavern (not far from his Bloomsbury lodgings), where the original gathering of headmasters was to take place; he gave lectures, took a Sunday School class and was ordained. His examiner on that occasion was Dean Stanley and when in 1859 a friend suggested to Mitchinson that he should apply for the headship of the King's School at Canterbury, it was partly owing to Stanley's support that, though he had been a teacher for only two years, he got the post. Dr. Alford, Dean of Canterbury, was responsible for his appointment, and characteristically, when Dr. Alford died, Mitchinson persuaded the Governors (the Dean and Chapter of Canterbury) to build laboratories as a memorial to him and call them by his name.

The King's School was one of the oldest in the country but it was then suffering from the general apathy and lack of purpose common in the 19th century to so many Grammar Schools—Cathedral schools being if anything worse than most. Mitchinson's effect is formally described by a Cantuarian in the introduction of his Memoir;

> The time had come when the King's School required all a man's energy and wisdom to reform it, as it was to hold its place among the great schools of the country. Such a man was found in John Mitchinson to whom Canterbury owes as great a debt as Harrow to Vaughan or Rugby to Arnold. He traced the lines upon which it has steadily gone forward and attained a high standard of useful-ness. . . up to the present day. (July 1947)

More vivid is the physical picture of the man—his strong springy step, and the quick eye that took in everything; his flying gown and the sharp voice "which sent the monosyllable *Wha-at?* or *Qui-aet* ringing down the school with amazing effect"—those were the signs of a force which drove but also inspired. No doubt he ruled, certainly at the beginning, by fear. "The life of a lazy lad at the King's School was no bed of roses." He was a severe disciplinarian, quick-tempered and stern; corporal punishment was common, though with his expulsions he was not so free as, say, Arnold was when trying to raise the school's tone. But the individual was caned for mistakes—"Dr. Mitchinson regarded a bad mistake in an exercise as an affront to himself."—and right at the end of his mastership there was an attempt to chastise 50 boys who in 1873 had planned a runaway revolt. These offenders had been marked out at so many a day, but the Headmaster left before completion. Without acknowledging a sadistic tendency (but he was by temperament very hard, on himself no less than on others) one might well speak of compensation, remembering his small size and hard early life. But always in discussing "Victorian Headmasters" (so wrongly visualized under a stereotype) one should remember the accepted ways of the time. Mitchinson had not only watched (like Charles Lamb, earlier) a public flogging to blood in his own school-days, but he had passed by the bodies of criminals displayed after execution at Newgate. And against his ruthlessness in punishment, one should set his generosity both in money and of time. In his boarding house, the profits of which were expected to add to his income, he was continually allowing boys to come for reduced fees, or even free; one because his family was poor, another as the son of an old boy, a third—"with no reason given." This was kept quiet at the time but it was known of Mitchinson that "his liberality made him a poor man".

It was the same with the extra coaching which he would give privately (and this in an age when it was still a tradition at many schools to pay for private tutoring) either because a boy had slipped behind or because he was going for a scholarship—or for any reason that seemed good to him. Remembering his own struggles for a scholarship, he remained all his life keen to see that a boy who could profit from a University course should get one. His teaching was stimulating and even for a scholarship he did not "cram". Boys realized that he expected them to think out and do things for themselves, to strike out and find their own interests. Also, consonant with our own reaction against over-specialization, a boy taking a scholarship for the University, in classics, would not be dropping other subjects such as modern languages, mathematics and science. As to this last, Mitchinson had not only got laboratories built but he insisted on science being studied throughout the school—it is one of the myths about Public Schools that in *all* of them nothing was taught but the classics. At an early meeting of the Headmasters' Conference it was found that a large proportion of schools included science in the curriculum, and at least three Headmasters had taught it themselves—Percival, Grignon and Mitchinson.

In spite of his own limited experience in youth, he encouraged sport and athletics and he took part himself (though not in games) with that unselfconciousness that comes from concentrated interest and enthusiasm. Among the arts, his own interest lay in music, and a carol composed by him became part of the school Christmas service. But boys would be encouraged also in appreciation of architecture (with noble examples so close at hand) and of nature in practical studies.

There remains also a pleasant description of Mitchinson reading aloud to his House when it was too wet for them to go out, "his legs flung sideways over the chair arm, reading so clearly and merrily that the vivid tones of his voice constrained our attention", and of his bathing with them, "the spirit dominated the insignificance of the body and made it strong."

Mitchinson unlike, for instance, Thring, had little imagination and very imperfect sympathy with boys, especially with any form of revolt among them. And he seems to have none of the charismatic quality of some great Heads. But the boys recognized in him that quality chiefly necessary for a headmaster—integrity. He was also loyal in support of both his staff and his older boys. On one occasion his head boy was sought out by an angry parent, a military man whose son had been punished by the boy; this "Captain" threatened to knock him down. Mitchinson confronted the threatening Captain and told him to go, and, if he wished, to take his own boys away on the spot. Remembering Mitchinson's small stature (he was shorter than most of the Sixth Form), the story of the confrontation probably lost nothing in the telling. "Parent-teacher co-operation" was not so much sought after in those days but when, in defiance of the Head's prohibition, a parent took his son to the races on their outing, the boy was expelled. However, Mitchinson's severity did not prevent his numbers from rising; during his headship they more than doubled.

Teaching and building were the directions in which he found most need for reform. The conditions in which he found the boys living, he roundly stigmatized as "squalid". Even the Headmaster had no proper house. Mitchinson got the Governors (Dean and Chapter) to build a boarding house with cubicles in the dormitories, also Common-rooms for both masters and boys. More class-rooms were needed so that the Divisions—blocks of enormous classes, on the Eton model—could be broken up into manageable forms and the teaching improved. Money was not, as in so many places, the real difficulty but it was Mitchinson's perception of what was needed and his energetic and persistent pressure in convincing the Governors of this need and the importance of spending on it that loosed the springs of official spending and, following the Headmaster's own example, of private generosity.

Mitchinson had been a headmaster for ten years when he took the bold step which had such consequence—that of calling a meeting of other Heads. He tells how, when the Endowed Schools Bill was actually before Parliament, he saw that the Heads of the schools affected had not been consulted and that no one was doing anything about getting any common action. So, he tells the tale:

Although, therefore I was but an insignificant member of the craft I ventured to invite a considerable number of my brother headmasters to meet at the Freemasons' Tavern in London. The meeting was well and influentially attended; we discussed the bill, framed resolutions, and by deputation interviewed Mr. Forster, then Vice-President of the Council. [i.e. the Privy Council's Committee on Education— there was as yet no Ministry or Department of Education].

It was at the second meeting, presumably again convened by Mitchinson, to hear the result of the deputation, that Thring put forward to those assembled his invitation to attend the first *Conference* at Uppingham. Mitchinson, of course accepted. He had known Thring nearly ten years; the connection started in an interesting way when Mitchinson was, as he himself says, "a very young headmaster with a miserable tumbledown set of domestic buildings".

I had been invited over by Dean Sanders to preach for him in the Cathedral at Peterborough and to him I broached the question (of plans) adding that I had heard much of Mr. Thring's success at Uppingham and was disposed to go over and ask to see his buildings and arrangements. The dean encouraged me to do so, adding "You will find Thring the best of fellows and most willing to help you to the utmost of his power". . . I walked over from Manton, presented myself at the schoolhouse and stated my errand. I was at once welcomed and taken over one or two houses and shown everything.

Mitchinson greatly appreciated the welcome he got there and profited by what he saw at Uppingham and when he got his buildings asked Thring to come over. Thring was much touched because the young man thanked him for the "hints" he had got and called him (Mitchinson) one of the few honest men who had publicly and unreservedly acknowledged the extent to which he had picked Thring's brains. Mitchinson also much admired Thring's preaching and his ideas (when he could understand them) so it was not surprising that he was found travelling to Uppingham on that cold December day.

Beside the important part he had played in inaugurating the idea, Mitchinson made some impressive contributions on the first occasion. At this meeting, it was suggested that the Great Schools (the Clarendon Nine were meant) should next time be specially invited, as representatives from them would give the new association help and prestige. Characteristically Mitchinson took another view, (as did Thring): "I most certainly object to being tied to the chariot wheels of the great schools." Also, he considered that the new association should make no hard and fast rules as to schools being admitted but the Conference should decide on each occasion what headmasters were to be asked. On both these counts the rest eventually agreed with Mitchinson, and the principle of individual invitation (no reason required) remains current to this day.

After some 14 years as Headmaster, Mitchinson left Canterbury rather suddenly to become Bishop of Barbados in the West Indies. Here he had an energetic and stirring episcopate, giving much of his time to laying the foundations of a very effective educational system. This included a number of Secondary Schools through which an educational ladder led up to College and an English degree from the University of Durham. In his farewell to his diocesan clergy in 1881, he sadly but without bitterness considered his time as Bishop had been in many ways a failure; there must have been a great deal of conservative opposition which he could neither break nor come to terms with. One hopes that the real affection and gratitude shown in the many addresses of farewell to him relieved him of this feeling. It is not unlikely that he had felt the same about his work at the Canterbury school, for he hoped his successor in Barbados would succeed where he himself had failed, just as he believed that his successor at Canterbury had done with that School. To some extent this was true; Blore and his wife had given the School a confidence, ease, and graciousness that it did not achieve under Mitchinson. But in either case, it took a man of honesty, humility and courage to say so.

He returned to England to take up a post in the Diocese of Peterborough which, he insisted, must be something more than an Assistant Bishop; he became a Coadjutor. In 1896, however, he was elected Master of his former College, Pembroke, returning thus to more definitely educational work for the rest of his long span of 85 years, and dying in 1918. With the Mastership went then a Canonry at Gloucester Cathedral, an office which among other duties brought him again into contact with boys of a Cathedral school. Also his love of choral music, perhaps dating back to his early days at Durham, would have been satisfied. (Even in Barbados, he noted the pleasure that one particular Church gave him by its choral services.) As Canon at Gloucester he would have been officially present at the great west-country "Music Meetings"—the Three Choirs Festivals.

He is still remembered as a most conscientious holder of his office; he never omitted or curtailed his terms of residence, and he took seriously his duties of preaching and of teaching the Cathedral choristers and boys of the King's School who came to be prepared for confirmation. He had not altered greatly in this since his Canterbury days—he was severe, frightening, and generous. His gown still flew out behind him with his energetic movements. But he was as bald as an egg.

John Mitchinson never married. This lack of hostages given to fortune had enabled him to point out on his retirement from Barbados that the financial arrangements would have been quite insufficient for a family man. He made it clear that he himself had enough for his wants—and there are references again and again to his liberal contributions to relieve poverty, help education and establish church buildings. But he said firmly that the Barbadians must not rely on always having a Bishop who was unmarried and without dependants. One member of his family, however, was out there with him—his mother. (And, it seems, his aunt at times.) It is pleasant to think of the sea-captain's widow sitting beside the Governor (according to precedence) at official banquets or taking part in the pic-nic when Prince Alfred and his brother were being entertained by the Bishop and on a hot afternoon's drive the whole party dropped off to sleep. No doubt, like her son, Mrs. Mitchinson retained to the end of her life her strength of character and her north-country accent.

Daniel Harper

The second meeting of the Conference was held at Sherborne, so we should look next at the Headmaster of that ancient school, H. D. Harper.

Harper was an attractive, vigorous, character of great energy with a power of attention to detail which sometimes exhausted the readers of his memoranda. ("Too long to read", grumbled one of his Governors, of a proposal for a new building.) In person, he was a big man with a great head like a lion; fair hair and a square open face fringed with side-whiskers. He was not unlike Thring in appearance but his eyes lacked the latter's piercing, fanatical character. He had an enormously strong constitution and seems never to have gone sick. Like Thring, he knew exactly what he wanted from people; his staff for example were told that as he considered smoking "extremely injurious" and would not have it among the boys, masters were either not to smoke at all or only to indulge in places where the boys never came. Again, he told an applicant that though the boys he was going to take would try his patience by their stupidity, he was not to lose his temper and knock them about. He was prepared to fight for his own way; when the School Chapel had been built, he wanted the boys to worship there rather than in the Abbey (to which, in pre-Reformation days, the school had been attached, before its re-founding under Edward VI). His argument—like that of Dr. Butler at Shrewsbury who had been defeated on this point by his Trustees—was that they should participate in the service and hear sermons, including his own, appropriate to their age. For a long time daily Matins in the Abbey was insisted on, but Harper took the matter to the Bishop of Salisbury who gave judgment in his favour, and he got his way. Yet as a whole he got on well with his Governors and especially with the Patron, Lord Digby. "If managed", Harper is reported as saying, "his Lordship is inclined to be liberal." He was, to the extent of giving the School large grants from his land for building.

As a teacher, Harper, though competent, was not outstanding but he recognized the need for change and expansion in the curriculum. Although there was no provision from the foundation for any but two Assistant Classical masters, he managed to get a full-time science master appointed (and the charge to each boy of a guinea "for chemicals" indicates some practical work as well as lectures), also an Art master and one (with workshops) for Craft. Mathematics were well enough taught for the school to produce A. N. Whitehead (later F.R.S.), but Harper also appointed on the mathematical side J. Sterndale Bennett better known in music, which he also taught the boys. Harper added French and later German to the curriculum—the latter, together with science was taught by Dr. Muschaweck, a Pole from Munich. (A tradition seems to have grown up in Public Schools that any emigrant from Europe was competent to teach any European language.) To sum up, when Harper came, nothing was being taught but Latin, Greek, Divinity and a rather poor attempt at mathematics: he succeeded in getting written into revised statutes that instruction should be given also "in French, Mathematics, Arithmetic, English Literature, and Composition, Sacred and Profane History, Reading and Writing and such other sciences and Languages as the Governors should from time to time ordain".

In accordance with the ideas of the times, one of the new clauses established a Fund for Prizes and Exhibitions. It is not recorded how Harper dealt with one incident arising from his choice of recipients for these. A lady sought an interview in which she explained how disappointed her husband had been at his son's lack of success and she suggested that she should *buy* the boy a prize to avert his anger. Less vulnerable, though subject to present-day criticism, was Harper's effort to introduce visits from University Examiners to report on the work in general and to select the Exhibition candidates for Oxford and Cambridge. Exhibitions, he said, should be open to boarders and found-ationers (day) alike. Later came the Oxford and Cambridge Board Local examinations; Harper became Chairman of the Council for the Local Centre.

Sherborne, though designed to take a number of local boys free, was one of those charitable foundations whose reputation had gone further afield than its founders had ever contemplated. It was, like others, *schola libera, grammaticalis, regalis* and its numbers through the centuries had been extremely varied. The town boys—during the early part of the 19th century their numbers had remained at about 40—received free education which, rather to Harper's annoyance, included free text-books from the school. But whereas under the last Head but one before Harper there had been about 140 boys in all, by 1850 the numbers had sunk to under 70, and when Harper arrived though there were still 40 free foundationers, there were but two boarders, apart from those which he brought himself from his previous school at Cowbridge. (This practice of bringing along one's own boys on appointment to a new school instead of leaving them to be taught by one's successor was widely sanctioned; there are numerous examples—with no ill-feeling ensuing.) However, by the time of the Taunton Commission, Harper had over 200, and when he left there were 278 of which 240 were boarders. It was characteristic of the man's self-confidence that in 1860, when the railway was reaching Sherborne, Harper, though he then had but 40 boarders, built a house for 90 boys which soon filled up.

Naturally the feeling of the town was divided about this increase, but Harper never seems to have suffered from the unpopularity that such a change brought at Harrow or Shrewsbury. The desire to keep the school for their own local boys was weighed against the pride in the expansion, in numbers and reputation, of a respected and traditional institution, not to speak of the economic advantages to the town of an enlarged school. In such cases, the character and personal relation of the Headmaster to the neighbourhood must have counted for a great deal. The transition at Sherborne (where there were also other local educational foundations) seems not to have roused bad feeling. The change itself was not in doubt. After 15 years of Harper's Headship the Taunton Commission summed up the position: "If intended as a mere local school, it has completely outstripped the circle of such intention and outgrown the limits of its early constitution." The school's historian, contrasting the cramped and dilapidated buildings, the old-fashioned curriculum and the "system of finance stuck in a centuries old groove" with Harper's ample building, sevenfold increase in numbers, vastly extended curriculum and changed accountancy explains: "In short, he made Sherborne a Public School." Without any comment on the value, the fact must be accepted.

The Taunton Commission and the scheme of 1871 which followed the Endowed Schools Act, did everything to help this transition. The new scheme reduced the numbers of an unwieldy Governing Body and provided methods of continuity. It broke the connection which, as so often, had linked the school charity with an almshouse; it abolished (after the education of the present holders) the free education of local foundationers and substituted entry by examination open to all regardless of locality, and extended this open examination for school scholarships to the leaving exhibitions, to be available to all at any Oxford or Cambridge College.

Harper, perhaps with Thring's example in mind, had certainly been working for a non-local independent Public boarding school and he must have realized that Sherborne was a very different proposition from Uppingham. The King's School Sherborne had a longer history, a deeper tradition, and a wider reputation than Archdeacon Johnson's school. Thring had merely to build—though he had to fight his Governors to do so; Harper could never have succeeded in the more difficult task of *changing* without the co-operation of his. But it was a formidable exercise in tact and determination.

With the Commissioners so clearly behind him and his view coinciding so closely with the new schemes, it is difficult to see exactly why Harper had joined so enthusiastically with the many smaller schools to consider concerted action against the Taunton Commission. Thring,—and it was Harper who persuaded him to attend the first meeting—was really far more on the defensive than Harper. One can only think that Harper *believed* that the proposed Bill would result in unfair discrimination against the old Grammar schools and that had he been able to foresee the scheme of 1871 he might not have insisted so strongly on the meeting of March 1869 and on Thring's coming to it! But perhaps it was the meeting and the deputation ensuing, (and this surely must have included Harper) which really did bring about a considerable change in the attitude of Forster and of those behind the Bill which enforced the schemes.

Harper was clearly very different in outlook from Thring, though resembling him somewhat in temperament, having a more limited vision, a less profound conviction that he was always right. But he was complementary to the acknowledged leader; he was untiring in correspondence, clear and knowledgeable in matters legal and financial, an excellent Committee-man and of the utmost value to the Conference from the moment it started. When he became Chairman of the Conference's Committee he was described as one "whose robust and genial leadership each was glad to acknowledge". He was Thring's "good lieutenant", a part to which—though he was an undisputed monarch in his own school—he was admirably suited.

John Bradley Dyne

Dr. Dyne was a man of a very different stamp from most of his fellow-heads, though he achieved for his school, Roger Cholmeley's foundation at Highgate, the same success as they did, in numbers, reputation and scholastic achievement. He had preceded the majority of them in time as he started as Head in 1839, and he had an even harder task than most of them. For the school had only recently been extracted by a judgment of Lord Eldon's from a most humiliating and quite illegal position. The chapel, which was found in the judgment to belong wholly to the School, had become used as the parish church of the village of Highgate; the Headmaster was looked on primarily as being the parish priest, and the care of the School had been delegated to an almost illiterate Sexton. (The fact that S. T. Coleridge was one of the parishioners made things no better for the boys.) Naturally no classical learning had gone on for years, unless privately provided by the Master for his own boarding pupils. In fact, the teaching was being carried on under the Monitorial system as in an elementary school—which was what the place really had become. The last Master before Dyne "rarely visited the school" except for disciplinary purposes.

Dyne himself had been born at Bruton in Somerset, and educated at the King's School there (at that time of very good repute) and at Wadham College, Oxford. Here he became a Fellow and Tutor. Many Heads of this period had been Fellows of their Colleges, but it is not very clear why Dr. Dyne should have wanted to take on a school in such conditions. There were but 19 boys when he came in 1838; when in 1848 the first lists of boys were printed there were 102. It was perhaps the sign of an even more remarkable effort that within eight years the school had achieved an exhibition at his old College of Wadham and from then onwards a number of scholars went up, to Oxford first and by the 1860s also to Cambridge.

"Education" under Dyne meant chiefly the Classics with a little mathematics and with French and German, taught by a retired Prussian officer.* Remarkably (and absurdly) the grammar books even beyond this time were written *in* Latin or Greek; most of the Conference Schools had at least got beyond *this.* Work was graded not by marks but by "Letters"—from O (Optime) to P (Pessime). Not surprisingly in this background, "the boys' learning was assisted by a liberal distribution of stripes". Dr. Dyne looked out over the Big Schoolroom (which at his advent contained four forms) from a window in the Library above; this window rattled when he opened it with "a silencing

---

* By 1865 however, there were School Prizes both for Modern Languages and for English Literature.

effect". Later, he used to keep watch over the playground and pounce on "doomed adventurers whom he suspected of being malefactors"—once he unfortunately pounced on an Assistant Master. It was perhaps in keeping that the rules for fagging, drawn up by the senior boys, were approved by the Headmaster. All these traits may be summed up in a reminiscent paragraph by an old boy in 1890. He admits that he was "idle, mischievous and independent"—so the last quality may account for his views.

> A capable enough pedagogue not more than usually narrow-minded priggish and conventional. He was a type of the old-fashioned pedantic school, which looked on Oxford as the hub of the universe and thought the study of Latin and Greek the primary object of our creation. He despised modern languages and foreign countries. He believed thoroughly in the virtue of corporal punishment. A desperate swisher the Doctor, as I had cause to know, and not over-burdened with tact, judgment or impartiality. (E. H. Yates)

It is hard, though natural, that those who are most articulate about their schools are often the most critical since they were during their schooldays perhaps the most mature, almost certainly the most sensitive. It was probably also a mutual misfortune that Gerard Manley Hopkins should have been at Highgate under Dr. Dyne (D.D.). In addition to the contrast of their natures there was the difference in religious outlook. Hopkins was entering his High Church phase; Dyne had passed through his Oxford period during the ferment of the Tractarian revival and remained untouched by it.

In any case religion must have been a subject needing careful handling. By the Eldon decision the school (as well as meeting costs) was committed to make a very large contribution to the building of the parish church. So in spite of growth, money was very tight at Highgate. The School's own Chapel to which the family of Crawley, which had produced many of the Governors over the years, had largely contributed, was not consecrated till 1867. Yet in spite of the stringency Dr. Dyne established two boarding houses which soon filled up. Like other revived schools, Highgate soon needed new and extended buildings. Fortunately the sites which might later have presented a severe problem, gave no difficulty since at the School's foundation, Archbishop Grindal, then Bishop of London, had made generous provision of lands belonging to him. But Dyne also forestalled a rise in price by buying more than one piece of ground and conveying it to the Governors for School sports grounds.

A recent critical biographer considers that Dyne's eye was too often fixed on the main chance for him to be thought a truly great man. One instance given is his asking Fearon, an officer of the Schools' Inquiry Commission, to a school function shortly after the official visitation; Thring, he points out would never have dreamed of encouraging good relations with that influential body. (But Fearon was a Government Inspector and a man of some distinction; Thring had been visited by a young and mediocre Assistant Commissioner.) It might be taken as a generous gesture or as an unworthily sagacious move. Similarly, his invitation to the H.M.C. to meet at Highgate as early as their third year may show great enthusiasm or a fine sense of publicity; perhaps both. Admittedly one gets the impression that had Dyne lived to-day he might have left his Fellowship—supposing that he had ever taken it up—for a career not in the scholastic but in the business world. There is a touch of the tycoon about him. Yet the verdict: "He was of all men the fittest to come here at a time so critical for the School" (Preface to *The School Register,* 5th edition) may stand; it seems to sum up his worth.

Towards the end of his reign the position of Highgate School—the founder's name having as so often in such cases been dropped from the usual title—was sufficiently established academically and financially for wider interests to begin to develop. School societies began to be formed—in 1872, the Natural History and Debating Societies; the Cholmeleian Magazine in 1873. One should also put it to Dyne's credit that when in 1868 he received a cheque of £920 as recognition of his 30 years' work, he gave back some £600 to found prizes for the School.

Dyne lived on till 1893. He had found it impossible at times "to avoid offending individuals in pursuit of what he conceived to be his duty" but the School benefited from his work "for all time".

James Ind Welldon

Dr. Welldon, the outstanding Headmaster of Tonbridge, presided over that school for over 30 years (1843-75). D. C. Somervell, the historian, also historian of the school, says:

Welldon was not, like Arnold and Thring, a man of intellectual eminence, but he had in full measure the evangelistic fervour, the Roman "gravitas" which was in those days, and perhaps always, a more important element in successful Headmastership.

A curious verdict, especially as neither Arnold nor Thring is, nor wanted to be, remembered primarily as an intellectual. The slightly disparaging comparison of James Welldon, who was after all a Fellow of St. John's College, Cambridge with a double First (Classics and Mathematics), applies rather to his status *vis-à-vis* his predecessors at

Tonbridge, the Knox dynasty. Vicesimus Knox the First (1772-8) and the Second (1778-1812) with Thomas Knox following (1812-43) had ruled Tonbridge for over half a century. They were outstanding in intellect, yet after their departure the school still lacked the material and traditional stability which it needed to rank consistently with the great Public Schools. Under Welldon it acquired all the outward signs of Public School tradition as well as the reputation and confidence to continue thereafter its career in that body. It got a Chapel, prefects, an Old Boys' Association, a school magazine, a cricket XI with colours (and a considerable proportion of the timetable allotted to games, athletics and gymnastics) and the buildings, both classrooms and boarding houses, which enabled it to retain the numbers necessary to keep it in the category of a Public School.

Welldon had a stroke of luck in this. The school was managed by the Skinners' Company which administered the bequest of Andrew Judd and this included property in what had by 1842 become the railway-land of North London. Part of this was sold to make St. Pancras Goods Yard, with considerable advantage to the School. Welldon persuaded the Governors to build and buy land beyond their immediate needs— though, presumably as a result of this extension, the old Tudor building was destroyed in 1858. As they expanded, the numbers shot up from 42 to 147 (1844), to 163 (1858), and to 235 in 1875, the year of Welldon's retirement. They bought the land for five boarding houses; Welldon's brother, whom he imported in his second year and who as Second Master almost ran the school in partnership with him, took up a house at once. In the 1860s, the Taunton Commission regarded Tonbridge as predominantly a boarding school. But in fact the number of day-boys also increased, though rather because parents came to Tonbridge for the purpose of educating their children than because the local families themselves took advantage of the school's rise to scholastic fame.

Dr. Welldon himself seems hardly to have been intended by nature for a pioneer. Academically, his training was against it. Before coming to Tonbridge he had been briefly at Oakham Grammar School, then for seven years at Shrewsbury, first under Dr. Butler and then under the great teacher B. H. Kennedy. Welldon is referred to as "a strict master of the old school, who took every form once a month"—an exercise from which the cane was not absent. Yet "with some difficulty" (from the Governors? from staff?? from parents???) he did try to substitute other punishments such as impositions, for "the more forcible and more usual style. . . of the Rod." (One can gather from the style of the historian the kind of tradition he encountered.) And there are testimonies to his "acts of generosity" and to his warm-heartedness.

"He spoke ill of no-one. . . .and he tolerated his assistant masters long and kindly." One wonders what is behind that curious phrase.

Unlike many of his fellows at the Headmasters' Conference, Dr. Welldon showed little interest in any but classical studies. French and German were indeed taught, also some music and drawing, but little encouragement was given even to mathematics. He told the Taunton Commission that there had once been classes in Physical Science but that these were discontinued, the fees being too high (for the parents to take advantage of the subject?). Instruction in chemistry, although it was allowed to be "an important and delightful study," was also lacking.

In fairness, it should be noted that Welldon had been a Headmaster longer than almost any at the Conference, except the equally old-style Dr. Dyne of Highgate, and that he survived for only a few of the yearly meetings. (He had started teaching before Victoria came to the throne and had taken over Tonbridge ten years before Thring went to Uppingham. During his apprenticeship at Shrewsbury—the last school to be included in the Nine "Great" Clarendon list—he had been where the pioneering work had already been established in the early days of the century. It is remarkable that he should have done even so much to lead Tonbridge into a newer age. Yet he had the vision to see the need for this change and in his penultimate year he and his staff wrote to the House of Commons urging that the new scheme for the School's government, over which the Skinners' Company were dragging their feet, should be hurried on. He did not live to see it in action.

In temperament, Welldon was severe with himself as well as with others. He belonged to the school of early exercise and cold water, no tobacco, no drink—in spite of the brewing connection of his middle name. Of a brewer's dray that he encountered on a walk before morning chapel, he remarked: "The Devil always gets up early in the morning"—a trait he himself had in common with the Evil One. A more human characteristic was his abominable and illegible writing. Though he did not, as was averred, write with a barge-pole, he did use a quill pen, and the nib was usually split. But perhaps the personal act by which we may remember him with most pleasure is his planting, soon after his arrival at Tonbridge, of an avenue of chestnut trees.

William Spicer Wood

One suspects that in inviting Mr. Wood of Oakham to the Conference, Dr. Thring of Uppingham was moved by mere politeness more than anything else. He could not without inflicting a deliberate snub have ignored the head of a Grammar School only six miles away.

Yet except in a physical sense, the two were not close and their interests were clearly opposed. It could hardly have been otherwise. The two schools were "twinned" by the charter of the original founder and, with such a small catchment area of pupils, the rising reputation of one must always have meant the decline of the other. (The question in 1869 must have been more of money and reputation than of pupils; Thring in 1865 had but half a dozen day-boys and over 260 boarders.) Thring in evidence to the Taunton Commission quoted the traditional saying: "Uppingham up, Oakham down; Oakham up, Uppingham down." He omitted to add that in the 18th century it was said: "The school of Uppingham is not, nor hath been of equal reputation with that of Oakham." But the scales now swung the other way and Thring had supported, if not inaugurated, an idea which would have put an end to Oakham as a Grammar School, let alone as a Public School. Thring's version was that after he had been Head for three years,

> the then Headmaster (i.e. Wood) joined me in petitioning that something might be done to alter the relations of Oakham and Uppingham. He saw that what was going on was likely permanently to depress the school at Oakham and he thought it would be better to make it a middle class school or to make it a preparatory school to Uppingham. I believe I am quite justified in saying that, for it was a public thing, but he may have changed his mind.

On being questioned further, Thring said that "some arrangement of that kind" was formally laid before the Trustees who "told us it could not be". Thring's biographer says Dr. Wood approved the idea of becoming a second grade school; Oakham School's historian, a subsequent Head, thought otherwise. Considering that Dr. Wood had successfully carried on the tradition, recently revived by his predecessor, of sending a very fair proportion of his boys to the University, equally with Uppingham in the days before Thring, the latter's vision of a "modern" school or a "feeder" for Uppingham seems mere wishful thinking. It got him the reputation of a bad neighbour.* However, the Oakham Grammar School was still there and Dr. Wood came to the first Conference—a matter of some pride to his successors.

It is not easy to learn much about Wood as a person, though he began as a Cambridge man of great brilliance whose successes were still remembered 60 years later. He took the remarkable high double honours of 7th Wrangler and 4th Classicist besides gaining the 2nd

---

* When it was rumoured that the Governors were considering the possibility of *Uppingham* as a middle grade commercial School, Thring was of course furious.

Chancellor's Classical Medal in 1840 and the Chancellor's Medal for "an English poem of excellent quality" and other University prizes. He became a Fellow of his College, St. John's, but two years later vacated the Fellowship on marriage and took the headship of Oakham in 1846. He was evidently a good classical teacher and his mathematical ability also improved the study on this side of the School. He also extended the curriculum so as to prepare boys for the examination of the Indian Civil Service, a new opening when, in the mid-century, competition superseded entry by influence or purchases into the old "John Company". It was a forward-looking move by Wood away from the traditional preparation solely for the profession of parson or teacher.

One advantage Wood seems to have had over Thring; he got on well with his Governors. In 1853 for example they decided to rebuild and spent the, for this Trust, not inconsiderable sum of £4,000 on a house for the Headmaster with a boarders' wing, later added to by Dr. Wood himself. This was opened in 1858 and numbers went up at once to 66. At the time of the Taunton Commission Wood had 80 boys in his own house; the 2nd Master had 20 and there were 30 day-boys. The lists of Oxford, Cambridge and I.C.S. successes was considered very presentable; athletics had also been developed and the tone was good. So was the local reputation of the school and its Head:

> Before the time of the present headmaster it is said the school was in bad repute and had not a high tone; at present everyone speaks well of it . . . the Head Master appears to have won to a considerable degree the confidence and goodwill of everyone connected with the school, whether trustees, parents, or old pupils. (Taunton Report)

It is from an old pupil that we get the testimony of the "affectionate esteem" in which his long succession of boys held him and of his "unwearied devotion as teacher and to the care which he ever exercised. . . to advance their spiritual, moral and mental development". It is an ordinary enough tribute for a retiring headmaster, but these words were written some thirty years later at his death in 1902.

For whether from competition with a much greater man or because towards the end of his 30 years in the school the Headmaster lost his grip, the high level of success was not maintained. The school's record is sad:

> Dr. Wood was a broken schoolmaster; he had lost his wife and his eldest son; he had seen his hopes in the School destroyed; he had latterly advised parents not to send their sons. His last entry in the Register is dated April 1875. Only two boarders and five day boys of his time are found in the new Register opened in the following year.

He obtained a pension and a living from his College and was Rector of Higham near Rochester till 1896. He retired to Bath where he lived to be 84, leaving a son to carry on his work as a clergyman but not as a Headmaster.

Dr. Pears

It is said of Stewart Adolphus Pears that on his first visit to Repton School, where he was to remain for 20 years, he was overwhelmed by the desolation of the physical surroundings in which he found himself. "He sat at a table with his head sunk upon his hands in the attitude of a man appalled by the magnitude of the task he had set himself."

Dr. Pears' previous experiences would not have seemingly fitted him for the task—that of pulling up this small, limited and in many ways backward Grammar School to take a respectable place among the body to be classed as Public Schools which were to form such a solid top-section of nineteenth century education. He was more of a scholar than many of his fellow Heads; he had been sent to Zurich by the Parker Society for material on the Reformation and had found and edited a volume of Philip Sidney's letters. He had acted as private tutor to the Marquis of Ripon's son; he was a Fellow of his Oxford College, Corpus Christi, and in 1844/5 its Dean, and he had gained theological prizes. He had gone on to a Tutorship at Durham University where he married the daughter of a noted astronomer and Professor of Mathematics, Dr. Chavallier. It was not till 1847 when he was 32 that he became a schoolmaster, going then to Harrow where Vaughan, whose reforms he evidently admired, was Headmaster. Pears stayed for seven years, becoming a housemaster and teaching classics. For this he seems to have had a gift, which he carried over into his new school—that "of carrying a pupil with him in the perception and appreciation of the beauty of style or the importance of the matter of every author whom he touched".

The most personal sketch of Pears as headmaster comes from an old boy, G. M. Messiter, who was later on his staff:

> Dr. Pears was a born ruler. . . He never made use of the old flogging block and seldom applied the cane; we rarely saw his scarlet robes, and some of his most impressive addresses were delivered at three o'clock call, when he had simply strolled up the yard. . . As he stood by the central desk in Big School (not on the raised platform at the end) the call proceeded not a sound being heard . . . then would follow in the quietest of terms, the rebuke he had come to administer. One Tuesday we were told that the day before some farmer had reported that Repton boys had been riding sheep on the

previous Sunday. Before the address had ended we all felt that the School had disgraced itself, though the speaker had hardly raised his voice at all, and his only action was that of twirling the School key round a finger as he spoke.

In person, he was rather tall, thin and distinguished-looking with aquiline features, eyes grey and rather short-sighted with a grave air and great dignity, natural but enhanced by his rigorous control. He seems to have begun quietly, though numbers, which he found under 50, soon started to increase. The tercentenary of the school was celebrated in 1857, three years after his arrival, and he used this occasion with its distinguished gathering (Dr. Vaughan coming up from Harrow as Preacher) as a jumping-off ground for the school's advance.

As so often, the first improvement needed was in buildings. When Dr. Pears arrived, the majority of classes were still being taken in the one "Big School", just as they appear in Ackerman's illustrations of Winchester etc. at the beginning of the century; as they had been at Rugby when Dr. James dispersed them in the 1770s. Pears had actually to build new classrooms at his own cost and then persuade the Governors to put up others, including a Sixth Form room. At the tercentenary, a school chapel was planned, and opened two years later. Pears was responsible for the building of boarding-houses to be staffed by the masters, the original system of "tabling" in the village having been the only alternative to becoming a private pupil with the Headmaster. Now, as at Uppingham and elsewhere, the masters themselves began to feel secure enough to put their money into acquiring houses permanently or on long lease, while some houses were school-owned.

Repton was not one of those schools where a new Headmaster introduced science into the curriculum—with or against the goodwill of the Governors; Pears' experience of it as a school subject may have been unfortunate, for he believed it consisted of cramming boys with facts instead of encouraging them to work and make judgments for themselves. But he encouraged extra-curricular studies, e.g. botany, as he did drawing and music. He was himself (like Mitchinson) the Choirmaster (with unaccompanied part-singing) and gave boys opportunities for singing and for chamber music with his own family. There was some teaching of modern languages; for the belief that these could be satisfactorily taught by any Central European we may compare Rugby and Sherborne. Repton had a "polyglot Pole". The classics were supplemented by Ancient Geography and History but modern history and literature Dr. Pears expected to be studied outside the curriculum, e.g. as the background to a holiday task.

Dr. Pears had been Headmaster of Repton for fifteen years when he first attended the Headmasters' Conference, having already given evidence to the Taunton Commission. When in 1874 the Commissioners got to work on a scheme for the government of the school, he was able to persuade them to accede to the views about this which he had put forward seven years before. Up to then, the old connection of Repton School with Etwell Hospital—the twinning of a charity for the old poor and the young scholar—was still in force. The scheme set up the school with control over its own revenues and with its own Governing Body which included a member nominated by the head and staff. The local "foundation" boys and home boarders were to be provided for in a separate, elementary, school. (The next century saw a revised solution of this problem of local charitable endowment.) The usual arrangements about a Headmaster's responsibility to the Governors and for his own choice of his staff, now becoming common to all Public Schools, also became part of the new scheme. Pears just stayed to see this scheme established. He had been away ill and returned for the last week of the summer term, 1874, taking the last call-over and shaking hands with his 260 boys. His valediction was modest:

> I came with a very high ambition and a very high ideal and I have not departed from it. I shall, as long as I live, expect to see this school grow greater and better . . . I cannot help regretting that I have lost opportunities which a younger and better man would have improved. . . .

He did not live long and died at sixty of *angina pectoris*. It was characteristic of his concentrated interests in the scholastic world that on his last attack he exclaimed: "This is what Arnold—and Messiter—died of!"

Albert Henry Wratislaw

A. H. Wratislaw has, quite apart from his considerable achievement in the history of the two schools of which he was Headmaster, an independent place of his own—a full page—in the Dictionary of National Biography.

He had also an interesting family history. His grandfather* was Bohemian, a Count of the Holy Roman Empire who had been attaché to the Austrian Embassy in Paris—Bohemia, now part of Czecho-Slovakia, being then in the Austrian Empire. He was there at the time of Marie-Antoinette's wedding but fell under suspicion of revolutionary ideas and had to leave. He came to England about 1770 and became

---

* See . p.52.

French master, first at King Edward VI School at Birmingham and then at Rugby under the pre-Arnold Dr. James. The family grew up in Rugby and perhaps their gradual Anglicization can be illustrated by the Christian names of three generations—Count Marc-Marie Emanuel; William Ferdinand; Albert Henry. Two of the Count's sons became masters at Rugby; William Ferdinand was a solicitor. In 1839 he brought a case against Dr. Arnold, then Headmaster. The ground of the complaint was that Arnold deliberately neglected the education of the younger children when they were sent to school and the reference was to Albert Henry's brothers. As the boy himself had been sent to Rugby when only seven, and others similarly, it is not surprising that Arnold took the line that this was too young for a Public School and that he would not cater for that age. (The case went against the Headmaster but his reasoning was in effect accepted as a principle for Public School life.) Young Albert Henry survived, however, and went on to Cambridge in 1840, first to Trinity, then to Christ's where he graduated as 3rd Classic and became a Fellow and Tutor in 1844. Five years later (perhaps also before) he visited Bohemia and began the study of Czech—language, history and literature—at Prague, becoming in this a distinguished scholar. A long list of publications, many being translations, includes *Lyra Czeche-Slovenska* (Bohemian poems from MS.), *The Adventures of Baron Wenceslaw Wratislaw of Mitrowitz, what he saw in the Turkish Metropol*. . . *The Life of St. John Nepomucen*, and *The Native Literature of Bohemia*, a book based on four lectures he had given at Oxford on the Ilchester Foundation. This last book was published in 1877 but though he worked on Czech studies all his life, he published but little during the years of his headships. His last work was *Collection of Sixty Folk-tales* of his own translation with introduction and notes, in 1889. He also wrote two pamphlets on the need for University reform, and *Notes on the Difficulties in Scripture* while still teaching, and after he retired *A Life of John Huss.*

But his record as a Headmaster also bears comparison with anyone's for he succeeded not once but twice in raising the standard, numbers and status of an old Grammar school that had fallen away. The first was at Felsted, the Tudor foundation of Lord Rich. This had been of outstanding reputation in the early 18th century; Defoe noted its ancient foundation and referred to it alongside Eton, Winchester, Westminster and Canterbury. But for many years, and particularly under its last Headmaster, it had fallen away in numbers and seemed to have lost its spirit. The Governors, at that time a conscientious body, were concerned about this and were prepared to support the new Head in his reforms. These included giving better pay and conditions to the staff, and setting up boarding houses which they could run. Those typical, solidly-built Victorian blocks appeared rather earlier there than in most Grammar-turned-boarding Schools, and the boarders came in to fill them. Wratislaw also got a London architect, Henry Clutton, to make alterations to the School house and he himself bought the furniture and such things as blinds, in his attempt to modernize the place., Felsted was at the time considered to be very modern and progressive.

Wratislaw was at Felsted for five years, from 1850, and when he left his work was kept up by his successor, Grignon (q.v.) who was also among those at the first Headmasters' Conference. He married, in 1853, Frances Gertrude Helm of High Wycombe, and they had a family of nine children. The eldest, William George Cayley, was drowned as a boy of 15 while boating with his tutor and family off the Isle of Arran but the others were successfully reared and established. In 1855 Albert Henry resigned from Felsted, his reason being discreetly given in the D.N.B. as "health" but it is evident that the real cause of his departure was the Governors' delay on financial grounds in building a house suitable for a married man with a growing family.

Wratislaw then went as Headmaster to the King Edward VI school at Bury St. Edmunds. Here, owing partly to a religious controversy enflamed by his predecessor, he again found a good old foundation half-empty. It is a curious comment on the ups and downs of school reputations that he should consider leaving Felsted—which has stuck to its position on the H.M.C. throughout the years since 1869—for Bury St. Edmunds which dropped out, having become first a Direct Grant and then a Voluntary Controlled school under West Suffolk.

Wratislaw seems to have been a conscientious and successful headmaster with a talent for administration and attention to detail. "He liked everything in its place" was a family comment and he was very fair, though a disciplinarian who did not spare the cane—even in his own household. He persuaded his new Governors to raise the almost nominal fees and to put salaries on to a more workable basis, including capitation fees for the Head. He organized a House system at Bury St. Edmunds and he introduced science as a curriculum subject. Other actions, such as installing gas, instituting uniform, and re-organizing the discipline of Sunday church-going, are examples of the varying administrative improvements needed, and after the Taunton Commission's Report, there was a new scheme of administration to be passed, based on an earlier draft by the Charity Commissioners. Wratislaw was successful in getting this accepted and it continued to be worked up to 1945. He retired from Bury St. Edmunds in 1879 and became Vicar of Manorbier, in Pembrokeshire.

He had always been a keen naturalist and he was particularly knowledgeable about fungi. (This resulted in his eating, successfully, all kinds of unusual "mushrooms", to the amazement of his family and pupils.) He taught his children, girls included, to know the Latin names of plants, and gardening remained an interest. His first wife had died while he was at Bury, much mourned by the School, and he married again. Albert Henry's branch of the family seems to have been well-off and till 1900 owned the large house in Rugby where he was born. He is said to have undertaken the payment of mortgages or debts for the less successful members. By 1889, his eyesight was failing and he retired from his Vicarage. He was one of the first to go to Germany as a patient to have a cataract operation, but he died at Southsea in November 1892.

The double-cultural background of his family enabled him to play a really important part in the revival of the literature of Bohemia, little known at that time, and the study of Czech was given an impetus by the number and scholarly merit of his works. He left to Christ's College quite a large number of books in Czech, many of which he had received from their authors. His translations, whether of poems, tales or historical works, were prefaced by literary, historical or folklorist introductions, and in all these fields this scholar-headmaster held a reputable place.

Wratislaw was a very faithful attendant at the H.M.C. meetings, though he did not often contribute to discussion. Perhaps it was characteristic of his own interests as a scholar that he advocated the teaching of Hebrew in the Sixth Forms of schools, expecially to help boys who would later need this for taking Orders. This study was added to the curriculum of at least one H.M.C. school (Repton) and though we may now commend him more for stressing the importance of science, his suggestion shows a present-day understanding of the need to cater for the individual boy at what we regard as A-level.

William Stanford Grignon

The story of W. S. Grignon is a sad and rather puzzling one. His career as Headmaster of Felsted ended when he was 52 and he lived to be 83 without going to any other school or taking another academic post. Considering the circumstances of his departure, one's mind turns to a possible breakdown, but if he had one, he recovered and supported himself by taking pupils in a country vicarage. He seems also to have been active in the world of examinations, as he had already done some of this work and was known at Cambridge, and besides the Classics he could have examined in French, which he spoke like a native. More than ten years after he left Felsted, he produced a very competent statement—about the school (giving details of the arrangements he used to make for day-boys, of whom there were very few) and though he wrote moderately and judiciously, he ended with the sentence: "As for the local Trustees under the scheme of 1851, they were worse than useless", which sounds as if he had never forgiven them. Yet the school of which he had been Headmaster for nearly 20 years, and from which he was extruded in circumstances which raised a serious correspondence in *The Times* and references in a House of Lords debate, proceeded after his death to collect subscriptions for a Hall opened in 1910 and named after him. His portrait was installed there, and so late as 1931 a new Hall was opened* in the presence of his daughter Miss Adelaide Grignon, then nearly 80.

Grignon was appointed to the Elizabethan foundation of Lord Rich (who had converted it from a chantry to a Grammar School) after its revival had been started by A. H. Wratislaw (q.v.). This revival had been hindered by lack of buildings which the Trustees (Governors) had agreed, and were enjoined by a Scheme in 1851, to put up. These should have included adequate houses for the Head and for taking boarders; Wratislaw had left chiefly because they did not. When Grignon was appointed, the Trustees were the more anxious to honour their commitments. Buildings, including a house for the headmaster, were begun about 1859 and the last instalment of this plan was finished by 1867. During all this time, the new intake of boys followed hard on, or overstepped, the provision made for them; "applications exceed admissions by four or five to one", commented the Taunton Report.

William Grignon (of Huguenot descent but born in Jamaica where his family had estates) had been educated in England, first at a private school in Islington, afterwards at King's College School and then at Trinity College, Cambridge. Though a scholar and a First-class Classic, he just missed a Fellowship. He was for a time a private tutor in Cambridge, helped by good family connections, then taught at Brighton College, becoming later the head of a Collegiate school at Sheffield. He had been ordained and married, but lost his young wife at the birth of their only child, and he went to Felsted as a widower with a sister to keep house for him. He was very competent scholastically, being a very good classicist, a fair mathematician and a fine linguist; also according to the Taunton Commission's Report he himself taught science. He was an excellent teacher, short of stature but of tremendous energy, and devoted to his boys. That they returned this feeling is clear from the way they rallied round him in his trouble, and the inscription on his presentation clock probably does represent a more than formal

---

* The first having been destroyed by fire.

appreciation:. . . "in grateful remembrance of his unfailing care and disinterested kindness during his head-mastership."

His great fault seems to have been his inability to delegate, when the time came to let go some of the great variety of jobs arising from the large increase of school numbers. This was the obverse of the qualities of self-reliance and competence which enabled him to do so much. For instance, in 1863 when there was a crisis in the accounts, he took over, and with great success, the work of "House Steward"—in effect, Bursar. This should have been the temporary answer to a necessity, but five years later he was still doing the work, on top of his teaching, settling in his influx of new boys and masters, and carrying out the general duties of headmaster.

As everywhere, scholarship and buildings were the first sign of progress on which expansion—which here meant also the enlargement of school life—set the seal of merit. The higher standards made worth while the establishment of Junior (School) and Senior (University) Exhibitions; school prizes also began to be endowed. But there was also an expansion of interests. The Shakespeare Society, which Grignon founded, led to theatricals; a boys' School Committee led to the founding of a well-run Debating Society (minutes still survive); there was a choir and, as early as 1874, a school orchestra. Felsted was among the first half-dozen schools to respond to the appeal for the Volunteer movement (i.e. "Corps."); Grignon was active in arranging for this, and he also made a place for games and athletics. (But he showed his real understanding and sympathy for the boys in *not* over-organizing their leisure time. G. C. Coulton, the mediaevalist, mentions the freedom of their holiday afternoons.) *The Felstedian* was started in 1873. All these elements were common to contemporary Public Schools but at Felsted they seem to have come into being very naturally, the boys being inspired but unforced. Also in accordance with the trend were the buildings; the Victorian School House—looking exactly as one might expect—must have marked for many the arrival of Felsted as a Public School on a par with any represented at the earliest Headmasters' Conference.

Grignon held the loyalty of his boys and, like Thring, the support of most parents. His relations with his staff may not have been wholly harmonious. With the Trustees, a breach certainly appeared and the actual row which led to his dismissal was triggered off by a quarrel with an assistant master. A virulent correspondence ensued, with extraordinary and baseless accusations against the Head, whom the Trustees only lukewarmly supported. In Grignon's words, this support "was accorded grudgingly, shabbily and without a sign of that goodwill which eighteen years of ill-paid but strenuous work for the school would have ensured me from men of generous mind." This seems a true assessment, but Grignon was unwise enough to include it in a letter to parents acknowledging their support, and he later complained to them of his inadequate salary—£500, but with no profits to be made from boarders, owing to the school's arrangements. In the end, the Trustees exercised their legal right of dismissal, without having allowed him to put his own case, and the Bishop of Chelmsford, to whom he exercised his right of appeal, endorsed the sentence, also without a hearing.

In the outside world, Grignon had no lack of supporters. There was a blast in *The Times* (November 1875) from Fellows of Trinity, Cambridge, and others, including Thring: ("All of us have had ample opportunities of knowing Mr. Grignon and. . . can testify to the excellence of the work he has done for the last twenty years.") But "this act of tyranny and injustice" was not only censured as a private wrong. A letter also appeared signed by the Headmaster of every school represented at the first Conference, pointing out the bad educational effect of Grignon's dismissal and asking that the Charity or Educational Commissioners should see that a clause was inserted in every new scheme providing for a hearing for the defence and noted in the contract of all subsequent headmasters. Their advice was, in general, heeded—but this did not help the dismissed Head of Felsted.

How, after this tragic crisis, did Grignon spend the rest of his life? One might have hoped that the Jamaican estates would give him financial security (he did once take a voyage out and negotiated the sale of some part of these)—but the Trustees had refused him a pension and he certainly died a poor man. (He left all his small estate to his daughter; one hopes she received a competence during his life.) However, he did get a legacy which freed him from the drudgery of tutoring. He retired and they lived with friends in the then village of Willesden for many years. Also, this competence enabled him and his daughter to travel which, to judge from the accounts she left of these holidays, formed their greatest pleasure. He died in 1907 at Torquay, the announcement noting both his Jamaican connection and his 20 years' Headmastership of Felsted, now over 30 years back.

This harking back was not surprising. Grignon had given the school a new character and status. True, he could build on the work begun by his predecessor, but when he came Felsted was generally still regarded as Preparatory, a feeding school for the Great Public Schools. He had caused it to stand on its own base and to flourish in scholarship, sport and reputation. Feeling that this rise was due to his own efforts it was not surprising that he resented being directed by the Trustees over the internal administration of the school. His dismissal was followed by a period of depression in numbers, but the foundation he had laid enabled the school to survive. Like so many of the first attenders of the Headmasters' Conference, he is one whose name has gone down as "the School's second Founder."

The last words of his memorial tablet sum up his fate:

ONE SOWETH, ANOTHER REAPETH:

Augustus Jessopp

The Rev. Canon Jessopp seems to have gone down in Norwich tradition primarily as a literateur and a beau. Yet Dr. Jessopp, during his 20 year Headship did effect a real improvement and change of status of Norwich School. Also his attendance at the first and subsequent conferences with other headmasters may well have been a reason why a local school, with a history of most uncertain progress, established itself in the H.M.C. and has there continued.

Yet at the end of his life—over thirty years after he had ceased to be a Headmaster—it was rather as a "lettered cleric with interests extending widely outside his own profession" that Canon Jessopp earned three-quarters of a column in *The Times* obituary. He had, for instance, written with generous sympathy of the ills of the workers in rural parishes—that was in the days of Joseph Arch and the first organization of agricultural labourers—and he did his best for village life in his own, at Scarning, near Norwich. Cottages, a village hall, Church repairs and so on were set on foot during his incumbency. If he was sometimes at cross purposes with his neighbours, as has been suggested, it may have been because he came late to parochial work, having spent his best years with his school. Moreover, he was not Norfolk-born, though that county became the subject of his historical and archaeological activity.

For the past occupied him no less than the present. He was on the County Committee for Norfolk for the *Victoria County History*, and he himself wrote the article on Ecclesiastical History in Vol. II. His publications, from the religious works of John Donne (which he edited in 1855; ahead of his time, one imagines) to articles in the D.N.B. on important Elizabethan statesmen—all these justify the esteem in which he was held in the scholastic world. His mild form of humour may be judged by his recreations which he described as "visiting his parishioners, grumbling at the weather, cultivating apples and potatoes and driving an old horse till his lamented death." His own lamented death occurred in 1914 at the age of 90.

One might have thought this cultivated cleric out of place at the

Headmasters' Conference, but he attended regularly and contributed occasionally. His life before that event does not seem to have been very remarkable. Born at Cheshunt, educated perhaps by his father, later at St. John's College, Cambridge, he graduated without great academic distinction. Before he went up, he had spent three years in a merchant's office at Liverpool, and after his ordination (1848) he married the daughter of a naval captain there. They lived childless but happy for 50 years, and the school chronicler refers to her as "the loved Mrs. Jessopp", and implies that though plain she was exactly the right wife for her husband, sharing his many interests. Jessopp spent some years as a curate before taking the headship of the Grammar School at Helston, Cornwall, where he stayed five years.

The School at Norwich, when he came to it, was in a poor way. The numbers were down, there was but one boy at the University; no books, registers nor other records were being kept. It had had a varied career since it was given its charter and name under Edward VI. One of its headmasters had been the eminent Dr. Samuel Parr* (after his own school had failed), while the latest, Jessopp's immediate predecessor, had in effect been dismissed for the brutality of his punishments. It was firmly local-based and regarded by the citizens of Norwich as intended for the education of their own sons at little or, more often, no cost, whereas the Governors (Trustees) endeavoured to provide a living wage for the Master and staff by encouraging boarders and raising fees. Not long before 1859 when Jessopp came, there had been about 90 boys, but he found under 30, not counting some boarders whom he brought from Helston with him. The school was indeed "at a very low ebb".

Dr. Jessopp's effect was probably first felt on the academic side. When five years later Mr. Hammond, Assistant Commissioner of the Taunton Commission, examined the boys, he pronounced them "well-educated and well-mannered youths" and said the school was in advance of others he had met with in the district during the course of his inspection. His main criticism of the headmaster was that he had a tendency to push the more intelligent boys—perhaps this is what the school historian meant by calling him "intense, as a master". Yet his praise was "an inspiration" and he was generous of his time—especially to young scholars of history. Hammond did not think him sufficiently "distant"; perhaps his own interest in the subjects taught made him ignore with leniency those who were not scholastically minded. His portrait shows a serene expression on his good-looking face, and the general verdict was that "there was not a mean thing in him."

His obituarist comments: "His tenure at Norwich (where George

---

* See pages 34, 77.

Meredith's elder son was among his pupils) was uneventful and from the fact that he seldom if ever alludes to schoolmastering in his subsequent writing it may be assumed that it was not altogether to his taste." This is hardly fair. The fact that he had more than doubled his numbers by the date of the Taunton visitation, and that they continued to increase in spite of difficulties of cramped class-rooms and insufficient dormitories, shows that his headship was being successful. He went up to 100 in 1870 and reached his peak of 127 two years later; numbers then dropped away though he never had less than 70. About the time of his appointment, the Governors, acceding to the demands of the citizens, set up a Commercial school, virtually independent of the Grammar School, with a separate Head. This cannot have helped Jessopp, especially as this school (which had 220 boys in 1864) was also described in the Taunton Report as "the best I have met. . . with much better accommodation than the Grammar School."

Jessopp did not find that the burden of mastership prevented him from working on and publishing his historical studies. He contributed to *The Nineteenth Century* magazine and, besides his work on Donne, published several Essays and *One Generation of a Norfolk House.* This chiefly concerned one Henry Walpole who became a Jesuit in the 16th century. (It was while he was occupied on this, at Mennington Hall, that Jessopp professed to have seen the ghost of a former cleric there.) By 1879, however, he or the Governors realized that his school work was taking second place to his writing, and he resigned, taking a local parish. His historical and antiquarian activity continued, also such writing as *"Random Essays", "The Trials of a Country Parson"* and, more seriously, a *History of the Diocese of Norwich.*

In his old age distinctions accrued. He became a Fellow of St. John's Cambridge, also of Worcester College, Oxford, and an Honorary Canon of Norwich Cathedral. One year he was Select Preacher at Oxford, where his handsome presence and his sonorous voice made him "an imposing figure". In 1901-2, he was Chaplain to King Edward VII. He got a pension of £100 in recognition of his services to archaeology and one from the Civil List of £50. When he gave up his parish, he sold his library and his letters which showed his connection with several literary men during his long life. He retired to Norwich, "loved and regretted", only three years before his death.

George John Blore

What seems always to have been remembered above all about George Blore was his gentleness, courtesy and thoughtfulness. In this he was a distinct contrast to many of the Heads at the Conference and not least to Mitchinson, whom he succeeded at Canterbury.

Blore's first headship, actually his first school, was Bromsgrove, Worcestershire. His own education had begun at the private school, Eagle School at Hammersmith, a very remarkable place which produced several of the headmasters he must have met later—among others H. Montagu Butler and his brother A. G. Butler, Ridding of Winchester and Warre of Eton. Blore went on to Charterhouse (then still in London) and to Christ Church where he eventually became a Student (i.e. Fellow) and Tutor. His high honours in classics, law, and history testify to his broad interest in the humanities even if he was less academically brilliant than some of the other heads considered here. He was also a fine cricketer. His father, Edward Blore, F.S.A. (1787-1879) was a well-known, not to say fashionable, architect. He had drawn plans for the exterior of Scott's Abbotsford, and was Special Architect to William IV and Queen Victoria in the early part of her reign. The family seems not to have wanted for money and Canon George Blore died, by school standards, a rich man.

His Bromsgrove headship (1868-73) was not spectacular, not at least compared with that of his predecessor who had been described as "a prince of schoolmasters" and the number of his boarders went up only from 50 to 70. But he was a great consolidator. The Taunton Commission had suggested considerable improvements in the constitution and management of the school which were embodied in a scheme later agreed by the Education Commissioners. Among other changes the scheme substituted unrestricted scholarships in the main school for an old charitable Trust under which a few foundation boys of the Blue-coat school—known as the "Blue Chaws" and looked down on by their middle-class schoolfellows—had been taught on elementary lines in a squalid outhouse under a system which benefited nobody. A civilised man like Blore must have been thankful to have this scandal abolished—and fate rewarded him the next year by sending him among new scholars "the son (A. E.) of Edward Housman, solicitor." For it had needed a good deal of tactful negotiation to induce the former Trustees and the Patron (descendant of the Founder, who used to have considerable say in the School's affairs) to agree to the reforms. Blore persuaded them to sign, and the scheme was sealed in February 1869, being probably among the first of 235 new schemes to be worked.

Though he was not long at Bromsgrove, no account could show more clearly Blore's happy temper and successful relations at the school than these words spoken on his last Speech Day there:

Schoolmasters and boys are natural friends. I have never made firmer friends than at Bromsgrove. I have lived very much among the boys and known them individually. I have never heard a word which has caused me pain.

Such a sentiment must have been rare a hundred years ago; the statement of it would be uncommon even now. No wonder Canterbury was agog in 1873 with reports about the "angelic qualities" of the new Headmaster and his family. School monitors at both schools joined the family party on holidays and Mrs. Blore's drawing-room with its civilizing influence became a centre of welcome in their family life.

At Canterbury Blore was "gentle, even lax"; his sympathy was ready, his preaching emotional (compared to Mitchinson's) and his religious feeling deep but unobtrusive. (It was said that the boys, especially those to whom he taught Greek Testament, realized from the burning of his desk candles down to their sockets how much time he spent in preparation for this lesson.) Corporal punishment grew less frequent and was used only for "grievous offences". There was also a positive and practical side to Blore's good-nature. One boy tells how the school choir used to bring in copy-books to the chapel services "for the better preservation of our Sunday trousers." Blore, observing this practice, provided a strip of carpet for kneeling on. Soon after his arrival too, the Sunday dinners were observed to be improving. When the first issue of *The Cantuarian* was brought out, Blore wrote an editorial statement for it. In his character as a patron of cricket he bought some ground now known as "Blore's piece", and an incident was long quoted which took place soon after he arrived at Canterbury:

Dr. Blore happened of a sudden during the time for preparation to require the services of a monitor and came himself to the nearest study to find one. The opening of the door revealed the inmates not seriously bending over their books but engaged in a lively game of stump-cricket. The culprits had nothing to say—and the Doctor stood equally speechless. The batsman of the study scored a century the next day, and the Head Master smilingly attributed his success to the practice which he had so unfortunately interrupted.

This all sounds like the tiny incidents of a Victorian school story and it is not surprising, especially after the reign of Mitchinson, that Blore was popular. But he was not one to exploit this popularity, not even with a view to increasing the size and prestige of the school which however he did maintain. After fifteen years at Canterbury his health began to fail and he left in 1886. Retirement evidently suited him and he lived till 1916 dying as a Canon of Canterbury at the age of 80.

As a rule there is not much to be said for the idea that Mr. Chips, if an ex-headmaster, should spend his last days at the school gates, but one feels that no-one could have objected to Blore. Perhaps he brought with him from Bromsgrove some of the gentle air of the West Midlands:

The country of easy livers
The quietest under the sun.

Robert Edward Sanderson

The reputation of R. E. Sanderson has been definitely though rather unfairly eclipsed by that of his great namesake of Oundle who lived later and had the advantage of a successful novelist (H. G. Wells) to write his life. And it is true that the earlier Sanderson devoted himself to one school, Lancing, and to the raising up of a tradition in that school, and had not the wider vision and farsightedness of "the great Sanderson".

Yet in his chosen field he clearly had much personal influence. It is not hard to find a laudatory phrase about any good Headmaster, but one must accept the man as remarkable on the evidence of Lord (Justice) Sankey who stated: "It would almost be enough to sum up (my five years 1880—85) in one sentence and to say that 'Sanderson was Headmaster' ". Another pupil again sums up superlatively: "All Sanderson's boys must ascribe to him a great part of what has been good in their after lives."

Lancing was a Woodard School, the first Public School of that religious denominational foundation, and dated from 1848. Sanderson, going there in 1862 found it an ordinary unremarkable little school and determined that a tradition should be created in tune with the religious (High Church) life and ideas which the Woodard Trust existed to promote. The fact that the Trust's originator was still active in connection with all the Trust schools might have made the Head's way precarious, but he seems to have had the necessary tact and loyalty. He concentrated largely on "a gradual amelioration of conditions, an improving organization, a growth of civilizing influence." Not surprisingly this began with the worship itself. The foundation of the eventual Chapel was not laid till 1868, but Sanderson introduced the playing of the organ and a surpliced choir at the services, and made a living thing of the ceremonies; for example of the Easter Eve procession which profoundly impressed the boys on the occasions when the school stayed for Easter. In the general school life, he fostered dramatic, debating and musical activities, promoting a Shakespeare Society and a Madrigal Society, as well as a Natural History Society. Scholarship also improved, though Sanderson was not an outstanding teacher. Unlike some of his contemporaries he did not try to inculcate learning by beating, though his devastating method of making boys listen to a verbal report by their teachers individually, before the Head, sounds like a most scarifying *viva voce* examination.

Not that he gave up corporal punishment, for example when it was discovered that a large number of the school were selling their clothes to one "Old Nosey" in exchange for his eatables, there was a mass beating of those who owned that they had done so. (But it is also on record that Sanderson improved the food.) Another outburst referred to his cancellation of the whole first edition of the Lancing College Magazine because it contained an ode of Horace "not in accord with modern taste" (i.e. that of 1877) in a translation by a member of staff of "most ingenuous frankness". In spite of such incidents, it is clear that his great success was in personal relationships both with staff and boys. The historian used the Victorian phrase: "he knew how to manage boys." Of course his numbers, though impressive for his time—were small by our standards: his highest was 300, in 1886.

The "peak years" for scholarships were considered to be 1865—74, but though science was taught it was not till 1885 that Sanderson started a Modern Side, designed especially for the boys who would go on to Woolwich and Sandhurst. There were also modern languages, German being taught by a certain Herr Fugger, incompetent in his lessons but enthusiastic about the orchestra! Sanderson's personality was felt in all, though towards the end of his 27 years he began to lose his strength, and did less teaching. When he was in his prime, Lancing was unique; "No other school could have been quite like it", but after 1890 its peculiar flavour faded.

"Sanderson was a competent classical and English scholar with a marked appreciation of exactness and precision; a theologian; a good preacher and not unskilled in music. Under him a high religious and moral tone was maintained as well as a high standard of scholarship. There was a great dignity both in his presence and manners, and to take a liberty with him seemed to be impossible."

A curiously impersonal summing up by the school's historian giving little idea of how deeply he was loved. Lord Sankey added tersely: "But this is not sufficient."
The effect of his work for the School is more precisely set out:

> He found it a small, haphazard little school, founded on a grand idea but uncertain as to its whereabouts and its direction. He softened its harshness, fostered its individuality, directed its energy, brought it out of a rather hazy mediaeval dream into nineteenth century reality, and left it a Public School with a tradition of its own.

Thomas Henry Stokoe

T. H. Stokoe seems to have been a typical schoolmaster-cleric. He put in thirty years as Assistant, Second Master, and then Head at different schools, and must have represented the three schools of which he was Head at the Headmasters' Conference. After his retirement in 1889 he took incumbencies in different parishes until his death, in Lincolnshire in 1903.

He was a north-countryman from Hexham with a well-to-do father, and went to Lincoln College, Oxford, where he got a scholarship and a double First. He also won a theological prize, was ordained, and eventually became D.D. Later in life he became an Hon. Fellow of King's College, London, Preacher at the Foundling Hospital and at Gray's Inn, and was remembered for drawing up courses for use in schools on both Old and New Testaments—thus dovetailing his two professions.

The first glimpse of him as a teacher appears to be early in 1859 when he applied for a mastership at Uppingham. Thring was much pleased with him, formed a favourable opinion of his quality, and accepted him almost at once. He then offered Stokoe a House, if—as was customary under Thring—the master would build accommodation for boarders; Stokoe accepted the terms but had to withdraw on account of his father—who presumably refused to put up the money (no explanation is given in Thring's diary, which is the source of this incident). Thring was deeply disappointed but thought him "a real good fellow" and it appears that he accepted him as a master none the less. At least we may deduce this from an advertisement in the *Bristol Times* two years later in which he is referred to as " late Assistant Master at Uppingham."

For the young man, evidently keen on experimentation, applied for a post in the newly-founded Clifton College. He was appointed as Second Master by the first Head, who unconscionably took another headship before ever the College got going, leaving Stokoe to open the "Preliminary School" in the summer of 1861. He was commended by the Governors for his "able conduct" of this pre-opening school, which already included boarders and day-boys, and he was re-appointed by the new Headmaster, Dr. Percival, under whom he served for two years. In 1863 he became Head of Richmond Grammar School (Yorkshire), and it was while he was here that he came to the first meeting of the Conference. It would seem that Thring invited him because of his connection with Uppingham, rather than on the merits of his own school, as this had been in a very poor state when he went, though it was certainly on the up-grade.

Stokoe's improvements had begun at once—as well they might. He arrived to find 15 boys only, very inadequate buildings, and a crisis in staffing. A new scheme had brought about a revised constitution and curriculum within a year of his arrival. By the end of his eight years' headship, the numbers had increased literally ten-fold and boarding houses had been put up as well as necessary additions to the old school buildings. A strong connection with the Universities had been established, with the foundation of a number of open exhibitions, and the acceptance of Richmond along with other Yorkshire schools as eligible for other scholarships earlier endowed. In this academic advance, the headmaster had been helped by the new scheme in so far as this enjoined examination by an outside examiner, and a wider curriculum. The subjects which had been laid down there included such diverse studies as General English Literature and Land Surveying, but Natural Science was not mentioned. Stokoe introduced it, and with it, a division into classical and modern sides; on the latter, science, as well as modern languages, was taught. The Taunton Report considered that one third of all the pupils were on the modern side (in 1864) and approved of the "bifurcation" which took place after the first year. They also thought well of the academic work as a whole and considered it superior to that in any other North Riding school.

Stokoe went in 1871 to the Reading Grammar School—which was almost immediately added to the H.M.C. list. There may have been family reasons for this as he was eventually buried at Sonning, and a memorial window to him was placed in Reading School chapel. In 1880 he applied for the headship of King's College School, London, and was chosen from nine applicants; the school was at that time very closely connected with King's College. As before, he got major improvements in conditions, (including playing-fields) and widened the curriculum to include a Commercial Class—he had already established a very successful "Matriculation Class". But he had hard work to establish a good tone, and during his headship there was a scandal about a terrible, indeed fatal, case of bullying with public censure of the lack of supervision. The headmaster was not apparently held responsible for this nor for the drop in numbers which took place in his time, but after nine years he "withdrew"—and perhaps this expression of the College historian is the right one—to the Rectory at Lutterworth.

He had always taken his pastoral duties very seriously and almost as soon as he came to Richmond complained that he had little opportunity of advising the boys "with proper force on matters affecting the religious and moral welfare of the school." He had got the Rector to agree to his using the parish church on Sunday afternoons for school services, which day-boys as well as boarders had to attend (they already went to the parish morning service on Sundays). In time the Headmaster became curate at the Trinity Chapel and eventually this became the School Chapel, the school having been given the right of nomination by Lord Zetland, who had already shown himself well-disposed to Dr. Stokoe.

Yet Stokoe, despite the good work he did early in his career (and the Richmond historian writes of the "magnificent recovery [of the school] when the foundations seemed securely laid for its development ... into one of the great Public Schools of the North"), never made a name for himself in the outside world. Nor did he manage to make his schools outstanding, in spite of his good work. At Clifton he enabled Percival to start that Public School at once on its successful career; at Richmond he raised the Grammar School in numbers, scholarship and general reputation to be "The Eton of the North"' But perhaps he did not stay long enough at Richmond to make its position invulnerable; at any rate a quarrelsome and litigious successor quartered the numbers and lost the school its status within little over ten years. It ceased to be represented on the H.M.C. Again, at Reading, his work brought the school within the orbit of the H.M.C. but later it faded out, reverting to (what it had of course been originally) a Grammar school, chiefly for local boys. At King's College he seems to have been a good organizer rather than an initiator; it was not he but his successor who succeeded in moving the school out to Wimbledon from "the cellars" of the College. It is difficult at this distance to judge the work of Thring's "real good fellow"; it may well have been personal rather than institutionally eye-catching.

George Butler

Liverpool College, from which Dr. George Butler came to the Conference, was a school of a different origin from those represented by the other Heads. It reckoned its age in decades, not in centuries, having been founded in 1840, with the idea of providing "a Public School education based on the principles of the Church of England", though it was open to and widely used by members of other denominations and faiths, as a day school in Liverpool. It had already acquired a character and its pupils regarded themselves as "Liverpool Gentlemen"—see the school's history under this title—as distinct from "Salford Lads" or "Manchester Men." Butler had been there three years when he was invited to the Conference.

One must admit that to a number of people in those days, George Butler would be, before all, the husband of Josephine Butler who from about 1870 was to devote her life to combating the evils of regulated prostitution. She particularly fought against the Contagious Diseases Act—a subject about which a well-bred lady and the wife of a clergyman was supposed then to know nothing, which she should shrink from and certainly not publicly interfere with. As the Butlers were a most devoted couple, his support meant "everything under

God" to his wife. One of the most touching chapters in her *Memoir* of her husband contains the passage where she let him know of the work she felt she must undertake:

> I went to him one evening when he was alone. . . I went in and gave him something I had written and left him. I did not see him again until the next day. He looked pale and troubled and for some days was silent. But by and by we spoke together freely and we agreed that we must move in the matter and that an appeal must be made to the people. . . And that good and noble man, foreseeing what it meant for me and himself spoke not one word to suggest difficulty or danger or impropriety in any action which I might be called to take. He did not pause to ask: "What will the world say?". His whole attitude in response to my words. . . expressed: "Go! and God be with you."

Canon Butler was in his own right an educator, and a member of a great scholastic family (of whom the present Lord Butler is one).* His father, George Butler senior, had been Headmaster of Harrow early in the 19th century, and his two brothers were respectively Headmasters of Harrow and Haileybury. Both were later respected members of the H.M.C., particularly H. Montagu Butler of Harrow who was for many years on the Conference's Committee. Perhaps George Butler was overshadowed by these also in popular opinion. He was, it seems, rather a self-effacing character: "modest and unpretentious" in words applied to him by Dame Millicent Fawcett in her *Life of Josephine Butler* "but he could in fact claim to great distinction as a classical scholar", as favourite pupil of Dr. Wordsworth and a winner of the Hertford Scholarship. (He only lost the Ireland because he had not put down his name as a candidate within the number of days specified, the question turning on the point whether or not Sunday was to be counted as a day.) Characteristic is one of the letters quoted by his wife:

> You know I don't like parsons. . . I shall never wear straight waist-coats, long coats and stiff collars. I have a longing to be of use and I know of no life in which I can be more useful than in education, my whole life having been turned more or less in that direction. It is a blessed office, that of teacher."

So a teacher he became, taking orders only some time after. He had been an undergraduate at Trinity College, *Cambridge,* but was transferred after two years to Exeter College, Oxford, as his father considered that his sporting friends were preventing him from working. After getting his degree he took pupils at Oxford, then held a Tutorship

---

* See Table I at p. 131.

at Durham University and returned to Oxford soon after his marriage in 1852. His work there included the introduction of geography, until then not studied as a subject in the University where the ignorance even of the dons in this field was remarkable. He also encouraged the study of art (Ruskin once complimented him on his drawing of mountains) and of modern languages. All these he fostered in the schools to which he went later. He and his wife fitted well into an active and intellectual group at Oxford (Jowett and Dean Stanley were among their friends) but her health suffered from the climate. Through the help of friends he was appointed Vice-Principal of the College at Cheltenham, founded curiously enough, about the same time as Liverpool College to which he went eight years later. He had by this time a family but he and his wife suffered a terrible shock from seeing their only little girl killed as she fell from a staircase while hurrying to meet them.

They removed to Liverpool in 1865 and he became the third Principal of Liverpool College which by this time had an almost international character: "Among its eight to nine hundred pupils there were Greeks, Armenians, Jews, Americans, French, Germans and Spaniards"* with the two sons of a Nigerian trader. The Taunton Commissioner (James Bryce) had commented rather critically both on the very restricted curriculum and on the line of demarcation between the Lower Middle and Upper Schools, which had social as well as educational implications.

Butler at once set about widening the curriculum to include the serious teaching of science—only a little zoology and botany had been mentioned by the previous Head. (Chemistry now became "very popular" but not, it seems, very practically taught.) Even more remarkably, he introduced the systematic teaching of Geography "political and physical" as an ordinary school subject. He himself lectured on geography as well as taking the religious instruction, and he published an *Atlas of Modern Geography* in 1872 and an *Atlas of Ancient Geography* in 1877. One of the most important things he could do for the college was to interest his eminent friends and connections in it. It was a great help to an institution, which though locally successful had not yet established its status and academic reputation, to become known to such men as Jowett, Stanley, and Darwin's cousin, Galton.

Academic successes were certainly gained but difficulties, which Butler never resolved, lay in the social complexities of the school. Liverpool College (as distinct from Liverpool Institute) originally

---

* M. Fawcett, *Life of Josephine Butler*, Private printing, London, 1927, p.38.

founded "for the education of the Commercial, Trading and Working Class", had developed particularly in its Upper School, which in effect catered for boys of a higher status and was winning a scholastic reputation for the College as a whole. Butler's view was that it "was not founded with the idea of giving a more genteel education to young men about to enter commercial life but to connect Liverpool College with the learned professions through the Universities." He was in favour of the "ladder" idea of advancing the poor, clever boy into the learned professions—but the ladder was not broad enough. The confusion of the original aim had been increased by the growth of Liverpool itself which tended to disintegrate the close-knit society of its trading community, and also by the Education Act of 1870 which led to provision of schools overlapping with the Lower School. Butler was not the man to cut across the complexities with a firm policy that would convince the Governors. For one thing, he had never really become reconciled to Liverpool itself, with its bricks and mortar, and, like his family, lived for the holidays which they always spent together in some country place—when he was not drawn into speaking for his wife's crusade. Towards the end of seventeen years he lacked the energy—perhaps had always lacked the self-confidence—to tackle the problems, personal, educational, and social, which beset the College. He resigned in 1882, putting his own case to the Governors:

> He spoke of the quality of the schools' teaching. . . of the number and variety of the University honours his pupils had gained. He mentioned. . . that three old pupils had become Mayors of Liverpool, as evidence that the local interests of the school had not been neglected. He pointed out that he had been offered other headships in his seventeen years at Liverpool but had declined them and now "in the last decade of ordinary human life" he purposed to take up ministerial work.

He was appointed a residential Canon of Winchester, dying there in 1890.

It is likely that Butler paid the price of his loyalty and charity and that his connection with and support of his wife's famous, and at the time notorious, struggle affected his career both locally and in connection with Public School headships (in spite of his statement) and ecclesiastical preferment. Perhaps, on the other hand, the lack lay in his own character and his overshadowing by his more forceful family and his wife. He did not make a great showing at the Conferences though at the first meeting he supported the idea that everything should be done to get the Great Schools (Eton, etc.) to join the Conference. This idea was strongly opposed by Thring who wanted them to come, if they came at all, only as equals. Butler was noteworthy many years later for suggesting that the Conference went into private session to discuss the report of the Church of England Purity Society, which it did. It may be that after all he identified himself more with his wife's work than with anything else.

HEADMASTERS OF THE FIRST CONFERENCE

		Dates of Headship	Life
Thring	Uppingham	1853–87	1821–1887
Mitchinson	Canterbury	1859–73	1833–1918
Harper	Sherborne	1850–77	1820–1895
Dyne	Highgate	1838–74	1809–1898
Welldon	Tonbridge	1843–75	1811–1896
Wood	Oakham	1846–75	1818–1902
Pears	Repton	1850–74	1815–1875
Wratislaw[1]	Bury St. Edmunds	1855–79	1822–1892
Grignon	Felsted	1856–75	1819–1907
Jessopp	Norwich	1859–79	1823–1914
Blore[2]	Bromsgrove	1860–73	1837–1916
Sanderson	Lancing	1862–85	1828–1913
Stokoe[3]	Richmond	1863–71	1835–1903
G. Butler	Liverpool	1865–82	1821–1903

[1] Also of Felsted.
[2] Also of King's School, Canterbury.
[3] Also of Reading, and King's College School.

To take even a glance at the diversity of these dozen characters is to wonder how they ever came together, let alone continued to meet with evident enduring pleasure. What, beside the original motive of defence, which after the satisfactory work of the deputation cannot have been so very strong, kept them together? Besides their differing temperaments and destinies, these men varied greatly in age and experience especially in their lengths of terms as Heads. Stokoe had gone to Richmond six years and Blore to Bromsgrove two years before the Conference, but Dyne had been a Head for over 30 years and Welldon for 25. He and Pears died not long after the Conference was established, whereas Blore, Grignon, Mitchinson and others lived on well into this century.

As to their characters, can any common factor be found, any quality or like views which would account for the respect with which they all came to be regarded in their schools and the fact that the majority are unhesitatingly referred to as "a second founder", "the man who renewed this school", "a great Headmaster"? In what did their greatness consist? To this, we shall return, but we might relate them to the one figure generally acknowledged to have been "great"—though it ought to be remembered that Arnold had by now been dead over a quarter of a century. To repeat, his summary of aims and priorities:

(1) religious and moral principles;
(2) gentlemanly conduct;
(3) intellectual ability.

These would certainly have been accepted by them all, though some seem to have put more emphasis than Arnold on a scholarship which would show results in University entrance and successes. But meaning, as Arnold did, by the first, a Christian basis, to this they all subscribed and most of them felt strongly about it. To "conduct" they would add a corporate feeling (Arnold might not have agreed), and a will to built up a fine tradition. Within this framework their emphases differed, in response to the particular needs of their own schools. Of these needs, physical, intellectual and moral, they were conscious far beyond their predecessors and they were determined to see them met. This comes out in their various contributions at the Conference. (It is only fair to say that later, the original group seems soon to have been overshadowed in discussion by the "new men" such as Percival and Jex-Blake as well as by the old stalwarts like Montagu Butler.) It is clear, though, that as at most conferences, it was the general talk, the discussion that does not go into the minutes, the cross-fertilization of ideas, which was of such tremendous importance. These men were tolerant, receptive and had a remarkable sense of proportion. They justified Thring's comment at the first meeting: "I never saw so little time wasted and on the whole so much good sense shown".

For they had, these Heads, a high level of intelligence, which has here been manifested by the monotonous regularity with which Firsts and double-Firsts, University prizes and College Fellowships have been (or could have been) mentioned. They knew how to use these brains. To take one aspect only; finance. Harper, Wratislaw, Dyne—to name a few at random, had to reconstitute entirely a system they inherited, in some cases centuries old, almost always irrelevant to modern conditions. Similarly, Thring was by no means the only one to have to insist on the power of "the Almighty Wall" and to have to devise new buildings himself. Mitchinson, Welldon and many others had to shake their Governors into an awareness of these new needs. The conventional picture of Big School, with a master and desk at each side and each end, seems to us to have nothing to commend it, but where schools, (masters, boys and Governors) had been brought up in this way they accepted the four hundred year old system without question. A Head needed to be clear, convincing and energetic to persuade the Governors to spend money on classrooms and equipment.

Such qualities these headmasters may be said to have in common with successful Heads of modern times. The taunt indeed is that now a Head must be primarily an administrator and a Public Relations Officer but these roles were important 100 years ago, even with schools infinitely smaller than they are now. But the Headmaster then had to be (and had the chance of showing himself to be, something in which so many are now almost deprived) a good teacher. To that actual indefinable quality there are testimonies in every school-history book—Mitchinson, Grignon, Pears and the rest brought stimulation, enthusiasm and skill to their classes. And it was not only in the Classics, be it remembered; the first two of these taught science also; George Butler taught that up-and-coming subject, Geography; Grignon, French; and most of them stimulated the reading of modern English literature and history outside school hours.

Scholarship, administration, teaching—to these were added what was later recognized as "pastoral care". Most—not all—put the care of the individual boy as their highest charge. That most also used corporal punishment (Dyne and Mitchinson fiercely enough to breed resentment) is not denied. But the trait best remembered in most of them was "liberality", a giving of their attention, of encouragement, of their time, and often actual financial help, to every boy whom they saw needing it.

To do all this needed unfailing energy. Many of them were faced with raising the standard of work, enlarging the curriculum, and extending the buildings to contain the enormously increased numbers. They differed in the details of their organization, in the kind of discipline, gentle or severe, that they adopted; in their forms of teaching and the curriculum they introduced; in the expression of their religious teaching, less or more emotional. But each Head sent through his school a pulsing drive which could be felt by boys, staff, parents and Governors. True, schools were not the only places where men of such energy could be found; it was a characteristic of life in industry, discovery and reform a hundred years ago that a wind of advance was blowing through it. There was an explosion of energy comparable with the population explosion of the century. (It reached education after a time-lag; may we yet hope to see as a concomitant of our own population explosion a much needed outburst of such energy in men and women?)

It put life into old and decaying schools and it vivified the co-operative organization which had sprung up from such a fortuitous beginning.

For if it was a very remarkable thing that the Headmasters ever came together in a conference, it was even more so that the Conference continued. The mid-century did indeed see the beginning and growth of many self-protecting associations, and the first banding together of the headmasters was definitely a league of this kind. Its subsequent development over the next 50 years has been excellently summed up by Dr. G. Baron.*

The Headmasters' Conference brought together the leaders of the most prominent schools. . . whilst by the end of the century the Headmasters' Association . . had enrolled practically every headmaster of a secondary school of note. The man working in some obscure county grammar school or some newly-founded municipal secondary school was brought into touch with the great figures of the day, heard them declare with passion their determination to defend their independence against the central authority and local authorities. . . and was strengthened in his own resolve to assert his authority over his school and its destiny. The headmaster remained no longer an isolated figure dependent only upon his school and his personal qualities. . . but was a member of a well-organized body of vigorous and active men who through the Conference and the Association constantly voiced their disapproval of any infringement of their authority and their autonomy. Thus when the Board of Education and the local education authorities eventually came into being they entered an area in which the chief advantage points had already been seized by well-organized and determined forces.

It remains here only to pose and not to answer the question of the Headmasters' Conference role to-day *vis-à-vis* the above-mentioned forces, to which must be added the political ones arrayed against it. One might have hoped that these military metaphors would have been as out of date as the terms sound. Certainly many outstanding and perhaps representative Heads have made very clear they wish to be considered as builders not fighters in the field of education; others like Nehemiah's men go about with both a tool and a weapon. But it is enlightening for any organization to consider its origins, and its originals. It would hardly be an exaggeration to say that the great force behind a century of Public and Secondary school education arose when Thring was so greatly pleased at meeting such "a very superior set of men."

---

* *Some Aspects of the Headmaster Tradition,* University of Leeds Institute of Education. Researches and Studies No.14, June 1956.

EPILOGUE

"Victorian Stereotype", or What makes a Great Headmaster?

The wheel has come full circle and the early travellers have arrived at Uppingham for the Conference—the dozen ranging from Mitchinson of Canterbury who braved the rigours of the train journey to Wood of Oakham, the next-door neighbour who had probably ridden the few miles over.

It is extraordinary that twelve such different schoolmasters were persuaded to attend their first meeting, and even more remarkable that it became an annual event. What was there in common between the future Colonial Bishop or the Cathedral Canon and the Norfolk antiquary, the Czech scholar, the quiet parson, not to mention their single-minded uncompromising Headmaster host? And besides these there were literally dozens of other Heads, many of them equally idiosyncratic; who in a few years would be joining the Conference and would continue to come to its meetings.

One thing at least they had *not* in common and that was the slightest resemblance to the stereotyped image which has since been created of The Headmaster. By 1914, Ian Hay in *The Lighter Side of School Life,* was drawing a satiric portrait of "the Headmaster of Fiction".

He is invariably called "The Doctor", and he wears cap and gown even when birching malefactors—which he does intermittently throughout the day—or attending a cricket match. For all we know, he wears them in bed.

He speaks a language peculiar to himself—a language which at once enables you to recognize him as a Headmaster... The "Doctor" invariably addresses his cowering pupils as "Boys" ... and if no audience of boys is available at the moment, he addresses a single boy as if he were a whole audience. To influential parents he is servile and oleaginous, and he treats his staff with fatuous pomposity. Such a being may have existed—may exist—but we have never met him.

Satire apart, there is a very general tendency to refer to headmasters in terms which suggest that there is still a fictional idea of what "the

Public School Headmaster" of almost any previous period was like. He was a fine figure of a man, bearded and gowned, commanding and unapproachable, whose word was law. He was learned, but in a narrow pedantic way, with no interests outside the classics and his school. He was without humour, though he might be persuaded to smile at some scholastic quip or, more grimly, at a sadistic joke. The tendency today at least, is to portray him as a power-loving, if not tyrannical, ruler who took pleasure in imposing his will on little boys in an unnecessarily harsh and cruel way, accompanied by a positive enjoyment of beating.

How are does the fictional picture fit the facts?

As to appearance, Headmasters unlike policemen do not have to reach a minimum standard in height—not even the most distinguished. Some were remarkably small—Keate, Thomas James, even Mitchinson, who "laid the egg" of the Headmasters' Conference. True, others were outstandingly tall and good-looking like Dr. Balston of Eton, or fine impressive figures like Percival or Temple. Thring was considered sturdy rather than tall, but was forceful in appearance, with his square jaw and piercing eyes. About Arnold, it is difficult to say. He was slight rather than big-built but the impression he made was through his whole personality rather than his physique.

Beards were worn, but by no means universally. Many fine faces (like Thring's or Harper's) were fringed. Of the twelve who attended the first Conference, by far the majority were clean-shaven. Possibly beards increased during the century; Montagu Butler and his brothers wore them, their father did not. Arnold did not. But it was then, as now, a matter of taste.

The attitude and sense of humour differed in headmasters as in ordinary men. Back in the 18th century, Thomas James did not think it beneath his dignity to share jokes with the boys. Samuel Butler also quipped—but these were rather scholarly jests. Thring, though a sense of humour was hardly an outstanding characteristic of his, never bothered about personal dignity in joking or sharing athletic pursuits with the boys. Neither did Mitchinson stand on his dignity, but then the future Bishop was hardly at any time a joking man. Arnold did not in any sense play games (though he watched them somewhat uncomprehendingly), but many of his pupils shared from time to time in his pleasant unconstrained family circle.

Tricky situations for Headmasters sometimes repeat themselves, even those we should consider unusual, and sense of humour changes; of both Thomas James and Dr. Pears it was told that they found on one occasion a donkey awaiting them in the class-room. The former met the schoolboys' joke with: "Take away the young Doctor but do not hurt him", the latter retorted with an allusion to bringing coals to Newcastle.

The reception of such witticisms must always be looked on with the suspicion of Goldsmith's couplet on the schoolmaster:

Full well they laughed, with *counterfeited* glee,
At all his jokes, for many a joke had he.

The sardonic joke was not wanting; it would take too long to explain the complicated context of Kennedy's:

T.I.B.I.—to thee, boy,
A flogging shall be, boy.

But to read the reminiscences of 19th century Heads and schoolboys certainly does not give the impression of a bunch of dry, humourless pedants.

Scholars most of the Heads undoubtedly were, and if the record of any one of them has been omitted here, it is only because repetition of prizes won and first-class honours gained by one distinguished man after another becomes wearisome. But narrow most of them were not; for example the early Butler with his pride in his Aldines and his dahlias became the fore-runner of countless book-collecting and gardening school-masters. Thring made it his business to widen his interests because "one boy is caught in one net and one in another"; he jumped hedges in their country rambles, and a box of his own wood-carving survives as an example of his attempts in craft. Arnold's interests in general social affairs was well-known; his liberalism was even notorious. And the truncated course of his professional lectures on modern history, with their numerous parallels of old and new, shows a remarkably wide view.

The accusation of harshness and sadism is often brought undiscriminatingly against "Victorian Headmasters", "Victorian" being used as a blanket word, emotive of cruelty and repression, for any Headmaster before the present century. (Many so-called Victorians fall outside her reign. Even Arnold had been at Rugby for two-thirds of his time there before the Queen came to the throne.) By the time Victoria actually arrived, more than a third of the way through the 19th century, English society, whatever wrongs it allowed to continue, was at least working towards more humane conditions. Was this reflected in the Public Schools? Moberly and Wordsworth at Winchester, for example, thought it was, and many, both of the Masters and pupils among those giving evidence before the Clarendon Commission stress that a kinder spirit was arising. There was less flogging; the gulf between boys and masters was diminishing; boys were less unkind to one another. In one way the mid-nineteenth century was a period of favourable balance. The tradition of the fierce beater was being overtaken by the new and kinder temper, but the numbers in the schools were not yet so large as to promote the loss of individuality and the lack of contact which tends to oppression on the one hand and violence on the other. Thring, whom his diary shows to have been sentimental rather than sadistic, put the matter vividly and precisely, saying that the Head who does not know his boys is, when he punishes them, simply acting as policeman for the master who does. (This had been Keate's dilemma—see p.97—he had to deal with the enormous numbers out of his great school who were sent him daily "on the bill".) Thring would never have more boys than he could himself know, so that with him—and with many even in the growing schools—a boy detailed for punishment was an individual, not just so much flogging material.

Naturally, Headmasters—like fathers, policeman, farmers, dons and other persons with similar responsibilities—varied individually in their kindness or harshness of usage. Some were outstandingly sympathetic, like Dr. Blore who followed the exacting Mitchinson at King's School, Canterbury, and like Sanderson at Lancing. Others genuinely believed that to spare the rod was to spoil the child. Yet others were faced on arrival with a school in which corporal punishment or expulsion seemed the only alternatives if they were to improve it, and only later could they allow mildness to appear. But to class all "Victorian Headmasters" together as great floggers or formidable disciplinarians is just stupid carelessness. Any serious writer should by now have got beyond the stereotype of "the Doctor and his Birch."

To take the positive side—were there any common characteristics which can be said to have made, in the late 18th and early 19th centuries, "a Great Headmaster"? The "superior men" of Thring's group and their predecessors are so different from one another that there seems only one quality which they can justifiably be said all to have had; every one was a man of energy—purposeful energy, consciously directed. The intelligence and scholarship and what Thring called the "style" of his fellows has been illustrated. They succeeded because each was clear about what he wanted to do—to put his school on the map, to improve its numbers, scholarship, conditions, reputation, or the religious quality of its pupils; he saw his aim or aims quite clearly. It was not a selfish aim, though many of them must have been human enough to believe that their own livelihood and reputation was bound up with their professional success. Thomas James' quaint comment on his somewhat unskilful successor might do for a number: "He seems to me still to pant after glory"—(letter, September 7th, 1794). Most, like Thring, Harper, and Mitchinson, were gluttons for work and, though in a few, like Butler and Elwyn, this energy was hampered by ill-health, they obstinately threw themselves into their chosen work in a manner well in tune with their countrymen in current English society.

For it was not enough that the Head should have this quality of energy, combined with intelligence and devotion. He must be not only "a man of parts" but a man of those parts acceptable to the age and appropriate to the circumstances in which he was functioning. That is, he must be outstanding in the qualities needed by *that* school at *that* moment, as well as having an understanding (intuitive, perhaps) of his own time. This peculiarity the men here portrayed clearly illustrate.

James of Rugby had the qualities, values and temperament appropriate to an era which was to pass with the Regency—perhaps even with the Napoleonic wars. He was urbane, cheerful, and socially easy-going. He had the usual appreciation of rank; he valued—and no doubt sought the company of—gentle and noble families, yet without any trace of servility. He made use of his well-placed friends, no more than was accepted but as much as was customary, to raise the social status of his little country school. His education and knowledge of his own merits seem to have given him an ease and a confidence which helped to make them valued. His classical scholarship was ample, so was his scriptural knowledge but he used the latter without the earnestness and emotion that gave later headmasters the power to inspire a spiritual revival. For this, the time was not ripe. To many parents it would have savoured of that suspicious quality, "enthusiasm". *That* would have frightened them off, whereas a school that was becoming both humanized and a nursery of "polite learning" they could understand. For a late 18th century Head it was best to be tolerant, pleasant, and civilized.

Samuel Butler was influenced by James' standard and type of scholarship and by his style of teaching—though in these he probably excelled his master—but was less assured and urbane. There was a thoroughness about *his* study of the classics which more than anything else was to make a success of his school. With him begins the long and visible series of notices of the school's distinctions won (in competition) at the Universities and on these he relied for justification of himself and his work. (Within half-a-century these notice boards had become ubiquitous; this emphasis on competitive success foreshadowed and kept pace with one important side of 19th century life.) Butler was a brilliant teacher and could communicate his standards, even his enthusiasms, to friends and pupils. The wonderful record of his Oxford (260) and especially his Cambridge (340) pupils was what gave himself the greatest satisfaction and his school the highest reputation.

Keate showed another side of life in the same century but one that was fast disappearing. His was a late anti-Jacobinism, a last important appearance in the scholastic world of that self-reliant spirit which had brought the country through the French wars. He embodied the farewell gesture of this assertiveness; he may have been blind to finer feelings but was unsparing of himself and disregarding of personal danger and discomfort. If he did nothing else, Keate underlined the mistakes of the past and the long-term ineffectiveness of solely repressive measures so clearly in his own person that he banked up enough resentment against them—though, curiously, not against *him*—to break open a gap for the waters of reform; a trickle first then a full flood.

Of Arnold as a man for his own season it is difficult to write; he has so obviously become the man for all seasons since then. Whether by his charismatic, legend-making personality or by the fortuitous coalition of a remarkable biographer, a famous novel, and other circumstances down to the name of a well-known sport, Arnold has become a symbol of a national institution—or of an out-dated type of establishment, according to how you look on the Public Schools. But *before* the legend, Arnold's main contribution, as vouched for by his contemporaries, was the bringing back into the schools of a moral earnestness and above all of Christianity. Of course religion had always been an element in education to which lip-service at least had been paid. It was to remain so long after Arnold, but he was the pioneer of an emotional and ethical revival for which, fortunately for him, the country was exactly ready. At a time of earnest Evangelicalism and of an exciting rise of the High Church movement, Arnold's call, unhampered by doctrinal controversies but backed by his sincerity and personal magnetism, was for Christian principles and conduct. It was particularly geared to the school; his appeal roused the idealism latent in adolescents and confirmed the endeavours of his hand-picked staff, who were to spread the message. In society as a whole, Godliness as well as Good Learning was beginning to be lauded.

It was partly the change from "Godliness and Good Learning" to Manliness (as set out clearly in Mr. Newsome's book under the former title) which made Thring so outstandingly the man for *his* own time—the mid-nineteenth century. But the meaning of "manliness" itself was changing; the stress was no longer, as with Arnold, on "grown-up-ness" as opposed to childishness, but on the stronger, so-called "manly" as opposed to "womanly" virtues. Not that Thring was at all anti-woman, even in education, but the form taken by his energy was assertive, expansive, even combative, in accordance with tendencies admired in the Victorian male. In his understanding of the importance of outlets for physical energy, in his awareness of social and moral problems and in his growing appreciation of the individual needs and capacities of his widely varying pupils he was ahead of his world, but not so far as to be out of sight of it. (On the first of these—provision for the physical side of school life, of which he made much more than Arnold—the scholastic world in the event caught up with Thring and literally out-ran him.) In his intuitive understanding of what was to be done, and in his drive and organizing ability to bring this about, Thring was a man of the mid-Victorian age. He showed this in a number of different ways: he was just in time to be regarded as a pioneer of school health (witness his evacuation of the school to the sea-side from fever-ridden Uppingham); he opened the boys' eyes to social obligations entailed by their privileges (shown in his fostering of the first "school mission", run by one of his Old Boys); he was the first real upholder of the equality of subjects in an enlarged curriculum, insisting that those who taught non-classical subjects were also "superior men". I have not found that Thring used the expression "muscular Christianity" but his values were akin to those of Charles Kingsley and Tom Hughes of that movement. Thring did not concentrate on "manliness' to the exclusion of other virtues, but he had a robust downrightness, he built on a strong religious foundation and he held an absolute conviction of the rightness of his own standards. This fitted in easily with the ideal of Christian manliness—it was also well suited to an age that had been congratulating itself in the Great Exhibition.

It would be tedious to pursue this theme of the appropriateness of each Headmaster to the immediate needs of his school and to the general trends of his time. Mitchinson and others, though less outstandingly successful than the great pioneers, had like them this energy and devotion which revived old schools from Felsted to Sherborne, from Tonbridge to Repton. Many not mentioned here are in their own schools celebrated as remarkable revivers, even "second founders."* Nothing has been said of Vaughan of Harrow, of Russell of the Charterhouse nor of later men like Moss of Shrewsbury and Haig-Brown who had the exacting job of uprooting a school and recreating it in new surroundings without which it could hardly have survived, nor of countless other "superior men".

For the work of restoration and revival did not stop in 1870. Fifty years after this, one of the later-renewed schools set up a finely-lettered memorial exactly expressing what it owed to its recent Headmaster. The words, which were in fact written about Sanderson of Oundle, might have been applied to almost any of those whose work and personality has been touched on here:

---

* An interesting example is Dr. West of Brentwood, who was at the original meetings of endowed Schools headmasters and supported Thring's idea of a re-union. But he expected this to be held in London and refused to come to Uppingham for the Conference, so can lay no claim to this act of pioneership.

TO WHOM GOD GRANTED GRACE
TO REVIVE THIS ANCIENT SCHOOL
WHICH IS ITSELF HIS MEMORIAL:
BY HIS VISION AND ENTHUSIASM
HE TRANSFORMED THE LIFE OF THE SCHOOL
PROMOTED ITS VIGOROUS GROWTH
AND ENHANCED ITS REPUTATION.

or, more generally and paradoxically:

"Let us now praise famous men"–
Men of little showing–
For their work continueth. . . . .
Great beyond their knowing

The Seal of Louth Grammar School

APPENDIX A

Mrs. Thring's Account of Montem

Mrs. Thring, who had driven up with her husband and a large family party from Somerset to attend the festival of which her son was the chief figure, writes the following account of the day's proceedings to a relative:–

My Dear Madam—The *Morning Post* which I sent you on Saturday as soon as I returned would give you a much better account than I can possibly do of the grand features of the Montem, still we think that you would like to hear our proceedings, which Gale desired me to give you. The business of the day begins very early, for before I was dressed at halfpast seven, I was called to look at one of the salt-bearers come to the lodging for his "salt", as the money is termed—a very handsome youth (the captain of the oppidans, a son of Mr. Piggott of Brockley Combe), dressed in a most splendid Spanish dress with hat and feathers. The captain of the college, the hero of the day, Edward, wears only a captain's uniform with a star on his breast to distinguish him, and he really did not look absurd, though so little. We went at nine o'clock to breakfast with Mr. Goodford, one of the masters, who, as such, has the power of admitting his party to the school yard, which cannot otherwise be obtained without a ticket from the headmaster. We then were taken to the College Hall, and soon after entered about 200 of the youths, all dressed either in fancy costumes or in scarlet, to breakfast, whilst a military band played and the whole area was filled with genteel people. Through Mr. Henry Woodhouse's introduction, we next got admission into the Provost's Lodge, and were in the first row of a line in a room through which the Queen and her suite passed, so that we saw her fully and closely. The Prince Albert is a gentlemanly, good-looking man, with a pleasing, but rather melancholy expression. After the Queen had passed we returned into the school yard, and had a front view of her from the open window bowing to the boys who paraded before her, cheering her most vociferously to the extent of their power. This done the procession of Etonians moved in rank and file to the mound at Salt Hill, and we got into our carriage and went up the road. The Queen passed us in her carriage quite close, and we arrived in time to witness the waving of the flag at the top of the mound by the boy ensign, and the renewed cheering the Queen. All the youths then went to the dinner given by the captain to the whole school, and as many private friends as he chooses to invite, and during their banquet the company adjourned to the gardens of the inn, where the band continued to play, and where you have again a well-dressed *mob.* We then returned to our lodgings, where we had ready for ourselves and friends abundance of cold chicken pie, etc., and from that time till eleven at night we had a constant succession either of visitors or boys to enjoy it. We took a turn, however, in the evening into the beautiful playing fields of the college, which are in themselves worth seeing, independently of the multitude of well-dressed ladies and beautiful fancy dresses of the boys. In the evening we saw these last to perfection, as between twenty and thirty came into our lodgings to supper at different times. The day was delightful for the purpose, and the collection the best ever made—upwards of £1,250; the expenses are enormous,—I believe £800. But still Edward is a lucky fellow, as he is now gone off to King's College, Cambridge, as a scholar, and goes on regularly to be fellow in course of time. It was a source of great gratification to us to find that he had not only secured the approbation of those in authority, but was likewise extremely popular with the juniors. We have, indeed, abundant cause for thankfulness, and are, I hope truly grateful for the blessings conferred upon us. . . . We all separated next day—Theresa, Gale and Theodore for town—Miss Hood, daughter of Sir Alexander Hood, whom we had taken with us, returned with me to Alford—Miss Thring to Clifton—Henry and Edward to Cambridge. . . Henry was very anxious that we should have gone to the installation at Cambridge, but that is. now postponed in consequence of the intended dissolution of Parliament, which will find employment enough for many of the visitors. . .

I enclose one of the copies of the Montem Ode,* written by a friend of Edward's, according to custom, in which he has remarked pleasantly enough on Edward's littleness. Will you please return it, as it is the only one I have.

---

*Any account of Montem would be incomplete which omitted mention of the doggerel verse here referred to as the Montem Ode. It was supposed to be the composition of a person (quite fictitious) styled the "Montem Poet." The ode was printed at the captain's expense, and distributed during the day, as a broad sheet ballad, by a man usually dressed in character, to whom the sale was a somewhat valuable perquisite.

Thring's Ode was written by a friend of his own class, his lieutenant for the day. A few lines will be sufficient to illustrate its character:—

> Step out, strut well, before such great spectators;
> Show off, smart lower boys, before your "maters,"
> You cock your chins up pretty well, but still
> You'd all of you be better for a drill;
> Though legs be cased in duck, and toes in boots,
> Our regiment is full of raw recruits;
> Eyes right though sisters giggle, "Don't you see, John,
> How you kick up the dust?" though Gov'nors wink,
> Threatening to draft you to the Spanish legion
> Unless you make your mark. But, pray, don't think
> That I would such aspersions fling
> Upon our stately, portly Captain Thring,
> That stern Caucasian chief, who rears
> Behind six files of mountaineers
> His proud, majestic figure;
> His well-bedizened retinue
> Almost, alas! obstruct the view;
> However well they be attired,
> Perhaps it were to be desired
> Their lord were rather bigger;
> But yet his purse—we hope—we know—
> Will beat in length his person,
> And ladies can't expect each beau
> To stalk as tall as Curzon:
> So drink his health and praise his feast,
> And, when the holiday has ceased,
> Say, one and all, with grateful heart,
> Thring has played well the captain's part.

Obviously Montem was a celebration which was likely to put a severe strain upon the character of a captain. One of Thring's old school and college friends writes:—

Edward Thring was the last but one of those who had the luck to be captains of Eton, or eldest of the foundation scholars when the triennial festival called Montem was held. I have known three others. . . all of whom suffered morally from being supplied with the inordinate credit given by innkeepers and shopkeepers to Montem captains, recipients of many hundreds of pounds collected as toll rather than free gift, and squandered on parasites or drink. He alone in my time escaped the evil effects of the absurd institution. He went through the summer school term as a schoolboy and the subsequent three years at Cambridge in perfect sobriety and purity. This did not strike me at the time; it was a matter of course. . . But afterwards when I learned why Dr. Hawtrey abolished Montem, I began to see the danger from which Thring's very strong character had preserved him.

The magnificence and extravagance of Thring's Montem, and the increasing popularity of the festival, which, in Dr. Hawtrey's words, made Eton on Montem day little better than Greenwich Fair, practically sealed its fate. After an ineffectual effort in 1844 to mitigate its worst evils, the authorities of the college decreed its suppression.

APPENDIX B

Marlborough College has been referred to as throwing a light on the development of "the Arnold Myth" so a note about it is added here. The Headmaster concerned (Cotton) does not fit into any of the groups discussed—he belongs rather to the category of "Arnold's men"; staff who went from Rugby to take up headships after they had worked under Arnold; outstanding examples are Percival of Clifton and Jex-Blake of Cheltenham. Cotton, like these, went to a new school.

Marlborough School (later called College) was one of the earliest deliberately founded schools intended as Public Boarding schools for educating boys—in this case particularly the sons of clergy—at moderate cost. The plan was thought of in 1842 and the school opened the next year with two hundred boys in a large coaching Inn and outhouses, formerly a stately home of the Seymour family. It was thought that by bulk buying, communal central feeding and other economies, expenses would be kept well down, so the fees were fixed at a minimum: £50.p.a. But for clergymen it would be only £30—and sons of the clergy were to form two-thirds of the entrants. Entry was through nomination by "Governors" who paid for this privilege; the venture as a whole was financed by obviously philanthropic shareholders. Not unnaturally, the financial difficulties were enormous and the whole institution almost foundered on these at one point though in the long run, after its first headmaster had left, it did pull round. But it was this initial cheapness that accounted for the soaring numbers, one cause of the educational difficulties which it took longer to overcome.

For the set-up seems to have combined every disadvantage except in the surroundings—a pleasant countryside with, at first, well-disposed neighbours. Because of the stringent economy there was considerable physical discomfort; the Council (Governors) were inexperienced; the staff old-fashioned and limited, and the Headmaster, "a Mr. Wilkinson, a clergyman", formerly Head of a smallish school in Kensington, was totally lacking in understanding or knowledge of a Public School and still more of the type of pupil he would have to deal with.

The boys poured in—two hundred on the opening day in August

1843; nearly all under sixteen, mostly sons of west-country parsons, tough, sporting and country-bred. If physical accommodation was inadequate, educational arrangements seem to have been even more so. There were no plans at all for leisure hours. Any boy could go into the town (unless forbidden as a punishment) or into the surrounding countryside or mouch about the buildings. There was a covered colonnaded "playground" for the wet and a large court in front of the mansion, railed off from the main road. But there was no playing-field and—as in the most traditional of the old schools—only one large schoolroom in which most of the classes were held. The few prefects, (those boys in the VIth who were over 16 alone seem to have been eligible at first,) had none but formal duties and the influence on them of the Headmaster, unlike that at Rugby, seems to have been negligible. In any case, one of Mr. Wilkinson's shortcomings was his inability to delegate to either his staff or the boys. Discipline was built up on the old idea of boy-master enmity; caning was constant and in public.

Clearly, after sixteen years of Arnold's influence, little of what we should now call Public School ideas had penetrated this new establishment. The boys made their own life—which might not, perhaps, have turned out much unlike an expanded Long Chamber had it not been for the country round which gave scope to, and at first absorbed, some of the energy of these sporting rambling country boys.* But such machinery as had been devised for organizing the school broke down entirely under the influx of more boys. Attracted by the low terms, another fifty fathers sent their boys that Christmas and by 1848 there were five hundred — building, hampered by financial stringency, vainly tried to keep pace with growth. After this, Marlborough's reputation, which started off finely, began to decline and the good-will of the local inhabitants had been dissipated. Tales came out about the utter lack of discipline, about bullying, about the roving, drinking, poaching, birds-nesting, rat-catching and even raiding of the farmers' poultry-yards and the local magnate's preserves. The most surprising story is of a boy who was handy with his knife being called in by two others to skin for

---

* One boy whom the life did suit excellently was William Morris, whc ranged the countryside studying churches and learnt about architecture in the Library—the one adequate educational element in the school. A recent biographer makes the conventional accusation that Morris was sent to Marlborough to be made into a gentleman, though why, if this was the object, a school filled chiefly with the sons of impoverished parsons should have been selected is not made clear. Mr. Thompson does add, however that the school was "too inefficient to do its corrupting job."

them a deer they had brought down. Games, as other schools were beginning to know them, hardly entered into these boys' lives; when some little boys clubbed together to get material for a "tip-&-run" type of cricket, they had difficulty in finding a smooth patch on which to play. The one sport really enjoyed was fighting—the qualities admired were courage and physical prowess.

Rowdiness and indiscipline by their very momentum increased and culminated in the "great rebellion" of 1851, breaking out on Guy Fawkes Day. Riot and disobedience continued sporadically till the end of term (there were two half-year terms ending at Christmas and in June); the next term saw the resignation of Mr. Wilkinson.

He was succeeded by the Rev. G. E. L. Cotton, a housemaster from Rugby who had known Arnold. He is said to have been the model for the "young Master" who appears chiefly in the penultimate chapter of *Tom Brown's Schooldays*, but this does not present us with a very exciting character as the latter seems to have been introduced mainly to glorify Arnold and to show that "The Doctor" had been the good and far-seeing power behind Tom's improvement. But he saw clearly what was needed at Marlborough and began by dealing firmly with the rambling and drinking without and the bullying within. And to tackle these problems he was to use two elements in Rugby life which would help greatly, both of which had been used by Arnold though not unduly stressed by him—the Prefects' authority and opportunities for games. Cotton was in the long run extremely successful and being followed after his six year term of office by Dr. G. G. Bradley, who had been at Rugby both as a boy and as a master, he could count on his ideas being carried further. The school improved financially, in due course; it rose in reputation and the decline in numbers was stayed and it soon came to the top of the list in scholarship; in the Clarendon Commission's evidence is a table of Oxbridge scholarships in which Marlborough with 29 scholarships leads Rugby with 26.

The point, however, of quoting this story, though only briefly, is to show that the situation at Marlborough required—or at any rate responded to,—those things which had grown up at Rugby as a result of Arnold, though Arnold himself evidently (to judge, for instance, by his lack of reference to them in letters and sermons) did not think them specially important. They were, at least, subordinate to his aim of producing a school of Christian gentlemen. Prefectorial authority, easy relations of staff and boys, expulsion of the frivolous, house-feeling, games and the team-spirit—these things (except the last) he used but valued chiefly as means of improvement, of hastening the boys towards development of the manly, grown-up character which alone was capable of Christianity. But to others they began to appear as ends in themselves and having appeared early at Rugby, they became regarded as a part of Arnold's mystique. When games, prefects, Houses etc. became popular because they fitted a particular situation, Arnold was credited with having invented them. It is no doubt too late to alter this belief, but now that educators are taking a long, hard, and disparaging look at much that has accrued to the Public School image, it is common justice to point out that Arnold is not responsible for it all.

BIBLIOGRAPHY

ACKERMAN, R. — The Public Schools of Eton, Charterhouse, etc. (Edited C. W. Trevelyan)
1958

ARNOLD, Matthew — Friendship's Garland
Smith, Elder 1903

BALSTON, Thomas — Dr. Balston at Eton
Macmillan, 1952

BAMFORD, T. W. — Thomas Arnold
Cresset Press 1960

BAMFORD, T. W. — The Rise of the Public Schools
Nelson, 1967

BEITH, "Ian Hay" — The Lighter Side of School Life
Foulis (Edinburgh) 1914

BINGHAM, J. — Our Founder
(Uppingham. Pr. Pr.)

BRADLEY, A. G. — A History of Marlborough College
John Murray 1893

BUTLER, Samuel (H. M. & B. P.) — Life and Letters. (Edited by Samuel Butler, his grandson)
John Murray 1896

BUTLER, Josephine — Memoir of George Butler
Arrowsmith 1896

CARLETON, John — Westminster School, a History
R. Hart-Davis, 1865

CRAZE, Michael — A History of Felsted School, 1564-1947
Cowell, Ipswich 1955

CUST, Lionel — History of Eton
Duckworth 1899

DERRY, Warren — Dr. Parr—The Whig Dr. Johnson
O.U.P. 1966

DILKE, Christopher — Dr. Moberly's Mint Mark (A study of Winchester College)
Heinemann, 1965

DOYLE, Sir Francis   Reminiscences and Opinions 1813—85.
Longmans, Green 1886

DRUETT, W.   Harrow through the Ages
King & Hutchings, Uxbridge 1935

ETONIANA   (Eton College)   Pr. pr.1904

EVERS, C. R.   Rugby
Blackie, Glasgow. 1939

FAWCETT, Dame Millicent   Life of Josephine Butler
Pr. Pr. London 1927

FINDLAY, J. J.   Arnold of Rugby. (His contribution to education.)
C.U.P. 1897

GILBERT, R. G.   Liber Scholasticus
Rivington 1829

GOULBURN, Edward Meyrick: The Book of Rugby School
Pr. pr. 1856

GOURLAY, A. B.   A History of Sherborne School
Wykeham Press, Winchester 1951

HANDFORD, B. W. T.   Lancing, 1848-1930
B. Blackwell 1923

HOLLIS, Christopher   Eton, a History
Hollis & Carter 1960

HOW, R. D.   Six Great Schoolmasters
Methuen, 1904

HOYLAKE, Geoffrey   Thring of Uppingham, The Man who made a School
S.C.M. 1946

HUGHES & DAVIES   Highgate School Register 1833-1964. 6th edition 1965
Castle Cary Press, Som.

KIRK, K. E.   The Story of the Woodard Schools
Hodder & Stoughton 1937

LAMB, G. F.   The Happiest Days
Michael Joseph 1959

ICELY, H. E. M.   Bromsgrove School through Four Centuries
Blackwell 1953

McCONNELL, James D. R.   Eton—how it works
Faber 1967

MACK, E. C.   Public Schools and British Opinion
U.A.T. London 1938

MAXWELL LYTE, H. C. A History of Eton College, 1440-1898
 Macmillan 1899

MOBERLY, C. A. E. Dulce Domum (Winchester)
 John Murray 1911

NEWSOME, David Godliness & Good Learning
 John Murray 1961

OGILVIE, Vivian The English Public School
 Batsford 1957

OLDHAM, J. F. History of Shrewsbury School
 Blackie 1952

OLDHAM, J. F. Headmasters of Shrewsbury School
 Pr. Pr. 1957

ROUSE, W. H. D. History of Rugby School
 Duckworth 1898

RUGBY School Report of proceedings respecting Rugby School before Rt. Hon. Lord Langdale (Wratislaw case)
 1839

STAUNTON, Howard The Great Schools of England.
 Daldy, Isbister & Co. 1877

SELFE, Lt. Col. Sydney Chapters from the History of Rugby School
 Rugby 1890

STANLEY, (Dean) A. P. Life of Thomas Arnold, D.D.
 (Hutchinson's Ed.) 1903

STOWELL, Hilda M. George Isaac Huntingford, Warden of Winchester College
 Pr. Pr. 1970

SUPER, R. H. Savage Landor
 Michael Elwin, N.Y. 1956

TEMPLE, Frederick et. al. Essays and Reviews
 1860

THORNTON, Percy M. Harrow School
 W. H. Allen 1881

THRING, Edward Diary, Life and Letters (Edited by George R. Parkin)
 Macmillan 1898

WENHAM, L. P. History of Richmond School (Yorks)
 Pr. pr. 1958

WAINWRIGHT, David Liverpool Gentlemen
 Faber, 1960

WOODWARD, Frances J.   The Doctor's Disciples
                O.U.P. 1954

WYMAN, Norman   Dr. Arnold of Rugby
              Robert Hale 1963

CHARITY COMMISSION: Reports: 1818-32
Digest of Reports on Schools and
Charities for Education
                  1842

CLARENDON COMMISSION: The Public Schools Commission
Report, 1864
              H.M.S.O.

FLEMING COMMITTEE :   The Public Schools and the General
Education System Report: 1944
              H.M.S.O.

TAUNTON COMMISSION: Schools Inquiry Commission
Report 1868
              H.M.S.O.

LEEDS, University of (Institute of Education) Researches and Studies
                  1956

BRITISH MUSEUM: Add.ms 34583-98. Correspondence
of Dr. Samuel Butler

RUGBY SCHOOL: (Temple library) Letters of Thomas
James
(Lawrence Sheriff's Charity)
Minutes of Trustees

SHREWSBURY SCHOOL: Minutes of Governors 1798-1838
UPPINGHAM SCHOOL: Diaries of Edward Thring
BRITISH PUBLIC CHARACTERS (Periodical)
                  1804

FRASER'S MAGAZINE for Town and Country
                  1842

BIRCH, William   The Schoolmaster (Poem) with
short memoir of Thomas James
            Rivington 1829

CHAPLIN, Edith   Memoirs of the Pyne and James
families (typescript)
               c 1920

HEADMASTERS' CONFERENCE. Reports (H.M.C. Office)

INDEX